Learning English

Green Line 2

Unterrichtswerk für Gymnasien

Herausgegeben von
Stuart Amor, Rosemary Hellyer-Jones,
Peter Lampater, Helmut Reisener
und Rolf W. Roth
sowie Werner Beile und Alice Beile-Bowes

Ernst Klett Schulbuchverlag
Stuttgart Düsseldorf Berlin Leipzig

Learning English - Green Line 2
für Klasse 6 an Gymnasien

Herausgegeben von
Stuart Amor M.A., Stuttgart;
Rosemary Hellyer-Jones M.A. und Peter Lampater, Ehingen (Donau);
Dr. Helmut Reisener Dipl.-Päd., Lüneburg;
Rolf W. Roth M.A., Idar-Oberstein
sowie Prof. Dr. Werner Beile und Alice Beile-Bowes M.A., Wuppertal

Beratende Mitarbeit:

Wolfgang Biederstädt, Minden; Klaus Büchler, München; Edgar Hilgers, Wuppertal;
Volker Strigl, München; Elmar Tegethoff, Hannover; Ann Thursfield-Stinglwagner B.A., Bonn;
Dr. Klaus Werner, Haßloch; Rolf-G. Wiele, Rinteln; Renate Zirn, Stuttgart

Visuelle Gestaltung:

Wolfgang Metzger, Mühlacker

Begleitende Tonträger zu diesem Band:

1 Compact-Cassette für den Lehrer und Schüler mit Lektionstexten und Liedern.
Beide Seiten besprochen, Klettnummer 58327.
Lieferung durch jede Buchhandlung oder, wo dies auf Schwierigkeiten stößt, zuzüglich Portokosten per Nachnahme vom Verlag.

1 Compact-Cassette für den Lehrer mit den Hörverstehenstexten, den Ausspracheübungen, den Rollenspielen und Versprachlichung von Bildgeschichten sowie Texten und Liedern aus ⟨*Merry Christmas*⟩ und ⟨*Reading corner*⟩. Beide Seiten besprochen, Klettnummer 58328.
Lieferung direkt an Lehrer, Schulstempel erforderlich.

Gedruckt auf Serena matt, hergestellt von den Cartiere del Garda
aus chlorfrei gebleichtem Zellstoff, säurefrei und ohne optische Aufheller.

1. Auflage 1 11 10 | 1996 95 94

Alle Drucke dieser Auflage können im Unterricht nebeneinander benutzt werden, sie sind untereinander unverändert. Die letzte Zahl bezeichnet das Jahr dieses Druckes.

Redaktion: Dr. Volkhart Weizsäcker, Redaktionsleiter; Peter Cole M.A., Dr. Gregory Fuller, Heinz-Peter Gerlinger, Verlagsredakteure

Umschlag: D. Gebhard, Korntal (Stuttgart).
Druck: KLETT DRUCK H. S. GmbH, Korb. Printed in Germany.
ISBN 3-12-583020-6 (Linson)
ISBN 3-12-583200-4 (Broschur)

Inhaltsverzeichnis

* Es werden bei jeder Lektion nur die wichtigsten kommunikativen Ziele der Texte und Übungen aufgeführt. Eine vollständige Angabe der Lernziele gibt das Lehrerbuch (Klettnummer 58323).

Die Texte, auf die sich die Hörverstehensaufgaben beziehen, sind auf der Lehrercassette (Klettnummer 58328) und im Lehrerbuch (Klettnummer 58323) verfügbar.

Zeichenerklärung

‹ › Stücke in Winkelklammern sind fakultativ.

S Das Stück ist auf Schülercassette (Klettnummer 58327) verfügbar.

L Das Stück ist auf Lehrercassette (Klettnummer 58328) verfügbar.

[ ] Die in rechteckigen Klammern stehenden Pensen können in Bundesländern, in denen ihre Behandlung in Klasse 6 nicht vorgesehen ist, als fakultativ angesehen werden.

weist auf die Hörverstehenstexte hin

Unit 1

⟨Photo page: Holiday postcards⟩

Borrowdale

Isle of Wight

Newquay

A The summer holidays

a) Holiday postcards

1 Come to the Lake District!

Why don't you come to the Lake District this year?

There are so many things to do!

Christine – David

You can climb mountains.
You can walk round the lakes.
You can look at interesting old houses and gardens.
You can visit quiet old villages.
You can sail on the lakes.
You can cycle thirty or forty miles a day.
You can stay at a camping-site – or at a hotel.

After her holiday in the Lake District, Christine says: "We climbed …" *Go on.*
But David says: "We walked …" *Go on.*

2 Peter's holiday pictures

Look at the pictures and talk about Peter's holidays.

to stay — to play — to look at — to walk — to climb

1. The Wilsons stayed at …

b) A page from Helen's diary

Friday, August 13th

Newquay, Cornwall

The weather was nice and we were on the beach again. We all had a great time. It was hot, so Mum and Dad stayed in their deck-chairs and did nothing all day. I wanted to go surfing with Ann, but she went off with some boys and went surfing with them. A dog rushed off with Mum's sun hat. Then Dad's deck-chair collapsed when he was asleep in it. Later we saw Ben MacDonald – he's here, too – and we all had ice-creams and lemonade. Ben dropped his ice-cream (typical!) and it went into my beach bag. When he tried to get it out, he dropped his lemonade in, too. – !

3 Yesterday

Example: Today is Saturday and the weather **is** bad, but yesterday it **was** nice.
Can you go on? Look at Helen's diary again.

1. Helen's sister Ann often **goes** surfing with Helen, but yesterday …
2. Sometimes it **is** cold on the beach in August, but yesterday …
3. Helen's parents usually **do** something on the beach, but yesterday …
4. Helen and her family sometimes **have** ice-creams at their hotel, but yesterday …
5. Helen doesn't usually **see** school friends in Cornwall, but …
6. Ben MacDonald often **drops** things. Yesterday …
7. Today the MacDonalds **are** at the camping-site. Yesterday …

4 Is that right?

Look at the postcards and the diary again.

Example: 1. Christine had a holiday at the seaside.
"No, that's not right. She had a holiday in the Lake District."

2. Christine and her family cycled up Great Gable.
3. Barbara's family stayed at a hotel at Barton-on-Sea.
4. Barbara visited the Isle of Wight with her aunt.
5. When they were there, a strange thing happened.
6. Helen's father collapsed when he was on the beach at Newquay.
7. Ben MacDonald was at Newquay, too.
8. He dropped his ice-cream on Helen's diary.

5 A day out

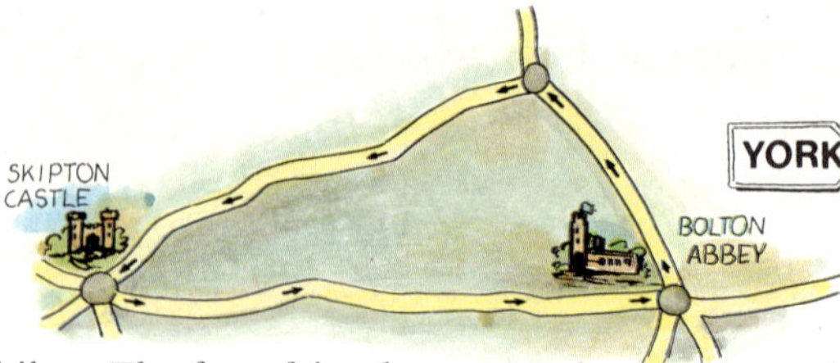

It is a warm Sunday in September. After breakfast Ronny *fetches* his bike from the garage, and *collects* Barbara from next door. Then they *go* to the Pearsons' house on their bikes. The four friends *want* to have a day out on the moors. Mr Pearson *opens* the van, and soon all the bikes *are* in. A few minutes later the van *is* on the way to the moors. Soon they *arrive* at Bolton Abbey.
First they all *look* at the Abbey, and half an hour later they *are* on their bikes. They *cycle* near the river, then they *turn* left and *go* down a quiet road until they *arrive* at Skipton. They *see* Skipton Castle immediately. They *visit* the castle, and then *cycle* back to Bolton Abbey. On their way they *stop* and *have* a picnic on the moors. They *stay* there for an hour and *play*, then it *is* time to get back to the van. They *have* a great day, but it *is* over too soon.

A week later, Ronny writes a letter to his cousin Daniel in London, and tells him about their day on the moors. He starts the letter like this:

Dear Daniel,
We had a wonderful day last Sunday. After breakfast I fetched my bike from the garage, and collected

Go on with the letter.

6 Do you remember?

Kevin and Kate are talking about last year, when they were 'new' in York.

Put in the verbs.

to arrive, to kick, to want (2×), to go (2×), to push, to listen, to rain, to be (3×), to climb, to open, to play, to laugh, to stay, to have (2×), to happen

Kate: Do you remember that first afternoon upstairs in Barbara's house? I … through that small window in the door, and … up to the attic!
Kevin: And then, when you … to get out, we … the door the wrong way.
Kate: Yes! Then I … so angry, I … the door, and it …!
Kevin: And do you remember what … when Mr Klein and Elke …, and we … all up in the attic?
Kate: Poor Mr Klein! But he … about it later.

Kevin: What about the day when we … to Whitby? We … a good time on the steam train, but it … cold on the beach! And then it … .
Kate: Timmy … to come with us. Do you remember? But then he … a cold, so he … at home after all.
Kevin: And the BBC … a record for him, and he … to it on Ronny's radio!

B Together again

The holidays are over, and the children are back at school again. Kevin and his friends are in 2B now. They are talking about their holidays.

Kevin: What did you do in the holidays, Christine?
Christine: We toured the Lake District on our bikes.
Barbara: What? Did you cycle all the way to the Lake District?
Christine: No, we didn't. We went there by train. But we cycled thirty or forty miles a day. There were lots of hills, so it was hard work. Did you go away, Kevin?

Kevin: Yes, I did. I went to Scotland for two weeks with my sister. We stayed on our uncle's farm near Perth. It rained a lot, but Kate and I learned to ride – that was great! Where did you go, Linda?

Linda: We didn't go away this year, but I didn't mind. We stayed at home and played a lot of tennis and went swimming every day.
Kevin: Hello, Ben. What did you do in the holidays?
Ben: Guess!
Kevin: Did you go to the Lake District, too?

Helen: No, he didn't. He had a caravan holiday in Cornwall. I saw him on the beach at Newquay. He dropped his ice-cream in my beach bag, and then he dropped his lemonade. Typical!
Ben: Oh, be quiet, Helen!

Barbara: Well, we went to Hampshire. We had a fantastic adventure at Carisbrooke Castle! When we –
Ben: Carisbrooke Castle? Where's that?
Barbara: On the Isle of Wight. It's a big old castle. A very strange thing happened to us there. When we –
Linda: There's the bell!
Barbara: Oh no! Well, it really was strange –
Ben: Mr Edwards is coming! Tell us about it at break, Barbara.

1 Answer the questions

Examples: 1. **Did** Kevin **go** away on holiday? – Yes, he **did**.
2. **Did** Christine **go** to Cornwall in the holidays?
– No, she **didn't**. She **went** to the Lake District.

3. Did Christine go to the Lake District by car?
4. Did Kevin go to Scotland?
5. Did he and Kate stay at a hotel?
6. Did they learn to swim in Scotland?
7. Did Linda go away?
8. Did she play a lot of football in the holidays?
9. Did Helen see Ben on the beach at Whitby?
10. Did Ben stay on a farm in Cornwall?
11. Did Barbara stay at home in the holidays?
12. Did she have an adventure on the beach?

2 What do you do in your free time?

1. Do you play football?
   Did you play football last week?
2. Do you sometimes visit your friends at the weekend?
   … you visit a friend last weekend?
3. … you often go swimming in the summer?
   … you go swimming yesterday?
4. … usually stay at home in the holidays?
   … stay at home last holidays?
5. … watch TV every day?
   … watch TV yesterday evening?

Yes, I do.
No, I don't. I …

Yes, I did.
No, I didn't. I …

3 Lovely weather for ducks!

Last weekend Linda went to the Lake District. She stayed at her aunt's and uncle's house. She went there by train on Friday afternoon and arrived in the evening. It started to rain immediately and didn't stop until Sunday afternoon. On Saturday they all went to Borrowdale and looked at Great Gable from the car. Then they went home and watched TV. Ugh! Football. On Sunday they toured the lakes – in the car. Linda went home on Sunday afternoon. She arrived back in York at 7 o'clock.

At school on Monday morning, Christine asks Linda about her weekend.
Christine wants to know

1. … where she went.
2. … where she stayed.
3. … if she went there by train.
4. … when she arrived.
5. … if it rained at all.
6. … where she went on Saturday.
7. … what they did after that.
8. … what they did on Sunday.
9. … when she went home again.
10. … what time she arrived back in York.

Ask Christine's questions and give Linda's answers.

4 Role Play What about your holidays?

C Did you know ...?

This is Ben Nevis, the highest mountain in Britain. It is 1343 metres high.

Karen Stevenson is the fastest baked bean eater in Britain. She can eat 2780 cold baked beans with a cocktail stick in 29 minutes and 59 seconds.

The biggest city in Britain is, of course, London. Over six and a half million people live there.

These are Shetland ponies. They are the smallest ponies in Britain.

The longest bridge in Britain is the Humber Bridge.

This is Luke McMasters, the heaviest man in Britain. He weighs 250 kilos.

More about Britain

- The Humber Bridge is 1410 metres long. No other bridge in the world is longer.
- 500,000 people live in Leeds. So London is much bigger than Leeds.
  100,000 people live in York. So York is smaller than Leeds, and much smaller than London.
- Great Gable, in the Lake District, is 899 metres high.
  Ben Nevis, in Scotland, is higher than Great Gable.

1 The longest river in the world

2 Clothes at a jumble sale

old / new short / long dirty / clean small / big

Look at all the clothes at this jumble sale.

Example: The brown cardigan is very old.
The green cardigan is newer than the brown cardigan.
But the red cardigan is the newest of the three.

Or you can say: The red cardigan is new ... *Go on.*

3 A rhyme: Seven questions

What's faster than the fastest car – much faster than a train?
What's bigger than the biggest lakes and rivers full of rain?

What's warmer in July, but colder in December?
What looks greenest in sweet May, but browner in September?

What's good to learn to ride on, but smaller than a horse?
What's the happiest day in all the year? – but just for *you*, of course!

What's older than a baby, but younger than a man?
Can you answer all these questions? Yes, I'm sure you can!

D The dark tower

"I was here with my parents two years ago," said Nick, when he, Barbara and Elke arrived at Carisbrooke Castle. "The castle's very interesting. The oldest parts are more than eight hundred years old, I think. I hope you aren't afraid of ghosts, Barbara."
"Of course not!" Barbara laughed. "Why?"
"Well, Charles the First was a prisoner here for a year before his execution. And people say his ghost still walks ..." "Don't listen to him!" said Elke.
They went through the entrance, and climbed up to the top of the castle wall. It was possible to walk all the way round. When they came down again, it started to rain.

"Let's go into the museum here until it stops," said Elke.
But Nick wanted to show Barbara the towers at the entrance.

So the two cousins rushed through the heavy rain and into the old building with its two towers. The windows inside were only very small, but there were lights here and there. It was very quiet.
They climbed up the stairs.

"Is there nobody else here?" whispered Barbara.
"A ghost or two perhaps," answered Nick.
"Oh, be quiet, Nick!" said Barbara.
They opened a door and went into a room. There were swords and old pictures on the stone walls. Suddenly there was a noise outside. Thunder! "I don't like it here!" said Barbara. "Let's go to the museum. I'm sure it's nicer there. We're so alone here."
At that moment the lights went out and it was suddenly much darker in the tower.
Barbara said nothing. She was afraid, but she did not want to show it. She pulled Nick towards the door.

They looked for the way back to the stairs, but suddenly there was another noise. It was not thunder this time. It did not come from outside.
"What was that?" whispered Nick, and looked behind him.

Barbara looked back, too. There was another door in the opposite wall. The noise came from there. Was someone behind it? Were they not alone in the tower after all? Barbara looked at the dark picture of Charles the First on the wall … Did his ghost really walk at Carisbrooke Castle? Perhaps in this old tower …?

Down at the bottom of the stairs, a door banged in the wind. Thunder sounded again, and then everything was quiet.

"Let's go," whispered Nick.

Then another noise came from the door in the opposite wall. A key turned and the door opened.

"Look!" Nick whispered. He sounded afraid. "Look at the shadow behind the door!"

Barbara looked. She wanted to speak, but she was too afraid. Through the half-open door she saw a strange black shadow on the grey stone wall behind. It looked like a giant's head.

The next moment a dark figure with an old lamp came through the door into the room and immediately turned towards the wall. Barbara closed her eyes, she was so afraid. She touched Nick's hand. How cold it was!

And then suddenly – the tower was full of light. A man was there. He was in front of a grey box on the wall. It was a fuse-box. He closed the fuse-box and looked at the two cousins. "Better with a bit of light in here, isn't it?"

The castle**'s** very old.
The castle **is** very old.

1 Comprehension

1. What did Nick say to Barbara about Carisbrooke Castle?
2. What was it like in the old building with the towers at the entrance?
3. Why did Barbara say, "I don't like it here"?
4. Why did Nick suddenly look behind him?
5. Why was Barbara afraid?
6. What did she and Nick see when the door opened?
7. Was Nick afraid in the tower? How do you know?
8. Were the two cousins surprised at the end? Why?

2 Linda's holiday plans

Linda wanted to do a lot of things in the holidays. Here is a list of her plans.
But she did not have time to do everything. *Say what Linda did, and what she did not do.*

1. Play tennis with Sue. ✓
2. Go to London for the day with Mum.
3. Visit Aunt Jane in her new house. ✓
4. Look after Ken's dog for two weeks. ✓
5. Repair my old teddy.
6. Answer Helen's letter. ✓
7. Look at my German words again.
8. Clean my bike. ✓
9. Help Mum with the shopping. ✓
10. Cycle to the sea with Sue and Penny.

3 At the Old Bell Hotel

Mr and Mrs Brown were on holiday with their three children, Wendy, Ann and Tony.
On the first day they arrived at the Old Bell Hotel ... *Go on with the story.*

Use these verbs to help you: to carry, to go, to say 'hello', to show, to say, to ask, to answer, to walk, to be ...
What happened at the end? Say what you think.

4 Last week at Newquay

When Ben and his family arrived at Newquay, Ben talked to another boy at the caravan-site.
Ask Ben's questions.

Ben: What ... ?
Alec: My name's Alec Jones.
Ben: When ... ?
Alec: We arrived here last week.
Ben: Did ... ?
Alec: No, we didn't! We had terrible weather here last week!
Ben: What ... ?
Alec: Well, we played cards a lot in the caravan. Then we went out in the car.
Ben: When ... ?
Alec: Oh, it started to get better the day before yesterday. We went for a fantastic walk that day.
Ben: Where ... ?
Alec: Look, I've got a map here. I can show you where we went.
Ben: And what ... ?
Alec: Yesterday? We stayed on the beach.
Ben: Were ... ?
Alec: Oh yes, there were hundreds of people on the beach.

5 Questions with 'do' and 'does'

The boys and girls in Kevin's class are answering a questionnaire about holidays. Here are some answers.

What do you do in the holidays? Name: Ben MacDonald

Do you	often	sometimes	never
go swimming?	X		
play football?	X		
play tennis?			X
read books?			X
ride your bike?		X	
go for walks?		X	
watch TV ?	X		

Name: Linda White

often	sometimes	never
	X	
		X
X		
X		
		X
X		
	X	

Name: David Fletcher

often	sometimes	never
		X
	X	
		X
	X	
X		
	X	
	X	

a) *First talk about what Ben does. Make a dialogue.*

Example: Does Ben go swimming in the summer holidays? – Yes, he does. He often goes swimming.

b) *Make your own questionnaire.*
Then ask your friends the questions, and answer __*their*__ *questions.*

6 Barbara's family in England

Grandparents:
grandfather (grandpa)
grandmother (grandma)
husband - wife
son - daughter
nephew - niece

1. What relation are William and Ann Smith to Barbara?
2. How many aunts and uncles has Barbara got?
   What are their names?
3. Who are Elke's cousins?
4. How many grandchildren have William and Ann Smith got?
5. What relation is Mary Klein to Nick?
6. Who are Mrs Klein's nephews? Has she got any nieces?
7. What relation is Charles Smith to Elke?
8. Who are Betty Smith's nieces?

William Smith says:
'Brothers and sisters
I have none,
But this man's father
is my father's son.'

Who is it?

7 The right word

Can you find the missing adjectives? Sometimes there is more than one right answer.

1. We can't play outside, because the weather's …
2. Don't play football in the street; it's too …
3. It was … in the old tower, because the lights weren't on.
4. I like museums. I find them very …
5. No two people are the same. We're all …
6. You're making too much noise. Please be …
7. When Ronny's …, he often shouts at Timmy.
8. You can do this exercise. It isn't …

8 Look, listen and say

[t]	lik**ed**, fetch**ed**, rush**ed**
[d]	listen**ed**, clos**ed**, climb**ed**
[ɪd]	visit**ed**, collect**ed**

He open**ed** the door‿and walk**ed** in.
It start**ed** to rain when we arriv**ed** at Newquay.
We push**ed** and pull**ed**, but nothing happen**ed**.
I want**ed** to visit Mike, so I fetch**ed** my bike.
Timmy's voice sound**ed** funny, and we all laugh**ed**.

⟨9 A game: When I went on holiday⟩

Do you know this game? It is not difficult if you find it easy to remember things! Everybody in the class takes turns. *Here is an example:*

Kevin: When I went on holiday, I packed a shirt.
Barbara: When I went on holiday, I packed a shirt and a hat.
Christine: When I went on holiday, I packed a shirt, a hat and a pound of sausages.
Ben: When I went on holiday, I packed a shirt, a hat, a pound of sausages and …

⟨10 Let's sing a song: The Grand Old Duke of York⟩

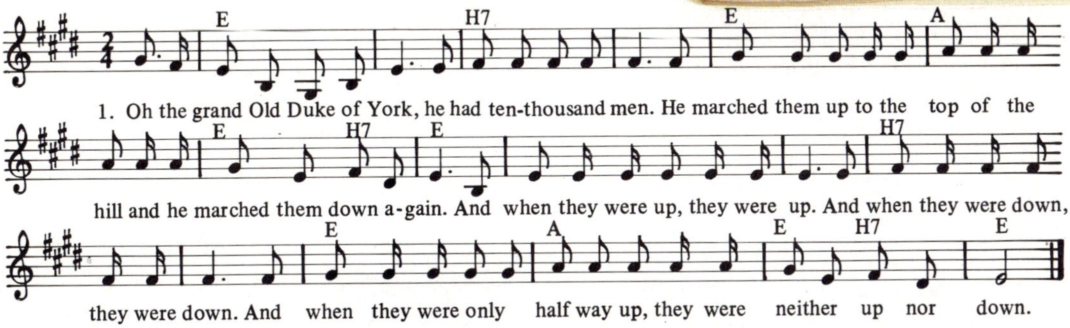

2. … They beat their drums … 3. … They played their pipes …

Unit 2

A Welcome to Nottingham

This is Broad Mar
the most modern
shopping centre ir
Nottingham.

The knitwear industry is one of Nottingham's most important industries.

The Robin Hood statue, near Nottingham Castle. Robin Hood is the most famous folk hero in Britain. His cruellest and most dangerous enemy was the Sheriff of Nottingham.

Nottingham is famous for its bicycles. These people work at a big bicycle factory in Nottingham.

Goose Fair, perhaps
thousand years old,
the largest three-day
fair in Britain. For
many Nottingham
children, these three days in Octobe
are the most exciting days in the yea

Nottingham is a modern industrial city, but it is a very old city, too. It was an important town in Robin Hood's time, but it was very different then.

Of course, Nottingham 800 years ago was not as big as Nottingham today. Now 300,000 people live in Nottingham, but then there were under a thousand.

The people were poorer than Nottingham people today. Their houses were not as clean and their food was not as good as it is today. Only a few people – like the Sheriff – were rich.

In those days nobody in Nottingham was as powerful as the Sheriff. He was certainly a more terrible figure than the Sheriff of Nottingham today!

Nottingham Castle was more important than it is now. Many English kings stayed there, and hunted in Sherwood Forest (it was four times as big as the forest today). But now the castle is a museum, and Sherwood is more famous for its tourists than for its deer.

1 The most famous in Britain

famous forest Britain	modern shopping centre Nottingham	important city Britain	famous building York	interesting museum York

Example: Sherwood Forest is a very famous forest.
It is the most famous forest in Britain.

2 More useful – or not as useful?

a)

Cars A fair Football A factory Old castles English Mount Everest	is are	more	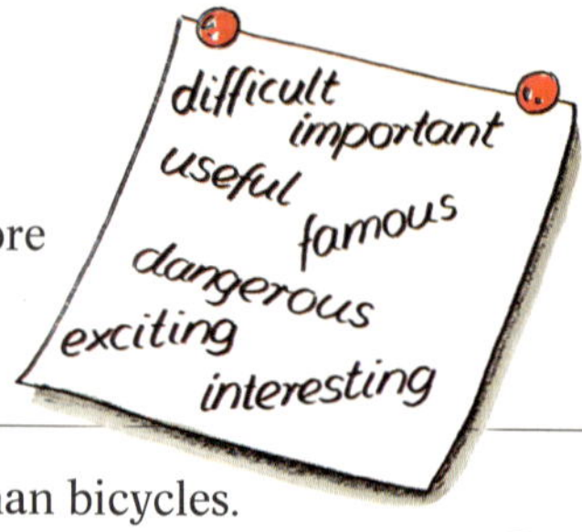	than	bicycles. a museum. tennis. a shopping centre. old houses. German. Ben Nevis.

Examples: Cars are more useful than bicycles.
or: Cars are more dangerous than bicycles.
Go on.

Have you got any more ideas?

b) *What do you think?*
Kevin, Kate and Barbara don't agree.
Kevin: I think football is more exciting than tennis.
Kate: Oh no! Football is not as exciting as tennis.
Barbara: Well, I think tennis is just as exciting as football.

Can you make two or three more dialogues like this?

3 Robin Hood and Nottingham

Examples: 1. The Robin Hood statue is not very **old**. (in Nottingham)
It is not *the oldest statue* in Nottingham.
2. But it is very **famous**. (in the town) But it is *the most famous statue* in the town.

3. Robin Hood is a **famous** folk hero. (in Britain)
4. The Sheriff was his enemy. He was a very **cruel** man. (in Nottingham)
5. He was a **rich** man, too. (in Nottingham)
6. He was very **powerful.** (in the town)
7. His house was **big**. (in Nottingham)
8. In those days the Castle was a very **important** building. (in the town)
9. It was a very **strong** castle. (in Northern England)
10. But after Charles the First's execution, his enemies pulled the castle down. The new castle is not an **interesting** building. (in Nottingham today)

4 Animals

Talk about these animals.
Examples: Deer are not as clever as dogs. Cats can be just as clever as dogs.

You can talk about your pets, too: Our rabbit is just as clever as the neighbours' cat.

B Robin Hood

Erroll Flynn as Robin Hood

The Major Oak in Sherwood Forest

Who was Robin Hood? History books do not really tell us anything about him. But British boys and girls all know something about him. They know him from books, songs, films and TV. For them, Robin Hood was someone in Sherwood Forest, with an enemy called the Sheriff of Nottingham.

But was there ever anybody called Robin Hood in Sherwood Forest? Do we really know anything about him? There are many old stories about Robin Hood. But in some stories he lived 800 years ago; in others he lived much later. Is there any truth in these stories? One thing is certain: the hero in all the stories was an outlaw. There were a lot of outlaws in those days. Why was that?

It all really started in 1066, when William of Normandy conquered Saxon England. The new Norman king and his men began to take everything from the Saxons – their land and their goods. All the forests now belonged to the King, so the Saxons did not have the right to hunt any deer in them. But the forest deer were the main food for many English people. So now they were often hungry. A hundred years later, the Saxons still hated the Normans. When the King wanted money, Norman sheriffs collected it for him from Saxon people. Some Saxons could not pay, so the sheriffs took their homes and goods, and made them outlaws.

Some of the old stories say Robin Hood lived at this time. They say he came from a Saxon family. When the cruel Sheriff of Nottingham took his house and land, he and his men became outlaws, and lived somewhere in Sherwood Forest. They robbed rich people and used their money to help the poor people of England.

1 Say why

Can you go on?

1. British boys and girls can tell you something about Robin Hood because …
2. We cannot be really sure if he ever lived – or when he lived – because …
3. In 1066 the Normans conquered Saxon England. The Saxon people did not like them because …
4. After that the Saxons did not have the right to hunt deer in the forests. This was cruel because …
5. Norman sheriffs collected money from the Saxons because …
6. Many people became outlaws because …
7. Some of the old stories say Robin Hood robbed the rich. He did this because …

2 The Normans in Saxon England

1066: William of Normandy conquers England and becomes King.
Nearly all English people live in or near small villages, and towns are still small. About 20,000 people live in London, the most important town. After London, York is one of the three largest towns; over 5,000 people live there.

1067: William makes plans for many castles in England.

1068: Work begins on Nottingham Castle.

Until 1217: All the English forests – like the New Forest and Sherwood – belong to the Norman Kings. Saxon people do not have the right to hunt in them.
The Normans take land and goods from the Saxons, and many Saxons become outlaws. Some go into the forests and live there. Perhaps one of them is Robin Hood.

Now say what happened. Use the past tense.
In 1066 William of Normandy conquered …

3 At the Sherwood Forest Visitors' Centre

Mrs Cook works at the Visitors' Centre in Sherwood Forest. She sells things in the shop there. Today a lot of children are asking for things about Robin Hood.

Philip:
Have you got any books about Robin Hood?
Mrs Cook:
Oh yes, of course. There are some books about Robin Hood over there.
(No, sorry. We don't sell any … about Robin Hood.)

4 At the supermarket

Mrs Bennett has got no time to go shopping today, so she gives Ronny a shopping list and some money, and he goes to the supermarket for her. Timmy goes with him.

Timmy: Do we need any crisps? I like crisps so much!
Ronny: No, Timmy. We don't need any crisps today. But we need some cornflakes. One big packet.

Timmy likes oranges, sweets, ketchup, chocolate and pineapple, too!

Go on with the dialogue.

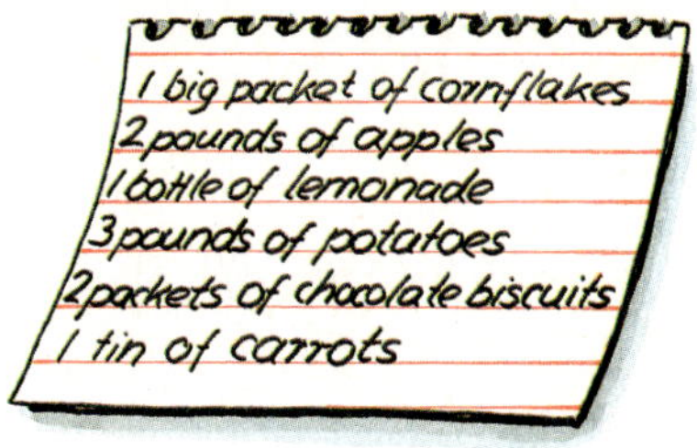

5 On the Nottingham road

a) *'something' or 'anything'?*

Robin Hood: Stop! Give me your purse!
Rich man: There isn't … in it.
Robin Hood: Let me see. Ah! But there is … inside after all. Ten pounds! Have you got … else in that bag there?
Rich man: Only … for my sister. I'm on my way to her house.
Robin Hood: All right. You can ride on.

b) *'someone' or 'anyone'?*

Sheriff: The Nottingham road is dangerous! Yesterday … robbed my neighbour on his way through Sherwood Forest. Does … know who did it?
Friend: Robin Hood, you can be sure! It can't be … else. He lives in Sherwood Forest now with a lot of other outlaws. … told me about them a few days ago.

c) *'somewhere' or 'anywhere'?*

Sheriff: Did you find Robin Hood and his men?
1st man: No, but we know they are … in Sherwood Forest.
Sheriff: Pah! I know that, too. Didn't you see them … near the Nottingham road?
2nd man: No, we didn't see them … at all.
Sheriff: Well, go out and look for them again. They must be …!

6 Tourists in Nottingham

Some tourists are talking together in the Old Market Square.
Complete the sentences with:

someone | anyone | something | anything | somewhere | anywhere

1. "Does … know where the Robin Hood statue is?" "Yes, it's … near the Castle."
2. "I want to have … to eat. Is there a nice restaurant … near here?"
3. "I can't find Robin Hood Street … on this map." "Well, let's ask … where it is."
4. "Can … tell me if there's a bus to Goose Fair?" "Sorry, I don't know … about the Nottingham buses. Ask … at that bus stop."
5. "I want to buy … to take back to my parents." "Try the Broad Marsh shopping centre. It's … between here and the station."
6. "Can you tell me … about Nottingham Castle? Do you know how old it is?" "Sorry, I can't tell you … about it. Ask at the Information Centre. It's … near here."

C Robin Hood and the black cloak

1. One day the Sheriff's men caught Will Scarlet, an outlaw in Robin Hood's band. They took him to Nottingham and brought him to the Sheriff. The Sheriff looked at the prisoner. "Take him to the gallows in the market square tomorrow!" he said to his men. "Let people see what happens to Robin Hood's men!"

Later that day, a poor farmer brought the news to Sherwood. Robin Hood's men wanted to go to Nottingham at once and rescue Will. But Robin said: "Wait! Will is a prisoner in Nottingham Castle. We can't get in there, the castle's too strong. We must think of something else."

2. Robin soon thought of a plan. Early the next morning, he started towards Nottingham. With him were his youngest and strongest men. They all wore long coats over their green clothes. And under their coats they carried swords or bows and arrows.

On the Nottingham road, they saw an old man in a dirty black cloak. Robin stopped him. "I see you come from Nottingham," he said. "Any news of Will Scarlet's execution? Do you know when it is?" "At twelve today," said the old man. "But Scarlet's not the only prisoner. The other is my nephew, John. He hunted deer in the forest once too often. They caught him again yesterday – for the third time. That means the gallows. He's got six children, too." "Wait," said Robin. "Could you sell me your cloak?" "This dirty old thing? You can have it for a pound!" "Thanks," said Robin. He put on the cloak and took out ten pounds. "For you and your family. Take it." The old man was so surprised that he could hardly speak. "God bless you!" he called at last, but Robin was already on his way down the Nottingham road.

3. At twelve o'clock the market square was full of people. Two men with ropes round their hands stood under the gallows. The Sheriff was there with twenty men. Only the hangman was missing.

"Well, where's the hangman?" the Sheriff asked his men.
"Nobody knows," said one.
"We can't find him anywhere," said another.
The Sheriff was angry now. He turned to the crowd.
"We need a hangman!" he shouted. "Well? Doesn't anybody here want to do the job? For five pounds? – For ten pounds?"
Nobody answered. Then an old man in a black cloak came forward. "I can do the job all right," he said.
At once there were angry shouts from the crowd. People picked up stones and began to throw them at the old man.
A woman took an egg out of her basket and threw it.
"Get on with the job!" cried the Sheriff, and gave the old man the money.

4. The old man did something to the ropes round the two prisoners' hands.
"Hurry up, man!" shouted the Sheriff. "What are you doing?"
"Tightening the ropes, Sheriff!"
But suddenly the old man threw off his cloak and stood there in his green clothes, bow in hand. The two prisoners threw their ropes down and ran into the crowd. "It's Robin Hood!" cried someone. At the same moment Robin's outlaws in the crowd took off their coats and ran to help him – some with swords, others with bows and arrows.

5. "Stop them! Kill them!" shouted the Sheriff, and his men ran forward.
The outlaws were not afraid, but the Sheriff had more men.
Suddenly Robin shot an arrow from his bow. It flew through the air and into the Sheriff's hat.
"Keep your men back, Sheriff!" cried Robin.
This was enough for the Sheriff.
A moment later he and his men were gone. Then Robin threw the ten pounds from his purse into the crowd. "A present from the Sheriff!" he cried.
The next moment Robin and his men were on their way back to the shadows of Sherwood Forest.

1 Comprehension *Answer the questions.*

1. Who was Will Scarlet? What happened to him one day?
2. How did Robin Hood hear the news?
3. Why didn't he and his men go to Nottingham at once?
4. Why did Robin stop the old man in the black cloak?
5. Why did Robin give him ten pounds?
6. Who was in the market square at twelve o'clock?
7. Why was the Sheriff angry?
8. What happened when the 'old man' came forward?
9. What happened when the 'old man' took off his cloak?
10. Why did the Sheriff suddenly leave the market square?
11. Where did the ten pounds in Robin Hood's purse come from?
12. What did he do with the money?
13. Why didn't anybody want to be the hangman?
14. Why did the Saxon people like Robin Hood so much?

2 John's story

That evening the old man's nephew, John, told the other outlaws about his adventures. "Yesterday I said goodbye to ..." *Can you go on?*

3 Let's compare things

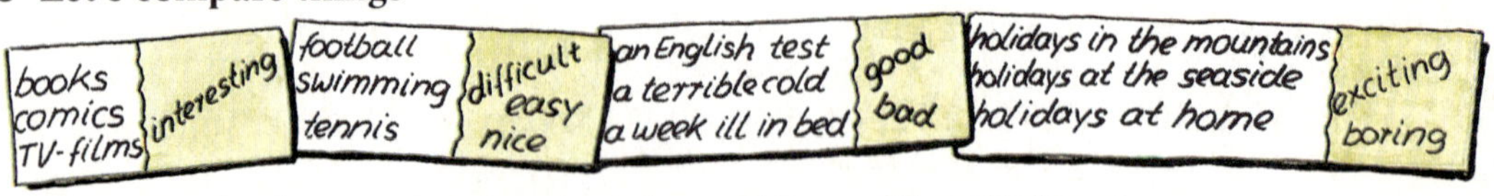

Barbara likes books. But Kate loves comics, and Ronny likes TV films best.

Barbara: I think books are better/more interesting/... than comics.
Kate: Oh no! I don't think so. Books aren't as good/as interesting/... as comics.
Ronny: Well, I like comics **and** books. But I think TV films are the best/the most interesting/... of the three.

What do you think?

good – better – best
bad – worse – worst

4 Saturday afternoon

When Ronny and Kevin go home from school on Friday, they talk about their plans for the weekend. Kevin has an idea. There is a film called 'William of Normandy' on at the Odeon cinema, and he wants to see it on Saturday afternoon.
So Kevin collects Ronny at half past one on Saturday, and the two boys go to the bus stop. They take a bus to the city centre. Then they walk to the cinema. They pay for their tickets and go in. Soon the film begins. It is a very good film. When it is over, they go to a chip shop near the cinema and have some chips and lemonade.
When they are in the chip shop, a man comes in. It is Mr Bennett! He sees the two boys at once. He gives them the money for their chips and lemonade, and takes them home in his taxi. On the way back Mr Bennett asks them about the film. "It sounds very exciting!" he says when he hears all about it. But the story is so exciting that Mr Bennett goes the wrong way and nearly takes the boys to the station!

All this happened last week.

When Ronny and Kevin went home from school last Friday, …
Go on in the past tense.

Be careful with these verbs!

hear	–	heard	[hɜːd]
say	–	said	[sed]
pay	–	paid	[peɪd]

5 Could you help me, please?

a) *Example:* *Barbara:* I can't find my pen. Could you give me a biro?
Elke: All right. But don't forget to give it back.

I can't find my pen.
This history homework is difficult.
I didn't hear what you said.
My pullover's in the kitchen.
It's not very warm in here.
The telephone's ringing.

Could you
fetch it for me?
close the window, please?
answer it, please?
help me, please?
say it again, please?
give me a biro?

Certainly. You're right, it's getting cold.
All right. But don't forget to give it back.
Sorry, I can't find it. It must be somewhere else.
Well, I can try. Let me have a look at it.
All right. But I don't think it's for me.
Why can't you listen? You never hear what I say!

b) *Now make some more dialogues with these ideas.*

1. The baby's crying …
2. There's somebody at the door …
3. The dog wants to go out …
4. There isn't any fruit in the house …
5. My bicycle's still outside, and it's raining …
6. I haven't got any money …

6 Word pairs

a) *Find the pairs. Who can find them all first?*
Example: Sunday afternoon.

1. Sunday	a) story
2. birthday	b) stop
3. exercise	c) case
4. lemonade	d) afternoon
5. ghost	e) salad
6. chocolate	f) party
7. model	g) hero
8. pencil	h) bag
9. plastic	i) plane
10. fruit	j) book
11. bus	k) ice-cream
12. folk	l) bottle

b) *Can you guess?*
Here are some more pairs.
English people often use them.

1. as easy as	a) a bird
2. as white as	b) a hunter
3. as cold as	c) toast
4. as strong as	d) the hills
5. as hungry as	e) A B C
6. as free as	f) a mouse
7. as old as	g) ice
8. as warm as	h) a horse
9. as black as	i) snow
10. as quiet as	j) night

⟨7 Listening comprehension: After a weekend⟩

Answer the questions.

1. Where are Kevin and Barbara?
2. What did Kevin do at the weekend?
3. What do you know about Kevin's relations?
4. Did the Pearsons go to Nottingham by car or by train?
5. Kevin didn't like Nottingham Castle much. Why not?
6. What else did the Pearsons do on Saturday?
7. Where did they go on Sunday?
8. What did they do at the Visitors' Centre?
9. What did Kevin hear about Robin Hood's tree?
10. What does Barbara think about it?
11. Did Kate climb the tree? What happened?

⟨8 Let's sing a song: Simple Simon⟩

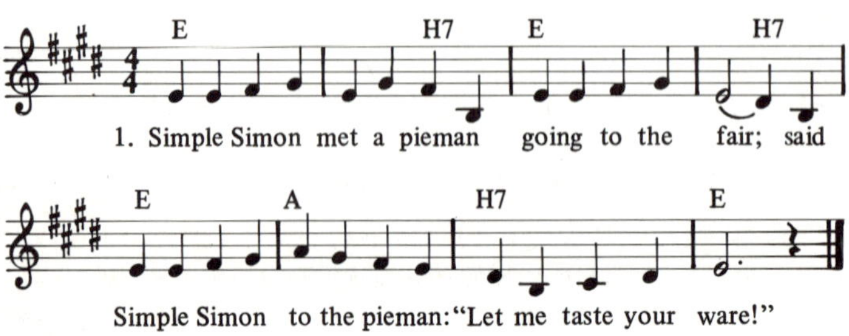

2. Said the pieman unto Simon:
"Show me first your penny."
Said Simple Simon to the pieman:
"Sir, I have not any!"

⟨Authentic Britain: Industry in Nottingham⟩

The knitwear industry in Nottingham

This is a miner in Nottinghamshire.

This man is working in the chemical industry in Nottingham.

Did you know ...?

- The world's largest bicycle factory is in Nottingham. Frank Bowden started it in 1887.
- One quarter of all British clothes come from Nottingham. The clothing industry in Nottingham began in the 13th century!
- 38,000 people live off the coal mining industry in Nottinghamshire.
- The knitwear industry is a very important industry in Nottingham.

William Lee of Calverton, near Nottingham, made his first knitting machine in 1589.

Unit 3

A The check-up

At the doctor's

Outside a hospital

1. One morning Mrs Bennett woke up with a headache and a temperature. She had a pain in her chest, too. She phoned the doctor and made an appointment. "Good morning, Mrs Bennett," the doctor said when Mrs Bennett came into his surgery. "What's the matter then?" "I feel really ill, doctor," said Mrs Bennett. "I've got a terrible headache, and a pain in my chest." The doctor took her temperature and examined her. Mrs Bennett was not very happy when she heard what the doctor said. "Well, I'm going to send you to hospital for a check-up, Mrs Bennett. Just for a few days. Take this prescription to the chemist's and get this medicine – it's for your headache. And then go to bed."

2. When Mrs Bennett got home she went straight to bed. In the afternoon the telephone rang. It was the doctor.

Ronny: That was the doctor, Mum. He says you can go into hospital tomorrow morning.

Mrs Bennett: Oh dear! Who's going to cook the meals?

Ronny: Don't worry, Mum. Dad and I are going to take turns.

Mrs Bennett: That's fine. But who's going to look after Timmy?

Mr Bennett: Mrs Klein can look after him tomorrow afternoon, and on Friday afternoon I'm going to take him to the Pearsons'.
Oh, here he is.

Ronny: Oh, no! He's got his doctor's set.

Timmy: Hello, Mum. This is just a check-up.
Open your mouth, please. I'm going to take your temperature.

1 How do you feel?

Mrs Klein is talking to Mrs Bennett on the telephone. *Give Mrs Bennett's answers.*

1. How do you feel?
2. What's the matter with you?
3. Did you go to the doctor's?
4. What did the doctor do?
5. What's the doctor going to do with you?
6. Did he give you anything for your headache?
7. When can you go into hospital?
8. And what about Timmy?

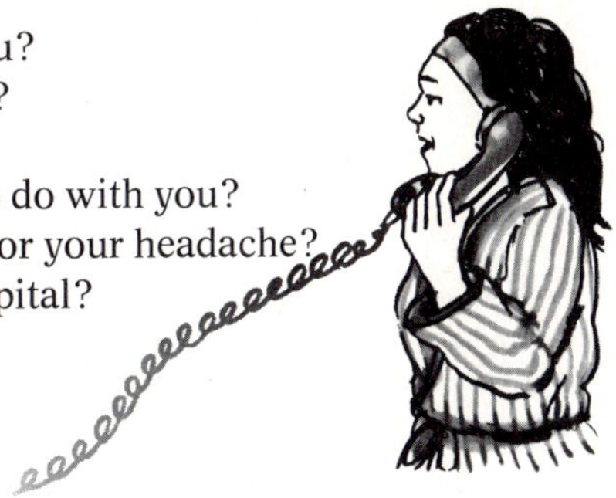

2 Before the check-up

Answer the questions.

1. Is Mrs Bennett going to stay in hospital for a week? – No, she isn't. She's going to …
2. Are the neighbours going to look after Timmy?
3. Why is the doctor going to send Mrs Bennett to hospital?
4. What is Mr Bennett going to do with Timmy on Friday afternoon?
5. When are the doctors at the hospital going to do the check-up?
6. Who is going to cook the meals?
7. Who is going to look after Timmy on Thursday afternoon?

3 Ronny wants to help

"Great!" thinks Ronny. "Mum is going to come out of hospital today! But the doctors say she mustn't do any work for a week. So I'm going to help her in the house."

I'm going to

do
look after
get
answer
go

the telephone.
lots of magazines for her.
all the shopping.
for lots of walks with Timmy.
Timmy in the evenings.

I'm not going to

play
make
have
forget

any noise at home.
Dad. He needs help, too.
football in the house.
any parties.

a) *Example:* "I'm going to do all the shopping." *Go on.*

b) OVER TO YOU The doctor says you mustn't go to school for a week!
Say what you are going to do/are not going to do.

4 What are they going to do?

Example: 1. Helen is going to write a postcard.

Helen–postcard

Kate–apple

Mr Pearson–van

The Bennetts–lunch

Two men–at Brimham

Mr Bennett–passenger to

Timmy–lemonade

Kevin–bath

5 Role Play At the doctor's

Read the dialogue and then act a scene at the doctor's.

Good morning, ... How are you today?
Hello, ... What's the matter?
Hello, ... How can I help you?
...

I don't feel very well, doctor.
I feel terrible.
I feel sick.
I've got a pain in my chest/my stomach/...
I've got a bad headache.
I think I've got a temperature.
...

Let me see what the matter is ....
Let me examine you.
Let me ....

You mustn't go to school today.
You must stay in bed.
You must go to hospital.
You must ....

Is it bad, doctor?
What have I got?
How long must I stay in bed?
...

No, it isn't bad.
You've got ....
Stay in bed for ... days.
...

Here's a prescription. Take it to the chemist's.
Here's some medicine for ...

Thank you, doctor. Goodbye.
Thank you very much. Goodbye.
...

B Keeping a pet

1. David Fletcher and his father are outside a pet shop in York. David is going to buy a dog with his birthday money. His friend Peter Wilson is with him because he has already got a dog – Bonzo.

David: There he is, Dad. In the basket. Do you like him?
Mr Fletcher: Yes, I do. But are you sure you can look after him, David?
David: Yes, of course I can. And Mum says I needn't pay for everything.
Mr Fletcher: No, you needn't. You must feed him. That's your job. But you needn't pay for his biscuits and dog food.
David: What about bones?
Mr Fletcher: Oh, yes – you must buy him a bone every week.
Peter: Big bones are all right, David, but you mustn't give him small bones. They can be dangerous.
David: May he sleep in my room, please, Dad?
Mr Fletcher: No, he may not. We talked about that yesterday. He mustn't go upstairs.
Peter: I can take Bonzo up to my room. He sleeps on my bed.
Mr Fletcher: Sorry, David. Not in our house.
David: Hm ... But ... All right, Dad. Let's go in and buy him.
Mr Fletcher: And then we must go to the post office.
David: The post office? What for?
Peter: The dog licence, of course!

2. Some people don't want a big pet, so they buy a budgie or a hamster.
Here is a leaflet about budgies.

Keeping a budgie

1. Your budgie must have fresh water every day, and fresh bird seed two or three times a week.
2. You must clean the cage and put in fresh sand every week.
3. You needn't wash your bird. He can wash himself, so buy a bird-bath.
4. Your budgie can't fly in his cage. Let him fly round the room. But don't forget to shut all the windows.
5. Be a good friend to your budgie and talk to him a lot.

1 Wrong again, Gordon!

A day later.
Gordon Gossip (Mr Gossip's son) knows all about David's dog.

1. David must pay for all the food for the dog.
2. But David's dad must feed the dog.
3. David needn't buy a bone every week.
4. He mustn't buy big bones. They can be dangerous.
5. The dog can go upstairs and sleep on David's bed.
6. You can get dog licences from a pet shop.

And he knows all about budgies, too.

7. You needn't give a budgie fresh water very often.
8. You needn't clean a budgie's cage.
9. You must wash your bird. He can't do it himself.
10. You needn't talk to your budgie. He can't understand what you say.
11. You may open all the windows when you let your budgie out. Budgies always come back to their cage.

Gordon has got it all wrong, of course. Can you correct him?

2 David's new dog, Nelson

When David got home with Nelson, he still had a lot of questions, so he asked his mum.
Ask David's questions and give his mum's answers.

Can I/we May I/we	take Nelson to the park? give him sweets? wash him every week? take him into York?
Must I/we	leave him here when we go on holiday? play with him outside? take him for a walk every day? make a bed for him? buy him a bone every day?

Yes, you can/may. Yes, you must. Yes, of course. No, you can't/may not. No, you mustn't. No, you needn't. No, of course not.	They're not good for dogs. We can buy a basket for him. In the garden, of course. Not on the road! Only when he gets really dirty. But be careful with him on the way to the park. Walks are good for dogs. You can take dogs to lots of camping-sites. He needn't have a bone every day! Think of all those people and cars there.

3 Ben's broken leg

Yesterday Ben MacDonald was late for school again. He rushed downstairs and …
Today he is in hospital with a broken leg. The doctor is talking to him.

Read the dialogue and put in 'may', 'must', 'needn't', 'mustn't', 'can' or 'can't'

Doctor: Hello, Ben. How are you today?
Ben: Better, thank you, doctor. … I go back to school soon?
Doctor: It's O.K., Ben. You … worry. With a broken leg you … go back to school immediately.
Ben: Oh, good!
Doctor: You … stay here until Friday. Then you … go home. But you … be careful for a few days.
Ben: … I watch TV in the TV room tonight?
Doctor: Well, all right, Ben. You … . But you … stay up too long.
Ben: But the football goes on until 10 o'clock.
Doctor: Football, eh? Well, of course you … miss that. If you … *play* football, then you … *watch* it. Have fun!

4 

The excursion to Brimham Rocks

Put in the missing words: on (2x), in, to (2x), from (2x), at (3x), for (2x), of, after, down (2x).

1. Last year there was an excursion … Brimham Rocks … July 18th for everybody … Kevin's class.
2. Brimham Rocks are … the moors, about thirty miles … York. Some of the rocks look funny.
3. The coach collected the children … the school and got … Brimham … half past ten.
4. First they all went … a long walk and looked … a lot of interesting rocks.
5. Then they sat … on the grass and had a picnic. "You can play … an hour now," said Mrs Griffin … the picnic.
6. An hour later David was … the top … Big Bear Rock and he couldn't get … !

⟨5 Just for fun⟩

McTavish put an advertisement in the newspaper: "Lost. Lucky, a small black dog. £10 for the finder." But nobody found McTavish's dog. So he went back to the newspaper office. He wanted to change the £10 to £15.
There was only a boy there.
"Where is Mr McGregor, the manager?" he asked.
"He's out."
"What about the assistant manager?"
"He's out, too."
"Well, where are they all?" he asked.
"Looking for your dog."

"You see? He's a different dog when he smiles."

C Kate's story

Kate wrote this story for her school magazine. Everyone said it was the best story in the magazine.

Tracy by Kate Pearson

1. At Mr Smith's farm in Fulford there was a new pony. At weekends I often cycled to the farm and helped with the hens and ducks. But the nicest animal there was Tracy, the pony. She always came over and said hello when I went near her field.

One day last summer I asked Mr Smith, "May I look after Tracy for you? I mean, brush her and feed her at weekends?" Mr Smith thought about it and then said, "I know what. We can take Tracy to my field near the school. Then you can see her every day. And you can give the other children rides on Saturdays." "Oh, thank you, Mr Smith," I shouted. "That's a fantastic idea."

2. The next Saturday I was with Tracy all day. I brushed her, talked to her and rode her, too. It was great. In the afternoon a lot of my friends came, and I gave them rides. Soon all the children at our school knew Tracy. They often brought food for her. Some brought apples, but most of them gave her bread, biscuits or even sandwiches. Tracy became very fat. I got angry with my friends. I told them, "You mustn't give her bread and biscuits. They're not good for her." After about six weeks Tracy was so fat that she didn't want to walk round the field any more. So there were no more rides. "What are we going to do?" I asked Mr Smith. "They mustn't feed her so much," he said. "We must put up a notice." So we put up a notice in Tracy's field. It said

PLEASE DO NOT FEED THE PONY!

But it didn't help.

3. One Saturday morning I got a shock. When I got to Tracy's field, she didn't come over to me. I called her, but she still didn't come. I ran over to her. She was in great pain and couldn't walk. I examined her legs. Nothing was broken, but her hooves were very warm. I was worried, so I ran to a telephone box and phoned Mr Smith. He was out. I tried the vet, but he was out, too! I told the vet's wife all about Tracy, and she said, "Don't worry. My husband is going to ring me in half an hour. I can send him straight to the field. Can you stay with Tracy until he comes?" "Oh yes," I said – and thought, "But how can I help her?" Then I remembered something …

4. Five minutes later I was in the school building. I found a bucket and four old pieces of cloth. I filled the bucket with cold water and hurried back to Tracy. She was still in the same place. I put the wet pieces of cloth on her hooves. The water was very cold, but she liked it. At 12 o'clock the vet arrived. He examined Tracy, and I told him why she was so fat. "Yes," he said, "it must be all those sandwiches. They're not good for ponies. Her hooves are badly swollen. That's why she can't walk." "What can we do for her?" I asked. "I'm going to give her an injection," the vet said. "Keep her hooves cold and wet. We needn't do anything else, thanks to you. That was a very clever idea with the cold water!" "Oh, thank you," I said. I was very happy. Of course, I didn't tell him where I got the idea from. It was in my book about ponies!

1 All about the story

1. Where was Mr Smith's farm?
2. What did Kate often do at the farm?
3. Which animal did she like best?
4. What did Kate want to do for Tracy?
5. Where was Tracy's new home?

Go on. Can you think of more questions about the story? Work in pairs.

2 Keeping a pet

On page 35 there was a leaflet about budgies. *Now work in groups and write another leaflet about dogs, hamsters or ponies. Say what you 'may', 'must', 'needn't', 'mustn't' do. Here are some ideas to help you.*

two meals every day
big bones
ill – vet
wash
brush every day
box or basket
car – window open
not in car on hot day

in a cage
not in a cold room – in a warm room
a piece of carrot or apple
fresh water every day
sand on the floor
clean paper in the cage
clean the cage every week
one hamster in the cage, not two or more together

enough room to run
apples
not bread or biscuits
talk to the pony
brush every week
ill – phone the vet

3 The camping-site leaflet

Nelson had a great time with this leaflet! Now David is putting the pieces together again. *Can you help him?*

Come to Lakeside Camping-site!
Have a lovely holiday in the Lake Distr ict.

You can •••
keep the campin g-site clean.
cook any meals We've got a good restaurant.
worry about the weather – there' s a games building.

You needn't •••
watch your dog. There's a farm near here.
stay in a tent or a caravan.

But remember :
You must ••
make too much noise at night.

You mustn't •
swim in the lake. It isn't too cold!
climb Great Gable. It isn't far from here
look after your child ren. We've got a children's playground.

4 Signs

Timmy doesn't understand these signs, so Ronny must tell him what they mean.

Go on. Use 'can', 'may' or 'mustn't'.

5 Words, words, words

Do you know what these words mean?
Talk about them.
Example: 1. When people are very ill, they go into *hospital*.
2. You can keep ...

1. hospital
2. cage
3. telephone box
4. vet
5. temperature
6. appointment
7. pet shop
8. shopping centre

6 The right medicine

Look at the pictures and tell the story of Ronny's German test. You can start like this:

One morning Ronny woke up early. ...

1. wake up – remember – idea
2. headache – take Ronny's temperature
3. in the kitchen – make tea – put some medicine in it
4. into Ronny's bedroom – take this medicine – every hour
5. drink – terrible
6. an hour later – come in again
7. give – another glass – jump – out of bed
8. run to school – get to school at ...

7 Look, listen and say

[w]	[v]	[f]
whisper	heavy	fat
wonderful	arrive	fantastic
worried	hooves	after‿all

That was a very clever‿idea.
The weather was nice. We had a wonderful time.
The friends visited the castle and had a fantastic adventure.
A budgie must have fresh water‿every day.

⟨8 Let's sing a song: The three crows⟩

2. The first crow was really very small,
Really very small,
Really very small,
The first crow was really very small
On a cold and frosty morning.

3. The second crow wasn't very tall . . .
4. The third crow couldn't sing at all . . .
5. The three crows, they fell off the wall . . .

⟨9 Riding a pony: The correct take-off⟩

take-off too early

take-off too late

take-off just right

⟨Authentic Britain: How to look after your cat⟩

Don't tie ribbons round her neck.

See that your cat can get some grass, it's her natural medicine.

She likes a clean plate and clean water; give her regular meals and no rabbit bones, chicken bones or fish bones.

Don't leave her out all night.

Give her a comfortable bed, for herself and her kittens.

Brush her often and dry her if she gets very wet.

ISSUED BY
RSPCA
WE RECEIVE NO STATE AID
Education Department, Causeway, Horsham, Sussex.

⟨Merry Christmas⟩

1 Christmas shopping

2 Christmas in Britain

Christmas Eve
1. The children go to bed and hang a stocking or two at the end of their beds.

2. In the night Father Christmas climbs down the chimney and fills the stockings with small presents.

Christmas Day
3. In the morning the children open their stockings. Then they go downstairs and open the bigger presents under the Christmas tree.

4. For Christmas dinner there is usually a turkey with roast potatoes. After that there is plum pudding. Sometimes there are coins in it, so you must be careful.

3 We wish you a Merry Christmas

1. We wish you a Merry Christmas *(3 times)*
   And a Happy New Year.

Chorus:
Good tidings we bring
To you and your kin,
We wish you a Merry Christmas
And a Happy New Year.

2. Now bring us some figgy pudding *(3 times)*
   And bring some out here.

Chorus:

3. We won't go until we've got some *(3 times)*
   So bring some out here.

Chorus

4 Making Christmas cards

People in Britain and America send lots of Christmas cards. Cards from a shop are expensive, but it is easy to make cards. *What you need:*

What you must do:
Fold a card in the middle. Draw a Christmas picture on it. If you want to, you can cut out the picture. Then decorate it with glitter.

What you can write inside the card:

5 The Bells

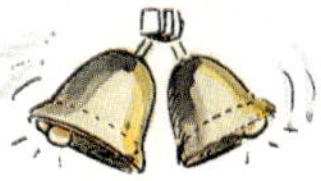

This happened a long time ago, some people say; others say that it didn't happen at all. What do you think?

It was Christmas again, and the townspeople were on their way to the church. It was a beautiful building. The only thing that was more beautiful, everybody said, was the sound of its bells. Only they never rang now. "But a long time ago they did," the old people said. "Our grandparents told us. And they will ring again when someone gives Jesus the right present for his birthday." That was why everyone was excited. Perhaps this year … "Yes, this is the year! This time the bells will ring again," many of the important townspeople said. "Our presents this year are more expensive than ever."

"Hurry, Eddy. We're late," Don, already 16, said to his little brother. It was dark and the road was bad. "We must put our present on the altar." They were poor boys, and the three small coins in Don's hand were a lot of money for them. "Yes, Don. Our present to Jesus," the little brother said. And then it happened: Don fell over a stone. "Ouch! My leg!" he cried. "Now I can't walk very fast. Eddy, you must go on alone and put the coins on the altar. Promise." "Yes, Don, I promise," Eddy said and hurried on.

Inside the church, the townspeople – one by one – went to the altar with their expensive presents, and waited … but the bells did not ring.

Eddy was out of breath when he arrived at the church. He hoped he was not too late and ran towards the big door with the three coins in his hand. Suddenly he heard a voice. "Please help us," it cried. Eddy stopped. He turned and saw a woman in rags. She held a small child in her arms. "My child is hungry," she said, "and I've nothing to give him." Eddy looked at the child. Then he thought of his promise. For a moment he did not know what to do. "Here." Eddy gave her the three coins and she thanked him with her eyes. Eddy did not go to the front door then. "I promised, and now Don will be very angry with me," he thought.

Inside the church it was quiet. Then, suddenly, there was a sound. The bells? Yes, they began to ring, and their sound *was* more beautiful than anything in the world. The people looked up. They wanted to see who was in front of the altar, but there was no one. They only saw a small boy, as he hurried in through the side door.

Unit 4

⟨Photo page: Bicycles and cars⟩

Outside a cycle shop

A cycle test at a school in York

Checking the oil and the water

A A morning's work

1. It is Saturday morning and the Bennetts are working on Mrs Bennett's taxi. There are a lot of things to do. Ronny has got a check-list.

Mrs Bennett is changing the plugs.

Mr Bennett is cleaning the inside.

Ronny is fetching a bucket of water because they are going to wash the car, too.

What about Timmy? He is climbing Mount Everest. So all the Bennetts are busy.

2. *Half an hour later.*

Mrs Bennett has changed the plugs.
The engine sounds much better now.

Mr Bennett has cleaned the inside.
It looks new again.

Ronny has fetched the bucket of water and they have washed the car. It is clean now.

Timmy has climbed Mount Everest.
The air is very thin up there.

3. Ronny looks at his check-list.

Ronny: Let's see if we've finished the job.
Have you checked the oil and the tyres, Mum?
Mrs Bennett: Yes, I have. They're O.K.
Ronny: What about the ash-trays, Dad? Have you emptied them?
Mr Bennett: I certainly have. I always do that first.
Ronny: Good. You've cleaned the inside, I can see that.
And we've all washed the car. ...
Ah! We haven't polished the chrome yet.
Mr Bennett: Oh no! Let's forget about that. I've done enough for one morning.
Timmy: So have I.

1 What have we done?

Ronny looks at his check-list again. *Who has done what? What does Ronny say?*

I Timmy Mum Dad We	has hasn't have haven't	climbed washed cleaned changed fetched done emptied checked polished	the ash-trays. a bucket of water. the inside of the car. Mount Everest. the oil and the tyres. the chrome. the car. the plugs. enough for one morning.

2 Mrs Bennett's taxi

Put in the verb. Then put the sentences together.

1. Mrs Bennett has … the plugs.
2. Mr Bennett has … the ash-trays.
3. He has … the inside, too.
4. Mrs Bennett has … the oil.
5. Ronny has … some water.
6. They have … the car.
7. Timmy has … Mount Everest.
8. Mrs Bennett has … the tyres, too.
9. They haven't … the chrome.

a) The chrome doesn't matter.
b) There's enough oil in the engine.
c) The air's very thin up there.
d) Now they can wash the car.
e) All four are O.K.
f) It's very clean.
g) They're clean now.
h) The inside looks new again.
i) The engine sounds better now.

3 Helen's birthday party

a) *A week before the party*

1. Has Helen asked everybody yet? – Yes, she has.
2. Have they all answered yet? – No, they haven't.
3. … Ben answered? – …
4. … the party started yet? – …

b) *A week later*

5. … Helen's friends arrived? – …
6. … Helen opened her presents yet? – …
7. … they played any games yet? – …
8. … Helen tried her birthday cake yet? – …

c) *10 o'clock in the evening*

9. … the party ended yet? – …
10. … they finished all the food? – …
11. … Helen and her family washed up? – …

B The Road Safety Officer

Kevin and his friends are excited. Mr Edwards, Kevin's form master, is excited, too. Next Friday afternoon the children in his class are going to take a cycle test. Mr Haig, the Road Safety Officer, has come to the school this afternoon. He wants to tell them about the test.

First they stay in the classroom and he talks to them about the rules of the road. Then they go outside. When the children have collected their bikes, they all go over to a corner of the playground.

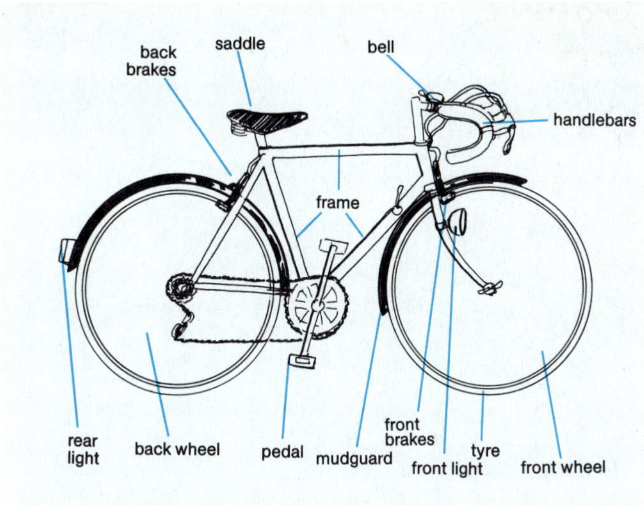

Mr Haig: I see you've all brought your bikes with you.
Mr Edwards: Oh yes. They sometimes forget their homework, but they never forget their bikes.
Mr Haig: Well, before we check the bikes, are there any more questions?
Helen: Where are you going to hold the test?
Mr Haig: Right here. We've marked the lines, so you can all practise.
Barbara: Can we start now? You've shown us what we must practise.
Mr Edwards: Wait a minute, Barbara. We haven't seen your bikes yet.
Mr Haig: That's right. The important things are: Have you tested the brakes and the lights? Have you checked the handlebars and saddle? …
Mr Edwards: And just for Ben: Have you cleaned your bike?
Ben: I'm going to do that tomorrow, sir.
David: There's a big scratch on my saddle. Does that matter?
Mr Haig: Not really. The height of the saddle is more important. But what have you done with your mudguards?
Mr Edwards: Yes. Why have you taken your mudguards off, David?
David: Because … it's faster without them.
Mr Haig: Well, please try to get them on before Friday. This isn't a test for speedway bikes.

1 Comprehension

1. Why are the children in Kevin's class excited?
2. Why has Mr Haig come to the school?
3. What does Mr Haig talk about in the classroom?
4. Where do the children take their bikes?
5. Where is Mr Haig going to hold the test?
6. What must the children check?
7. What is the matter with David's saddle?
8. What has David done with his mudguards? Why?

Helen's pencil case

the boys' bikes

the top of the tower

2 The cycle test

Say what happens.

1. Today is the day		the road.
2. Mr Haig has come from the centre		their saddles.
3. Kevin's classroom is at the back		York.
4. That's where they talk about the rules		the playground.
5. Things like: Don't ride in the middle	of	the school.
6. And: Don't hold on to the back		the cycle test.
7. After that they go to a corner		a bus or a van.
8. Mr Haig checks the height		their bikes.
9. But he doesn't worry about the colour		the road.

3 On holiday

Put the sentences together into one sentence. 'Of-genitive' or 's-genitive'?

Example: The **MacDonalds** are excited. Their **holidays** start today.
The MacDonald**s'** holidays start today.

1. Are the sleeping-bags in the **car**? – Yes, they're in the **back**.
2. Where's **Ben**? His **things** are still upstairs!
3. There's the **caravan site**. Now we must look for the **owner**.
4. Can you see that big **building**? His office is on the **left**.
5. Not that **caravan**, please. I don't like the **colour**.
6. The **Browns** have got a **motor caravan**. It's very nice inside.
7. That **hill** looks very high. Do you know what its **height** is?
8. Our **neighbours** have got a **dog**. It wakes us up every morning.
9. Look at **Mr Brown**! His **deck-chair** has collapsed.
10. Our **holidays** are nearly over. Today's the **last day**.

4 What have they done?

to bring	brought	brought
to come	came	come
to see	saw	seen
to show	showed	shown
to take	took	taken

You can find more irregular verb forms on page 191.

All the children have brought their bikes to school.

David has taken off his mudguards.

a) *Example:* Kevin … his blazer. (to take off)

Kevin has taken off his blazer.

1.  Helen's father … nothing all morning. (to do)
2.  The children … some apples for Tracy. (to bring)
3.  David … a ghost. (to see)
4.  Linda … some nice photos. (to take)
5.  David … Nelson. (to feed)

b) *Now use the list of irregular verbs on page* 191

6.  Kate … a letter to her cousin. (to write)
7.  Christine … a key. (to find)
8.  The Kleins … to the cinema. (to go)
9.  Peter … a present for Bonzo. (to buy)
10.  Ronny and Timmy … a model plane. (to make)

5 Please, sir!

It is Friday afternoon. The children are so excited that they all talk at the same time.
What do they say? Use the present perfect.

Example: Helen: Where's Mr Haig? I … him. (not to see)
Where's Mr Haig? I haven't seen him.

1. *Linda:* Mr Haig … yet. What are we going to do, sir? (not to come)
2. *Kevin:* Has anyone lost a key? I … one. (to find)
3. *Christine:* Look at my bike, sir. I … a new front tyre. (to buy)
4. *David:* I … my mudguards back on, sir. (to put)
5. *Tony:* We … all … our bikes, sir. Aren't you surprised? (to bring)
6. *Barbara:* I … the rules of the road. Who wants to test me? (to learn)
7. *Ben:* Oh dear. I … to clean my bike. Does that matter, sir? (to forget)
8. *Jenny:* I think I … my bicycle-pump. Have you seen it, sir? (to lose)
9. *Ronny:* Perhaps Mr Haig … to the wrong school, sir. (to go)
10. *Mr Edwards:* Help! I need my ear-plugs. Who … them? (to take)

C The stolen bike

1. All the children in Kevin's class passed the cycle test. "Let's have a party," cried Ben. So they all cycled to a chip shop and had a great time there.
It was almost six o'clock when they left. Suddenly David shouted, "Hey, where's my bike? Has anyone taken it?"
"No, I haven't," they all answered.
"I've looked everywhere, but it's not here," he said. "Someone has stolen it. What am I going to do?"
"You must report it to the police," said Barbara. "Let's go together."
At the police station David told the policeman all about his bike.
"People have reported a lot of stolen bikes in the last month," the policeman said, "but we haven't found the thieves yet."

2. The next morning David went round to see Kevin and Kate. "The police haven't got time to look for bikes," David said.
"We want to help you," said Kevin. "Perhaps we can find your bike."
"I know what," said Kate. "We can go out and look for your bike here in Fulford."

Two hours later they met again at Kate's house. "Well, where have you been, Kate?" David asked.
"I've checked all the bikes in the shopping centre," Kate said.
"I've walked up and down at least twenty roads, but I haven't had any luck," said Kevin.
"And I've examined all the bikes in York Road," said David. "My bike is gone, and that's that."

3. One afternoon, at about five o'clock, Kevin was on his way home from the school camera club. Outside the Minster Snack Bar he saw two bikes. One of them was the same size as David's bike. The frame was a different colour and the handlebars were different, but there was something about it! What was it? Yes, it was the saddle. The side of the saddle was scratched, and David's saddle was scratched, too. Was this David's bike? "I can phone the police," Kevin thought. "Or I can go to David's house. Or I can wait here." But just then the door of the snack bar opened and two young men, one of them very small, came out. Kevin could hear the men's voices, but they did not notice him. "O.K. then. Back to work," one of them said. They got on the bikes and rode away.

4. Kevin followed the men on his bike. They rode through the centre of Fulford. Then they turned left and went down a dark street towards the river. They came to some old factory buildings and went into one of them. Kevin was afraid, but he wanted to see what was inside. He went over to a broken window and listened.

"How many bikes have you picked up this week?" a big man asked.

"I've got six, and Jimmy has got five."

"Good," said the big man. "Have you done the job on them yet?"

"Yes, we have," said Jimmy, the small man. "We've painted the frames and changed the handlebars, too."

Kevin knew enough. He rushed to the nearest telephone box. Ten minutes later two police cars arrived. The police arrested the three thieves. They also found parts of stolen bikes and cars and a lot of car radios in the old factory.

David was very happy when he got his bike back from the police. "Thanks again for your help," he said to Kevin. "My bike looks different. ... Not the old scratched saddle, of course. I'm going to keep that for luck!"

1 Comprehension

Only two of these sentences about the story are right. Correct the others.

1. Nobody in Kevin's class passed the cycle test.
2. After the test the children cycled home.
3. They left the chip shop soon after six o'clock.
4. Barbara went to the police station with David.
5. The next morning Kevin and Kate came to David's house.
6. They wanted to report David's stolen bike.
7. Kate looked for David's bike in York Road.
8. One day Kevin was on his way home from the Minster Snack Bar.
9. He saw two bikes. The frame of one of them was scratched.
10. Kevin followed the men to a bicycle factory.
11. Kevin rushed to a telephone box and called the police.
12. David wanted to get a new saddle for luck.

2 Grabbit the bicycle thief

Look at the pictures and say what Grabbit 'has just done' and what he 'hasn't done yet'.
Example: 1. Grabbit has just seen a bike. He hasn't stolen it yet.

1. see/steal
2. steal/get home
3. arrive home/change handlebars
4. change handlebars/paint frame

5. paint frame/test lights
6. check bike/take to shop
7. leave shop/find another bike
8. steal/police: arrest

3 David and Nelson

Example: 1. What does Nelson *want to* do every afternoon? (play with David)
"Nelson wants to play with David every afternoon."

2. What does he *like to* do? (fetch sticks)
3. What does he *try to* do? (catch them in the air)
4. What does he sometimes *start to* do? (run too soon)
5. What has he *learnt to* do? (bring them back to David)
6. What does David always *remember to* do? (feed Nelson)
7. What does he sometimes *forget to* do? (brush him)
8. What does he *want to* do? (teach Nelson some new tricks)

4 Food and drink

a) *You know lots of words for things to eat and drink, so this quiz should be very easy.*

1. Many people eat them for breakfast. They come in a box.
2. You get it from an animal and you can drink it.
3. Two pieces of bread and butter, and something else between them.
4. You can eat it and it's also a colour.
5. You usually have three of them a day – the first is breakfast.
6. People in Britain often eat them with fish.
7. It comes in a lot of different colours. It's good to eat when the weather's hot.
8. It's red and you can put it on chips.
9. People in Britain drink lots of this in the morning, in the afternoon and in the evening.
10. You can get them from the butcher's. They are good for dogs – but not for people!

10–9 Very good   8–7 Good   6–5 Not bad   4–0 Don't you like food?

b) *Now you go on. Can you say what these things are?*
a strawberry; a bar of chocolate; fruit salad; eggs; a picnic.

Example: a strawberry: It's a red fruit, smaller than an apple.

5 Role Play Have you seen it?

Read the dialogues and act one of the scenes.

Have you taken my pencil/biro/exercise book/…?
Do you know where my German book/ my … is?
Hey – my ruler/… is gone! Have you seen it?
…

No, I haven't.
No, I haven't taken your pencil!/ … .
No, I don't know where your … is.
Sorry, I don't know.
No, I haven't seen it.
…

Well – can you help me look for it?
Where can … be?
Where did I put it?
…

Yes, I can. Let's look over here.
Did you put it in …?
Have you looked for it in the hall/…?
Isn't it in your …?
…

O.K., thanks. Let's see now. Ah – here it is!
Hm. Yes, perhaps I put it in … . Thank you.
No, I haven't. That's a good idea.
Yes – it is! Thanks very much.
…

6 Don't forget Looking after your friend's pets

You are looking after a friend's dog and parrot for a few days. Here is your check-list.

1 Play with Rex. ✓
2 Take him for a walk.
3 Open a tin of Doggofood for him.
4 Give him some water.
5 Brush him. ✓
6 Clean Polly's cage. ✓
7 Change her water. ✓
8 Give her fresh bird seed.
9 Talk to her. ✓

a) You have already done some of the things ✓ when your friend rings up.

Friend: Is everything O.K.?
You: Oh yes, everything's fine.
Friend: Have you played with Rex yet?
You: Yes, I have.
Friend: Have you ... yet?
You: No, I haven't. I'm going to do that later.
Friend: Have you ...?
Go on.

b) Can you remember everything without the check-list? *Shut your book and say how you are going to look after Rex and Polly* **tomorrow.** (I'm going to ...)

c) You are looking after a friend's cat/rabbit/pony. *What are you going to do?* OVER TO YOU

⟨7 Listening comprehension: Bikes⟩

a) Ben wants to ask David about two things and tell him about one thing. *Listen to the cassette and find out what they are.*

b) *Now listen to the cassette again and find out*
1. ... what David says when he answers the phone.
2. ... if David has got his bike back from the police station.
3. ... what David's bike looks like.
4. ... what David is going to take to eat.
5. ... when they are going to check their bikes again.
6. ... where they are going to check them.
7. ... what Ben can now do on his bike.
8. ... what David thinks about the English homework.

8 Look, listen and say

[ʃ] **sh**adow, sta**ti**on, Engli**sh**,	The **sh**op-assistant sells **sh**oes in the Engli**sh** **sh**op.
[tʃ] **ch**ildren, ki**tch**en, hopsco**tch**	The **ch**ildren fe**tch**ed **ch**airs from the ki**tch**en.
[dʒ] **G**erman, a**dj**ective, villa**ge**	The **G**ermans had a stran**ge** adven**t**ure in the villa**ge**.
	They bought **ch**ocolate and a **ch**eap lun**ch** down by the bea**ch**.
	She **ch**an**g**ed the **ch**eap **j**eans because they were too **sh**ort.

⟨9 Let's sing a song: Riding in my car⟩

2. Engine goes brrm-brrm, *(three times)* Riding in my car.
3. Horn goes beep-beep, ...
4. Wheels go round-round, ...
5. Brakes go screech-screech, ...
6. Radio blares yeah-yeah, ...
7. Riding in my car, car, ...

'HAVE YOU EVER RIDDEN ON THE PAVEMENT?'
THINK ABOUT THIS....
DBL 123 X
DRIVERS WON'T NOTICE YOU!
....AND THIS....
YOU MAY HURT SOME-BODY!
....AND THIS....
YOU CAN GET INTO TROUBLE!
....CYCLE ON THE ROAD OR CYCLEROUTE
RoSPA©
SEP/S244-1
Published by RoSPA, The Royal Society for the Prevention of Accidents.

Unit 5 A At Fulford School

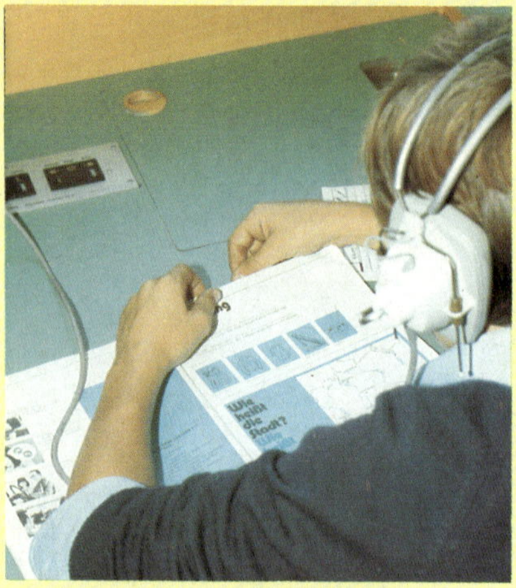

◁ 1. This is Kevin in the language lab.
French is the first foreign language at Fulford, and Kevin has to do more homework for French than for German. That's bad luck, because he likes German better.

2. These boys are playing rugby.
In this game, you are allowed to run with the ball in your hands. At Fulford the boys play rugby and football, and the girls play hockey.

3. All the pupils at Fulford have to learn to cook.
This subject is called Home Economics.
Ronny likes it. Sometimes he is allowed to cook a meal at home, too, but he is glad that he doesn't have to cook every day.

4. Fulford School has got an outdoor swimming-pool. The pupils can only use it in the summer term. If they want to go swimming in the winter, they have to go to the public baths in York.

5. Here is part of another letter from Ronny to his cousin Daniel in London:

-2-

Friday wasn't my day. First Kevin and I made too much noise in the French lesson, so we had to do some extra work in the lunch hour. That meant that I wasn't allowed to go to rugby practice at 12.30. Just my luck! Well, we finished our French in the end, but then afternoon school started. We made chocolate cake in Home Economics, and we were allowed to use the food mixer. Well, I wanted to

-3-

taste the mixture, so I put my finger in. Then some idiot switched the mixer on – and broke my finger!! Mrs Walker sent me to the doctor's. I didn't have to go to hospital. Of course it's my left hand. So I can still do school work. But I can't play the guitar. Typical! Well, at least I can still write to you.

Write back soon!

Ronny

1 Comprehension

Is that right? If not, correct what is wrong.

a) 1. The pupils at Fulford have to learn French as their first foreign language.
2. The girls at Fulford play hockey and rugby, and the boys play football.
3. Ronny often has to cook the meals at home because he is learning to cook at school.
4. The Fulford pupils can't use their swimming-pool in the winter.

b) 5. Ronny wasn't allowed to go to rugby practice on Friday because he had to go to a French lesson.
6. Ronny broke his finger when he switched the food mixer on.
7. He had to see the doctor at the hospital.
8. He can't play the guitar now, but he can still write letters.

2 More about Fulford School

Of course, every school has different rules, but Fulford is typical of most British schools. Pupils at Fulford …

1. … **have to** wear school uniform.
2. … **aren't allowed to** wear jeans at school.
3. … **aren't allowed to** bring radios or cassette-recorders to school.
4. … **can** have lunch at school, or they **can** bring sandwiches.
5. … **are allowed to** go home for lunch (if they live near the school).
6. … **have to** do homework every evening.
7. … **have to** stay at school until four o'clock every day.
8. … **don't have to** go to school on Saturdays.
9. … **have to** learn French as their first foreign language.
10. … **don't have to** buy their school textbooks.
11. … **are allowed to** play with tennis balls in the playground (but **not** with footballs).

And what about you?
Example: It isn't like that at our school. We **don't have to** wear school uniform.
or: It's like that at our school, too.

3 School again

Present	**Past**
You **have to** go.	You **had to** go.
Do you **have to** go?	**Did** you **have to** go?
You **don't have to** go.	You **didn't have to** go.
You **are allowed to** go.	You **were allowed to** go.

a) *Before an excursion*

The pupils in Ronny's class are going to go on an excursion over the moors to Whitby tomorrow. They are asking Mr Edwards some questions about it.

Make dialogues. Can you ask their questions, and give Mr Edwards's answers?

When Where What Why How long How much money	do we have to aren't we allowed to are we allowed to	take swimming things? stay at Whitby? be at school? wait for the coach? take with us? wear?	School uniform, of course. Because the sea is still much too cold! At nine o'clock. Don't be late! Until three o'clock in the afternoon. Don't take too much. A pound is enough. In front of the main building.

b) *When Ronny's grandpa was at school:*

When I was at school, When I was a boy, When I was young like you,	I had to I didn't have to I was allowed to I wasn't allowed to	go to bed as late as you! go to school on Saturday mornings. go swimming in the winter. swim in the river in the summer. learn any German. wear uniform, too. ride my bike in York because there weren't many cars. learn to cook at all!

4 At home

a) What **do you have to** do at home? What **don't you have to** do?
What **are you allowed to** do? What **aren't you allowed to** do?

Examples: "Do you have to go shopping?" "No, I don't usually have to go shopping."
"Are you allowed to stay in bed late on Sundays?" "Yes, I'm always allowed to do that."

go shopping
cook the meals
go to bed early on Saturdays
make the beds

look after your little brother or sister
help at home in the holidays
buy food for your pet

b) OVER TO YOU *And what about your brother/your sister/your best friend?*

B School lunch

FULFORD SCHOOL CAFETERIA	
MENU	
FRIDAY FEBRUARY 25th	
SAUSAGES	50p
FISH FINGERS	50p
IRISH STEW	50p
BEANS ON TOAST	40p
. . .	
VEGETABLES:	
PEAS OR CARROTS	20p
MASHED POTATOES	20p
CHIPS	20p
. . .	
CHOCOLATE PUDDING	20p
VANILLA ICE-CREAM	15p
STRAWBERRY ICE-CREAM	15p
CHEESE AND BISCUITS	15p
. . .	

a) *Outside the school cafeteria*

Helen: What's for lunch today? Sausages! No, I had sausages yesterday. I'm going to have Irish stew, with mashed potatoes and peas.
Christine: Irish stew? Ugh!
Helen: You should try it. It's really good.
Christine: No thanks. Now, let me see. Fish fingers with chips – or beans on toast? Oh dear, I like both of them.
Helen: Well, which are you going to have? I know. Be a devil! Have both.
Christine: Hey, that's an idea.

b) *In the cafeteria*

Helen: Hm. What pudding are we going to have?
Mrs Wood: Well, dears, we've got chocolate pudding and ice-cream today. Which would you like?
Christine: I'd like chocolate pudding, please. That's my favourite pudding. And a big glass of milk, please. I'm thirsty.
Mrs Wood: Here you are. A nice big plate of chocolate pudding! And here's your milk.
Helen: Ice-cream for me, please. And a cup of tea.
Mrs Wood: Which ice-cream, dear? Strawberry or vanilla?
Helen: Oh – vanilla, please.

c) *Twenty minutes later*

Helen: Hey, Chris, what's the matter?
Christine: Nothing really. I just feel so full!
Helen: I'm not surprised. You shouldn't eat so much pudding after beans on toast *and* fish!
Christine: Well, that was your idea!

1 Comprehension

Answer the questions.

1. What is on the menu for Friday, February 25th?
2. Why doesn't Helen want sausages?
3. Does Christine like Irish stew?
4. What does she like?
5. Which of these things does she choose? Why?
6. What else do the two girls have?
7. What is the matter with Christine after lunch?
8. Whose fault is it?

2 In a cafeteria

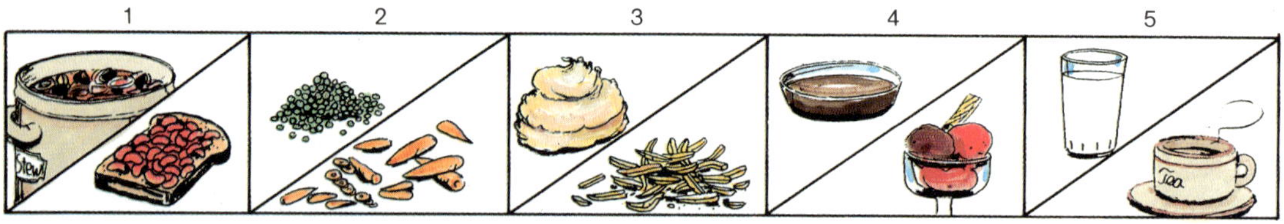

Make dialogues. Use this example to help you:

1. *Kevin:* Look, there's Irish stew or beans on toast. Which are you going to have?
   Ben: I don't know. I like both./Irish stew. I don't like beans./ I'm going to have beans on toast. Which do you want?
   Kevin: I'm going to have the same as you./… I don't like …/I'm going to have …

3 Question time

Complete the questions with 'which' or 'what'.

1. "… time is it?" "Half past three."
2. "I've made two cakes. … do you like better?"
3. "…'s for lunch today?" "Fish – or vegetable stew. … do you want?"
4. "I've got a new pullover." "… colour is it?"
5. "… language do you like better, Kevin? French or German?" "German."
6. "Right or left? … is the right way?"
7. "… day is it today?" "Thursday."
8. "… vegetables are you going to have? Peas or carrots?"
9. "…'s your favourite food?" "Sausages and chips."

4 Helen always knows best!

I feel so full!	Well …	look after your things better!
I can't understand this French exercise.		go to the doctor's!
I haven't finished my homework yet.	You should	eat so much!
I've got a terrible headache.		wake up in the lessons!
Two of my felt-pens are missing.	You shouldn't	stay in the swimming-pool so long!
I'm so cold, I can hardly feel my fingers!		be so slow!

5 Role Play What would you like?

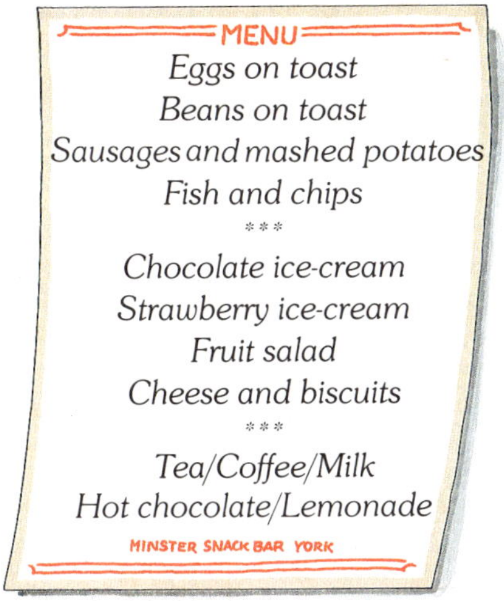

You are having lunch at the Minster Snack Bar with a friend.

What are you going to have?
What do you want to eat?
What would you like?

I'm going to have …
What about you?

I'd like …. And after that let's try the …

Yes, let's. I'm hungry.
Oh no. I don't like …!
I'd like …

All right. And let's have a cup of …/a glass of …

No, let's …
Good idea.
Not for me. I'm not thirsty.

⟨6 Waiter!⟩

"Waiter! What do you call this?"
"It's bean soup, sir."
"I don't want to know what it's been – what is it now?"

"How did you find your steak, sir?"
"I looked under a chip – and there it was."

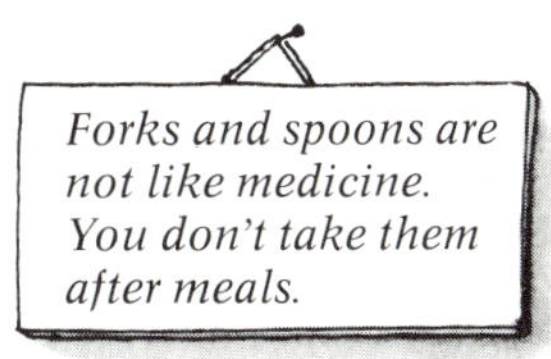

⟨7 Let's sing a song: Cockles and Mussels⟩

2. She was a fishmonger,
But sure 'twas no wonder,
For so were her father and mother before,
And they each wheeled their barrow
Through streets broad and narrow,
Crying, "Cockles and mussels, alive, alive-o!"

Chorus: Alive, alive-o! Alive, alive-o!
Crying, "Cockles and mussels,
Alive, alive-o!"

3. She died of a fever,
And no one could save her,
And that was the end of sweet Molly Malone,
But her ghost wheels her barrow
Through streets broad and narrow,
Crying, "Cockles and mussels, alive, alive-o!"

Chorus: Alive, alive-o! etc.

C Have you heard?

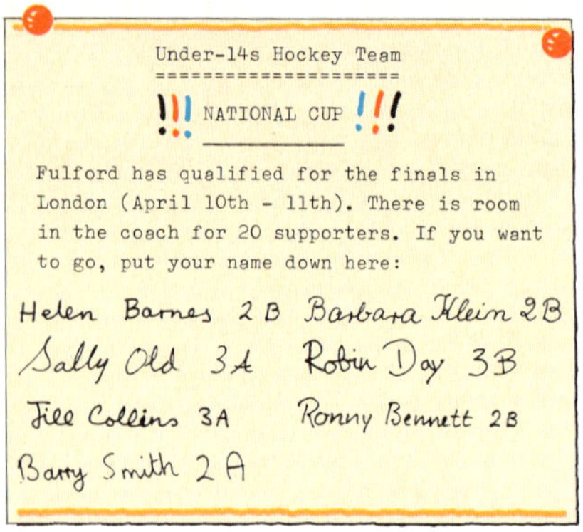
Under-14s Hockey Team

!!! NATIONAL CUP !!!

Fulford has qualified for the finals in London (April 10th - 11th). There is room in the coach for 20 supporters. If you want to go, put your name down here:

Helen Barnes 2B
Barbara Klein 2B
Sally Old 3A
Robin Day 3B
Jill Collins 3A
Ronny Bennett 2B
Barry Smith 2A

Christine: Have you heard the news about the Under-14s hockey team?

Kevin: Everyone has! I heard about it at lunch. Linda told me.

Ben: What? What news?

Helen: Haven't you heard? About the National Cup, of course. Our team won against Queen Margaret's yesterday.

Ben: Oh.

Christine: So now we've qualified for the finals. They're in London in April. And I'm in the team! That is – I'm a reserve.

Helen: And there's room on the coach for supporters. I've put my name down already. Have you, Barbara?

Barbara: Yes, I have. I put my name down before lunch.

Ben: Well, I can't go anyway.

Helen: Why not?

Ben: We're going to move to America in March. My mum and dad told me about it last night. My dad has to go over next week, and we're going to follow.

Kevin: Fantastic!

Christine: But bad luck that you can't come with us.

Ben: I call it good luck. I don't want to go to London in a coach full of girls!

1 Comprehension

Answer the questions.

1. Has Kevin heard the news about the Under-14s hockey team?
2. When did he hear about it?
3. What team did the Fulford girls win against yesterday?
4. Have the Queen Margaret's girls qualified for the finals?
5. How many supporters can go to London with the team?
6. Have Helen and Barbara put their names down?
7. When did Barbara put her name down?
8. What about Ben? Why can't he go with them?
9. When did his parents tell him the news?
10. Ben can't go to the hockey finals. Why does he call it good luck?

2 A week in the holidays

What has Ronny done this week?

Example:
"Has he cleaned his bike yet?"
"Yes, he has.
He cleaned it on Monday."
"And has he polished the chrome, too?"
"No, he hasn't done that yet."

3 At home and at school

Have you taken Bonzo out for a walk?		… on Saturday.
Have Kevin and Kate done their homework?		… last Monday.
Has Miss Price put the notice up?	Yes, I have.	… after tea.
Have you seen Barbara's new bike?		… last night.
Has Kate written to her pen-friend?	Yes, he has.	… before lunch.
Have you given Mr Edwards your essay?	Yes, she has.	… a few minutes ago.
Has Ronny bought a present for Dad?		… two days ago.
Have you read Grandma's letter?	Yes, they have.	… yesterday.
Have you learnt your French words?		… last week.

Example: Have you taken Bonzo out for a walk?
– Yes, I have. I took him for a walk before lunch.

4 A party at the Pearsons'

a) Kevin and Kate are going to have a party. Look what they've done.

Kevin has made a big chocolate cake. *Go on.*

b) A few days after the party, Kate writes to her German pen-friend.

Write Kate's letter. Start like this:

Dear Bettina,
Kevin and I had a party last Saturday. It was great! Eight people came.
Before it started, we were really busy! Kevin made a big …

D Come on, Fulford!

"Look out of the window, everyone!" called Miss Price. "We've left the M1 and we're coming into London now." The coach with the Fulford Under-14s hockey team was on its way to the finals in South London. Their supporters were in the coach, too.

"Great!" said Barbara. "Look out for Buckingham Palace!"

"We aren't anywhere near there yet, idiot!" said Ronny. "Hey, Chris, are you dreaming? What's the matter?"

"Oh, nothing," said Christine. She and Linda were the only ones from 2B in the team. Of course, Christine was only a reserve, but she was a bit nervous, even so. After all, the finals were a big thing.

"Have you seen Chris's hockey stick?" Linda asked. "She got a new one yesterday for the finals."

"What? But you're only a reserve, Chris!" laughed Helen.

"That doesn't matter," said Christine. "I can still use it back at school."

When they arrived at the sports ground, they met the other teams. In the first round the Fulford team had to play against St Anne's, a team from the South of England. The boys and girls from 2B watched at the side with the other Fulford supporters and the three reserves, Christine and two older girls.

When the match started, everyone was very excited. There were a lot of supporters from St Anne's, and they all had very loud voices, but the Fulford crowd made as much noise as they could. They jumped up and down and shouted:

"Two – four – six – eight!
Who do we appreciate?
F – U – L – F – O – R – D !
Fulford!"

"Come on, Linda!" shouted Ronny, when Linda had the ball. But then a St Anne's player got the ball, dribbled it towards the Fulford goal – and scored. The St Anne's supporters nearly went mad.

"We haven't got much chance," Christine said. "They're too good."

"Well, the game's only just started," said Ronny. "You needn't worry."

But at half-time, the score was 2–1 to St Anne's.

"Come on, Christine! You're on!"

Was that Miss Price's voice? Christine couldn't believe it. Someone pushed her forward, and a moment later she was in the middle of the game. And Sarah Wiley, one of the best players in the team, was out – with a leg injury. It was like a dream at first. Then there she was suddenly, near the St Anne's goal. Sue Evans had the ball.

"Out of the way, Chris!" Sue shouted and tried to score.

But Christine was too slow. The ball hit her hockey stick and bounced off. "Oh no!" she thought and looked away. "Did I have to start like that?"

But what was all that noise from the crowd? Christine looked again. Was it possible? The ball was in the St Anne's goal!

"Goal! Fantastic, Chris!"

"Come on, Fulford!"

The Fulford supporters shouted and laughed, they were so excited. So now it was two all, and everything was open.

After a time, Christine began to feel really good. She was not in a dream world now. The match was great, and she was glad she was in it. The score was still two all. Could they score another goal before the end? They had to! But there wasn't much time. There was Sue Evans again. She passed the ball to Christine, and Christine dribbled towards the St Anne's goal. A St Anne's player tried to get the ball, but Christine was too quick for her. She was near the goal now. This was her chance! Now or never!

"Come on, Chris!" her friends shouted from the crowd. And then …

"Goal!"

"Fantastic!"

"She's done it again!"

"Chris! You're the greatest!"

Then the whistle. "We're through to the next round!" Everybody ran onto the field. Miss Price was first. "Well done, Chris! And you were so nervous at first. How did you do it?"

"I don't know! I –"

"But **I** know!" shouted Ronny. "It was her new hockey stick! See, Helen?"

1 An interview

After the match against St Anne's, Sheila Smith interviewed Christine for the Fulford School magazine. *Can you give Christine's answers?*

Sheila: Well, Chris, how do you feel?
Christine: …!
Sheila: And how did you feel before the match?
Christine: …
Sheila: Oh, really? But you were only a reserve. When did you have to come into the game?
Christine: …
Sheila: And not long after that you scored your first goal. How did that happen?
Christine: …
Sheila: Did you still feel nervous later in the match?
Christine: …
Sheila: And how did you score your fantastic second goal?
Christine: …
Sheila: Great! Well, thanks for the interview, Chris. Oh, just one more question. I hear you've got a new hockey stick. When did you get it?
Christine: …
Sheila: Really? Well, let me take a photo of you with it!

2 Back to Fulford

After their match against St Anne's, the Fulford team had to play in the second round against Southgate Comprehensive, a London school …

Answer the questions and then tell the story.

1. Was Christine in the team this time?
2. What happened after five minutes?
3. Did Fulford win? What was the score? What did they say after the match?
4. What happened when they got to Fulford?
5. Why was David excited? What did Ronny say?
6. What did the school notice-board say? Were they still unhappy?

[3 Kate's things]

These are some of Kate's things.

Say what she has got.

Example: She's got two cardigans – a **blue one** and a **red one**.

4 When Mr and Mrs Klein were away

Last holidays Mr and Mrs Klein had to go to London for a long weekend. Elke and Barbara stayed at home. While Mr and Mrs Klein were away, Ronny came round to see Barbara.

Ronny: All alone without your parents? Not bad! But *don't you have to* go shopping?

Barbara: No, we *needn't*. There's enough food for the weekend.

Ronny: And what about meals?

Barbara: Oh, we *needn't* cook any meals. There's lots of cold food in the house. But we *have to* wash up after meals, of course!

Ronny: Bad luck! Well, how long *are you allowed to* stay up in the evenings?

Barbara: Well, we *mustn't* stay up too late. Mum says I *have to* go to bed at half past nine, but Elke *doesn't have to* go before half past ten.

Ronny: *Are you allowed to* ask your friends to come round?

Barbara: Yes, of course we are!

Ronny: What about TV?

Barbara: Dad says I *mustn't* watch too much TV. Well, I'm certainly going to watch the Saturday night film with Elke, but *I'm not* really *allowed to*!

Ronny: I'm not surprised. It goes on until 11.30. – Are your parents going to ring up while they're away?

Barbara: Yes, they are. We *must* listen for the phone on Sunday morning. I only hope they don't ring up too early!

Now say what the girls **had to** *do,* **were allowed to** *do,* **didn't have to** *do and* **weren't allowed to** *do, when their parents were away.*
They didn't have to go shopping. There was enough ... *Go on.*

	Present	Past
Du mußt ...	You **must** go. You **have to** go.	– You **had to** go.
Du mußt nicht ... / Du brauchst nicht ...	You **needn't** go. You **don't have to** go.	– You **didn't have to** go.
Du darfst ...	You **may** go. You **are allowed to** go.	– You **were allowed to** go.
Du darfst nicht ...	You **mustn't** go. You **aren't allowed to** go.	– You **weren't allowed to** go.

5 Let's set the table

a) Do you sometimes set the table at home? *Then you can answer these questions.*

1. Your family are going to have sausages and chips, and lemonade to drink. What must you put on the table?
2. Now you are all going to have breakfast: tea, toast, butter and marmalade. What must you put on the table this time?

b) *What is it?* 1. You need it when you eat meat, but you mustn't put it in your mouth.
2. You need it if you take sugar in your tea.
3. German people sometimes drink tea out of it, but British people never do!
4. It looks a bit like a plate, but you don't use it for food.
5. You can cut it, and it comes from milk. *(2 answers)*

6 Have they? Did they? *Past tense or present perfect – which is right?*

Example: 1. *Helen:* Where's Chris? I want to ask her something.
Ronny: (not – to arrive – yet) She **hasn't arrived** yet.

2. *Barbara:* Can I see your picture of York?
Kevin: (not – to finish – yet)
3. *Christine:* Has anyone seen Mr Edwards?
Ben: (just – to go – language lab)
4. *Ronny:* I'm going to have sausages. Aren't you?
Kevin: (to have – for lunch – yesterday)
5. *Helen:* Have another plate of chips! Be a devil!
Christine: (already – to have – two)
6. *Ronny:* Has your dad gone over to America yet?
Ben: (to fly – New York – last night)
7. *Barbara:* Did your rugby team win the match against Tadcaster?
Ronny: (not – to play – yet)
8. *Linda:* Is Sarah Wiley back at school yet?
Christine: (to see – playground – at break)
9. *David:* Did you learn any new songs at guitar practice yesterday?
Ronny: (not – to go – guitar practice – yesterday)
10. *Ben:* Where have you been?
Peter: (just – to be – cafeteria)

7 Words and their meanings

a) *Do you know the opposites of these words?*

First some easy ones:		*These are more difficult:*		*And these have more than one answer:*
rich –	to buy –	to pick up –	to shout –	old –
fat –	goodbye –	friend –	the best –	to start –
to like –	full –	to break –	to find –	right –
something –	to arrive –	to throw away –	never –	boring –

b) *Now say what these words mean, or make a sentence to show that you understand them.*

cafeteria to hunt playground cinema cup famous
cheese adventure relations pedal market

〈Authentic Britain: A trip through London〉

⟨Revision⟩

1 A story from Ireland

a) *Put in the right forms of the adjectives.*

1. Long long ago, in Ireland, there was a giant. His name was O'Connor. "I'm the … and the … man in Ireland," he shouted.
2. He could climb the … mountains and he could carry the … stones.
3. He needed … shoes than everyone else.
4. "And I can tell the … stories in Ireland," he said.
5. One afternoon, the people in the village rushed to O'Connor's house and shouted, "O'Connor! There's a giant from Scotland in the village. He says he is … and … than you.
6. He can climb … mountains than you.
7. He can carry … stones than you can.
8. He looks … than you.
9. And he says he can tell … stories than you."
   O'Connor began to be afraid of the giant from Scotland.

b) *Read what O'Connor and his wife did.*

"What can I do?" O'Connor asked his wife. She had a good idea. "Quick, jump into the baby's bed," she said. O'Connor's wife put the baby's bonnet on his head. Just then the Scottish giant rushed in. "Where's that little Irishman?" he shouted. "He's not in," answered O'Connor's wife, "but come and have a look at his baby." The Scottish giant looked at the 'baby'. "Let me out, let me out!" he cried. "I don't want to be here when this baby's father comes home." He rushed out of the house and ran away as fast as he could. The people in the village often laughed about 'O'Connor the Baby'.

2 What do you think?

Say what you think.

Examples:
German is more difficult than history.
Home Economics is the most boring subject at our school.
Football is just as dangerous as rugby.
Swimming is not as …
…

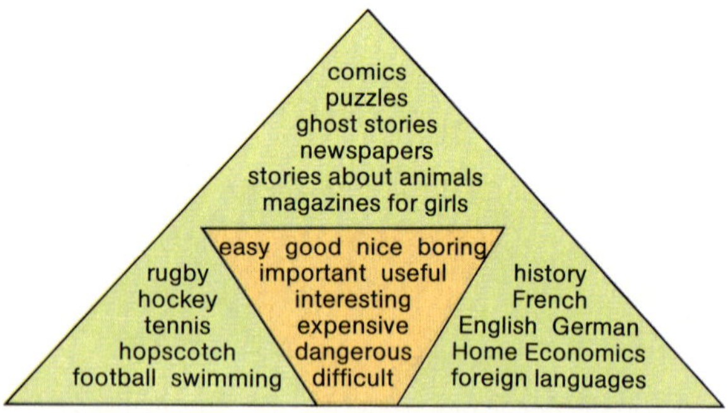

Just for fun

Father: Do you want any help with your homework?
Son: No, thanks. I can get it wrong without your help.

Jimmy: I'm going to work for a circus.
Mother: What are you going to do there?
Jimmy: I'm going to be a giant.
Mother: But you're too small to be a giant.
Jimmy: That's the idea. I'm going to be the smallest giant in the world!

Just for fun

Can you find the answers? If you can't, look for the answers on this page.

1. What has got a face but no legs?
2. What do you call a flying elephant?
3. Where do you take a sick horse?
4. When do you like school best?
5. Why can't the letter 'e' work?
6. Where does Tarzan get his clothes from?

3 Ronny's dream

Put in the verbs in the correct form.

1. Last night Ronny … a terrible dream. (have) 2. He … all alone in an empty van. (be) 3. He … the door, but he … open it. (push, cannot) 4. Then he … two women outside. (hear) 5. They … for a long time, but he … a word. (talk, not understand) 6. He …, but they … him. (shout, not hear) 7. Then he … Bonzo through the window. (see) 8. Bonzo … at the van, and suddenly the van door … open. (bark, be) 9. Then his father … in. (come) He … to play a game of cards with Ronny. (want) 10. They … for a long time, but Ronny … one game. (play, not win) 11. After that they … to a bus stop. (go) 12. They … all night, but the bus … . (wait, not come) 13. Early in the morning it … to rain. (begin) 14. The strange thing was that only Ronny … wet. (get) 15. And then Ronny … Timmy's voice. (hear)

4 Remember?

Ask your neighbour some questions. Here are some ideas to help you.

Example: Did you watch TV yesterday?
No, I didn't (watch television). I listened to records.

Can you ask any more questions?

A KITE   A JUMBO JET   TO A HORSEPITAL   WHEN IT'S CLOSED   BECAUSE IT'S ALWAYS IN BED   FROM A JUNGLE SALE

5 At the school cafeteria

a) Say what Mrs Wood is doing.
b) Say what Mrs Wood has done.

Examples:
1. a) Mrs Wood is putting the vegetables into the food mixer.
   b) Mrs Wood has put the vegetables into the food mixer.

6 People and their jobs

a) *Put in the verbs in the right tenses.*

1. This morning I ... a passenger from the station to his hotel. There are two more passengers for me at the station now, but I ... them yet. (take, collect)
2. The children ... just ... down in their seats, but I ... the engine yet. (sit, start)
3. I ... the hens anything to eat yet, but I ... the ducks twenty minutes ago. (give, feed)
4. A woman ... in and ... me these two prescriptions five minutes ago, but I ... the medicine yet. (come, give, make)
5. I ... the people in the village a lot of questions yesterday, but I ... my report yet. (ask, write)
6. I ... this little boy's temperature five minutes ago, but I ... that girl yet. (take, examine)
7. I ... just ... the exercise books, but I ... the exercise yet. (collect, correct)
8. I ... at the pony's legs, but I ... its hooves yet. (look, examine)

b) *What are these people's jobs?*

7 Find the words

Can you find the words? It's not difficult because they're all from Units 4 and 5.

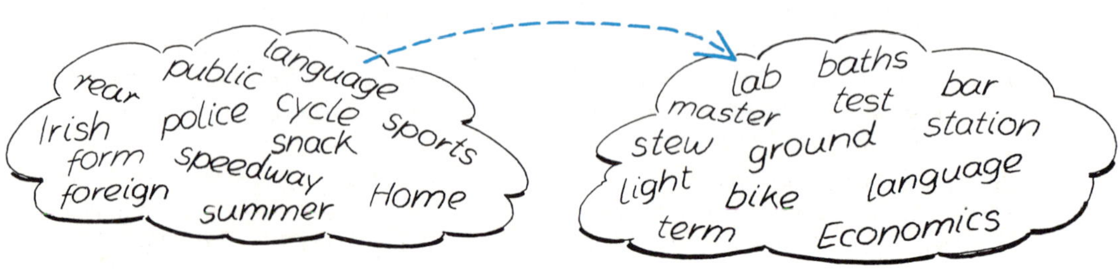

8 Dialogues *Put in the right words.*

a) *Sandra:* Have we got ... cornflakes, Mum?
Mother: There's a box in the kitchen. Bring ... milk, too, please.
Sandra: There aren't ... apples.
Mother: Oh yes, you're right. I didn't buy ... fruit yesterday. Here's ... money. You can buy ... apples or oranges on your way to school.

b) *Philip:* Has ... got my German book? I can't find it ... .
Linda: It must be ... in your room, Philip.
Philip: No, it isn't. ... has got it.
Linda: Look, there's ... under the chair over there.
Philip: That's a magazine, Linda. Hey, Dad, do you know where my German book is?
Father: There are ... schoolbooks on the kitchen table.
Philip: Oh yes, now I remember. Mum wanted to look at ... in my German book.

9 Shadows

Look at the shadows and say what you can see. Examples: Number one is the shadow of a guitar. Number two is Kevin's shadow.

10 In bed for a week *Put in the right words.*

Kate Pearson was ill, so she had to stay in bed for a week. When she got back to school, her friend Wendy asked her all about it.

Wendy: Hello, Kate. Nice to see you back. You ... tell me all about it. ... stay in bed all the time?
Kate: No, I only ... stay in bed from Monday to Thursday.
Wendy: ... you go to see the doctor?
Kate: No, I ... go to his surgery. He came to our house and examined me at home.
Wendy: ... take any medicine?
Kate: Yes, the doctor gave Mum a prescription, but she ... go to the chemist's. Kevin fetched the bottle of medicine for me. Sometimes brothers are useful! But the medicine is terrible. I ... take it three times a day.
Wendy: But aren't you better now?
Kate: Yes, but I still ... take the medicine every day. The bottle isn't empty yet.
Wendy: I ... take any medicine at all when I was ill last year.
Kate: Perhaps I ... go to *your* doctor next time! – Oh, look. It's nine o'clock. We ... hurry. We've got French. Why ... come back to school?

Unit 6

⟨Photo page: Heathrow⟩

The Heathrow tower is in the background .

One of the big terminals at Heathrow

An airport reception hall

Waiting for the next flight

A Oklahoma, here we come!

a) It is a grey, rainy March day. Ben and his mother have just arrived at Heathrow Airport in a taxi. Mrs MacDonald is nervous because they are late. She is sure they will miss their plane.

Mum: Please hurry, Ben, or we'll miss our flight.

Ben: No, we won't, Mum.

Mum: Yes, we will.

Ben: Don't worry, Mum. We've got nearly fifteen minutes.

Mum: Oh Ben, you're impossible. I still can't believe we had to go back just because you forgot your ticket.

Ben: Will we see any Indians at the airport when we land in Oklahoma City, Mum?

Mum: Ben! We'll never find our counter in time. And your father won't know what has happened to us. He'll be so worried.

Ben: No, he won't, Mum. We'll explain everything to him when we get there.

Mum: Ben, you know your father. He'll have a nervous breakdown *before* we get there.

What will happen? Will they miss their plane? Will Mr MacDonald have a nervous breakdown? Let's find out.

b) Mrs MacDonald has at last found the counter. Is it too late?

1 Comprehension

Is that right? If not, correct what is wrong.

1. Ben and his mother arrive at Heathrow Airport by train.
2. Mrs MacDonald thinks they will miss their flight.
3. They have only got five minutes.
4. They had to go back because Mrs MacDonald forgot her ticket.
5. Mr MacDonald will be happy if they miss their plane.
6. Mrs MacDonald goes to the wrong counter.
7. Ben isn't with her. He is late again.
8. Mr Pushy is the ten millionth passenger.
9. Ben wins a bar of chocolate.
10. Everybody is happy now.

2 "Will they remember me?"

On the plane Ben thinks about York. *Put in 'will' or 'won't'.*

1. My friends at school – … I ever see them again? 2. I hope they … forget me and … write to me. 3. Perhaps they … even send me a cassette. 4. And what about the rugby team? I … be there for the final. 5. … they win without me? 6. It … be easy. 7. And Grandma – she … see us every week now. 8. I know she … be unhappy. 9. But Mr Edwards? Well, I think he … be happy now. I was always late for his class.

3 From Heathrow to Enid, Oklahoma

Can you put these together?

1. When Ben flies to America ---	he will ask her for some lemonade.
2. When the plane takes off	he won't forget his old ones in York.
3. When the stewardess comes	he will be a little nervous.
4. When they get to New York	he won't know anyone at first.
5. When they arrive in Oklahoma City	→ he won't have to pay.
6. When Ben gets to Enid	Ben will write to all his friends in England.
7. When he lives in Enid	they will have to change planes.
8. When he has new friends in Enid	Mr MacDonald will be at the airport.

4 When I live in Oklahoma, I'll ...

Ben thinks that this will happen when he lives in Enid, Oklahoma.

wear/look like | ride/be | meet/play with | write/get | find/become

1. I'll wear a cowboy hat when I live in Oklahoma.
   I'll ... *Go on.*

5 Ben's flight to the United States

Look at the map, then answer these questions:

a) 1. Will the plane fly over the Atlantic Ocean?
   2. Will the MacDonalds leave London at 5 p.m.?
   3. Will they fly over Africa?
   4. Will they land in Chicago?
   5. Will they arrive in New York in the morning?
   6. Will their plane fly to Enid?
   7. Will they change planes in New York?

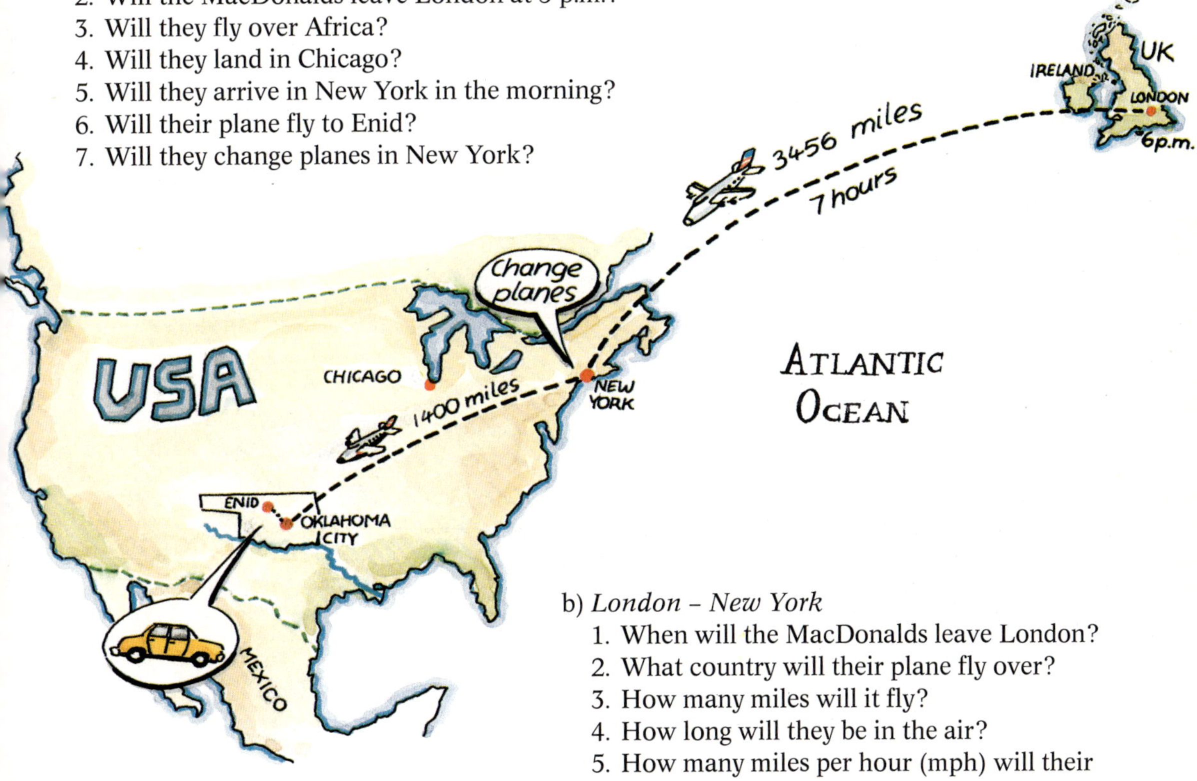

b) *London – New York*
   1. When will the MacDonalds leave London?
   2. What country will their plane fly over?
   3. How many miles will it fly?
   4. How long will they be in the air?
   5. How many miles per hour (mph) will their plane fly?
   6. Where will it land in the U.S.?
   7. What will they do in New York?

B Ben's letter

10 millionth passenger will live in Enid

UPI On March 22 Ben MacDonald, 12, went to Heathrow Airport in Lon- don with his ... arrived late but they did not miss their flight. In the end everything was ... Ben will with his ...

Ben MacDonald
425 Glenwood Drive
Enid OK 73701
USA

April 25th

Hello everybody,

Yes, it really is a letter from me. I wrote to you about a month ago. But I had the letter in my shirt and Mum washed it!!

My trip here was very good. I'm going to put a newspaper article in with this letter. That will tell you everything. I've taken some photos and I'll send them, too.

I really like it here. It's spring now and the weather isn't too hot yet, but it will be in the summer. And in the winter it'll be cold and windy. A few days ago we had a thunderstorm here and the thunder was so loud that I dropped 10 plates! (I don't have to help in the kitchen any more!)

Do you know what the people here say when you ask them the way? Things like: "... go north, then turn east and it'll be the big building on the south side." That's why I always get lost here.

Did you know that Enid is the wheat capital of the world? There are wheat fields everywhere and "prairie castles" - where they keep the wheat. It's very flat here. You can see for miles and miles - wheat fields and a big blue sky.

I've got a lot of friends here already. There's Peggy Whitecloud. She's a Cherokee Indian. And Ralph Jones. But my best friend is Harry Hopper. Harry is learning to do magic tricks and he can already cut a girl in two. He's a little crazy. We're going to open a lemonade stand this summer.

Mum says the postman will be here in a minute, so I'll have to hurry. Shall I send you more pictures? Please write soon and tell me all about everything.

Ben

P.S. In the autumn (they say "fall" here) we're going to buy a house and I'll have a BIG room then.

1 Comprehension

1. Why didn't Ben send his first letter?
2. What is he going to send with this letter?
3. What's the weather like in Oklahoma in the spring?
4. What does Ben say about the summer and the winter in Oklahoma?
5. Why did Ben drop 10 plates? Why isn't he unhappy about it?
6. What is Enid famous for?
7. What is Ben's best friend learning to do? What can he already do?
8. What are Ben and Harry going to do in the summer?
9. Why will Ben have to hurry with the letter?
10. Why is Ben looking forward to the autumn?

2 What are we going to do on Saturday?

Harry Hopper has made plans for Ben and himself for the next few days.

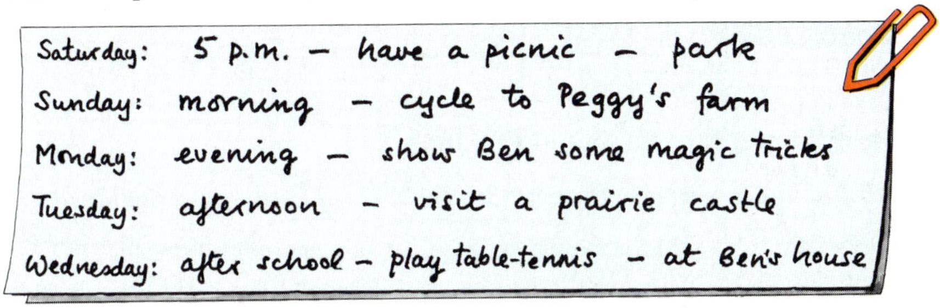

Ben wants to know what they are going to do.
Ask his questions and give Harry's answers. Work in pairs.

Ben: 1. What are we going to do on Saturday? *Harry:* We're going to have a picnic.
2. Where are we … … in the park.
3. When … … at 5 p.m.
4. What … on Sunday? …
Go on.

Talk about your plans for the next few days.

3 Mother's Day!

Example: 1. *Mum:* It's so cold with that window open.
Dad: **Shall I** shut it for you, dear?
Ben: **I'll** shut it for you, Mum.

Here's what Ben's mum says. What do Ben and his dad say?

2. Oh, my pullover is in the bedroom.
3. The "weather" will be on TV in a minute.
4. Where's my coat? I can't find it anywhere.
5. Look at all those dirty plates.
6. I've got so much ice-cream on my plate.
7. Oh dear! These bottles are so heavy.
8. But I don't know that card game.

C Looking at the weather

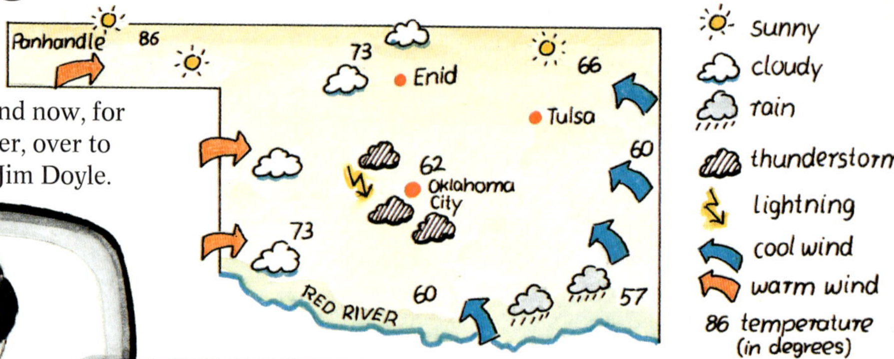

TV Announcer: And now, for tomorrow's weather, over to our Weatherman, Jim Doyle.

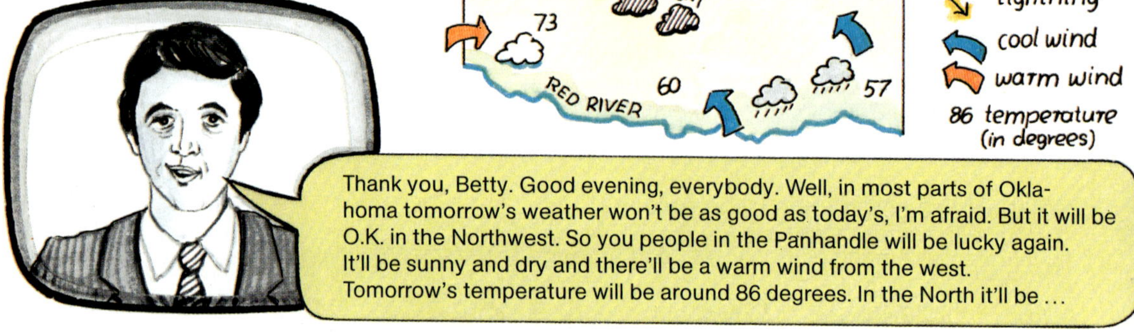

1 What will the weather be like in Oklahoma?

Go on with Jim Doyle's weather report. Say what the weather will be like

1. … in the North 2. … in the Southwest 3. … in Central Oklahoma
4. … in the East 5. … in the Southeast 6. … in the South

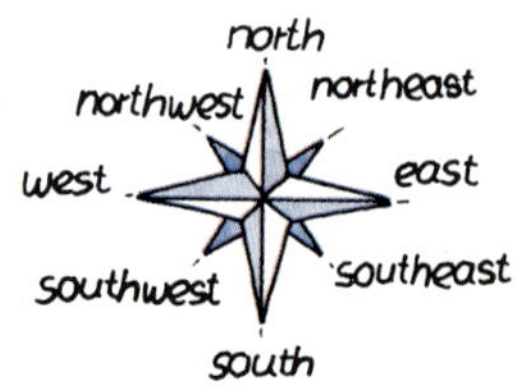

2 Hello, Jim – this is Mabel

Every afternoon from 3 to 4 o'clock, Jim Doyle answers people's questions on the telephone.

Look at the map and give Jim's answers.

1. *Mabel:* Hello, Jim – this is Mabel. We want to drive to the Panhandle tomorrow. Will the weather be O.K. there? *Jim:* Don't worry, Mabel. It'll be …
2. *Arnie:* Hi, Jim – this is Arnie. What will the weather be like in the Southwest? We want to visit my aunt there. *Jim:* …
3. *Ben:* Hello, Jim – this is Ben MacDonald. We live in Enid, but we want to visit Oklahoma City tomorrow. Will it be sunny there? *Jim:* …

Go on. One of you is Jim Doyle and the others ask him questions about the weather …

4. … in the South 5. … in Tulsa 6. … in the Southeast 7. … in Enid

3 And in Germany?

Now tell the class about the weather in your town/ in your part of Germany.

1. now 2. in the summer (usually/last summer/ next summer, I hope) 3. in the autumn
4. in the winter 5. in the spring

OVER TO YOU

D The bet

Beverly Snyder is in Ben's and Harry's class. She also lives in their neighbourhood. When the boys decided to open their lemonade stand, Beverly wanted to help. But the boys said no. No girls.

On Friday afternoon Ben and Harry told all the kids in their neighbourhood about their plans for the weekend. Everybody was excited. Especially Buddy. He was already thirteen and he often played tricks on people.

"What about the weather? I think it'll rain tomorrow!" Buddy shouted.

"Impossible! We talked to Jim Doyle," Harry laughed.

"We'll see," Buddy laughed back.

Then Buddy went over to his friend Pete. Beverly saw them and knew that Buddy wanted to play a trick. She moved a little closer. "... Pete, you must stand next to the house. And when I give the signal, you must turn on the water," Buddy said.

"Uhhh – what shall I do?"

Pete didn't understand, but Beverly did. There was a hose with a sprinkler on Harry's front lawn right where Ben and Harry had their stand. And when you turned the water on, it "rained". Beverly smiled but didn't say anything.

The next day nearly all the kids from the neighbourhood were at the stand. It was like a party. And then Buddy and Pete came, too.

"Looks bad. Rain," Buddy said.

"You're crazy. You've got rain on the brain," Harry laughed.

"Well, I'll bet you five dollars that you and your lemonade stand will get wet. Soon," Buddy said.

Ben and Harry looked up. The sky was blue and sunny. Then they looked at each other and said O.K. Buddy laughed and started to give the signal. But Beverly was suddenly there. She took Buddy by the arm and moved him over a little. Buddy pulled his arm away. He did not want to talk to Beverly now. Then he gave the signal with his head, and Beverly moved back.

And then it happened. One moment Buddy was dry and the next he was wet from head to foot. He shouted and jumped about like a wild thing. There was a garden hose in the tree above him, and water shot out of it. For a moment nobody understood anything. Then they saw Pete at the side of the house – and he looked very silly as he turned off the water.

"This is all your fault, Pete!" Buddy shouted.

"What's going on here?" Harry said.

"It's a good thing you have two garden hoses," Beverly smiled.

"Hey – Beverly switched the hoses and they didn't notice," Ben said.

And then the penny dropped for everyone: Ah! *Beverly* put the other hose in the tree above Buddy. And when Pete turned the water on, only Buddy got wet.

Everybody laughed. Only Buddy and Pete didn't. "That was a good trick, Beverly," Harry said. "Thank you, Harry," Beverly answered. "I think I'll collect *our* five dollars from Buddy now. And then *we*'ll get some more lemonade for *our* stand. O.K.?"

1 Comprehension

Everybody talked a lot about the lemonade stand after that. Here's what Peggy Whitecloud heard. *Can you help her with the facts?*

1. Ben and Harry asked Beverly to help them with the lemonade stand.
2. Everybody thought the boys' lemonade stand was a bad idea.
3. Buddy told Beverly about his plan.
4. Pete understood everything immediately but Beverly didn't.
5. Not very many people came to the stand.
6. The sky was dark when Buddy and Pete came.
7. Buddy got all wet because Pete forgot the signal.
8. Buddy lost five dollars because the lemonade was so good.

2 Looking into the future

Now say what you think will or won't happen in the future.

Examples: – I'm sure we won't have an English test this week.
– I hope/I don't think/perhaps we will ... homework ... *Go on.*

3 Facts about Ben – and you

- Ben will be thirteen next year.
- He will have English at 9 o'clock tomorrow.
- His summer holidays will start on June 1st.

Now let's look at some facts about you. *Can you answer these questions?*

1. How old will you be next year? (Your brother/sister?)
2. When will your summer holidays start?
3. Will you have English tomorrow? (German? History? ... ?)
4. How long will you be at school tomorrow? (The day after tomorrow?)
5. Will you have to go to school on Saturday? (Ben won't.)

Think of more facts.

⟨4 Trick no. 217⟩

5 What is Peggy going to do?

Peggy has got a lot of plans. *Can you say what she is going to do?*

Example: 1. On Friday afternoon she's going to play tennis with Ben.
2. On Saturday she … *Go on.*

6 Old Jeff

Old Jeff is one of Ben's new neighbours. He thinks he knows all about the weather. Ben and Harry are talking to him now.
Put in the correct form: 'There'll be'/'There won't be'/'Will there be … ?'

Ben: … any bad weather this weekend?
Old Jeff: Oh yes. … a lot of bad weather this weekend.
Ben: Oh dear. We want to go to a rodeo on Saturday.
Old Jeff: … a rodeo this weekend – only rain!
Harry: Listen, Ben. I'm sure there –
Ben: Are you sure … rain?
Old Jeff: Of course. … rain and storms and everything else, too.
Harry: Ben, I –
Ben: But look at the sky. There aren't even any clouds!
Old Jeff: That's right. But this weekend … lots of them. Well, I must go now, boys. Have a nice weekend.
Harry: Don't worry, Ben. … any bad weather. Old Jeff is always wrong.

〈7 Trick no. 1460: Cutting a girl in two〉

8 What are they going to do? What will happen?

a) *What do they say or think?*

1. *Ben:* **I'm going to** take off my T-shirt. Then I **won't** be so warm.
2. *Peggy:* I …… Spot. Then he … nicer.
3. *Harry:* I …
4. *Mr MacDonald:* I …

b) *Now say what they are going to do and what will happen.*

1. Ben is going to take off his T-shirt. Then he … *Go o.*

c) *Now look at these sentences. Put the verbs in the correct form: 'going to' or 'will-future'.*

1. Peggy's brother John is looking at the engine of his car. "I … it. It … better then." (to clean, to run)
2. Ben is looking forward to the 28th. "I … 13 then. We … a big party." (to be, to have)
3. Mrs MacDonald … Ben's dirty pullover. It … better then. (to wash, to look)
4. Beverly is at the bank. "I … some money in the bank every week. In a few years I … rich." (to put, to be)
5. Ben's dad is sleeping on the sofa. Ben is looking at him. "I … Dad. I hope he … angry." (to wake up, not to be)
6. Peggy is in her room. She … her bed. Her mother … happy then. (to make, to be)
7. Old Jeff is sure the weather … terrible this weekend. He … at home. (to be, to stay)
8. It is too hot in the house. Ben … the door. He is sure it … cooler then. (to close, to be)

9 Shall we have a party?

You and your friends want to have a party. *Make dialogues. Here are some words to help you.*

		Shall we	dance have do eat make drink listen to watch invite sing play start finish …	records games sandwiches a party folk songs TV lemonade … ?
	When What Where Who	shall we		
What	music games records	shall we		
How many	sandwiches …			
How much	lemonade …			

Of course.
Yes, that's a great idea.

No, I don't like …

On Friday/…

At 6 o'clock/…

Upstairs and Downstairs.

Let's …

Oh no, not again!

Example:

10  Have you been there yet?

Old Jeff and Ben are talking again. *Put in the verbs: 'present perfect' or 'simple past'?*

1. *Old Jeff:* Hi, Ben. ... the world's biggest prairie castle yet, boy? (you – see)
   Ben: Yes, I have. I ... it last week. (see)
2. *Old Jeff:* What about Frontier City, Ben?
   Ben: No, I ... there. (not be) We want to go there soon.
3. *Old Jeff:* I know you ... to Indian City a few days ago. (go) ... it, boy? (you – like)
   Ben: Yes, I did. It ... very good. (be)
4. *Old Jeff:* I see that you ... a cowboy hat. (buy) Where ... it? (you – buy)
   Ben: I ... it in Oklahoma City. (buy) Dad ... us there last week. (take) That's where I ... it. (get)
5. *Old Jeff:* Say, boy, how long ... here now? (you – be)
   Ben: I ... here for over a month. (be) We ... here at the end of March. (arrive)
6. *Old Jeff:* Over a month? ... to the Salt Plains in all that time? (your parents – ever – drive)
   Ben: No, they haven't.
7. *Old Jeff:* Well, I'm going to go there next weekend. You can come with me.
   Ben: Great. I ... a lot about them. (hear)
   Old Jeff: Good. The weather will be great then.
   Ben: Well, perhaps –

L 〈11 Listening comprehension: A cassette for Ben〉

Some of Ben's friends in England are making a cassette to send him.
Listen to them and answer these questions:

1. What did Ronny do with Ben's letter?
2. What will happen to the article about Ben?
3. What does Barbara think of Ben's photos?
4. What are Timmy's questions about Peggy?
5. What is Kate's question about Ben's new school?
6. What has the weather been like in England?
7. What is Kevin going to do?
8. Why will they have to finish the cassette later?

S 〈12 Let's sing a song: 500 miles〉

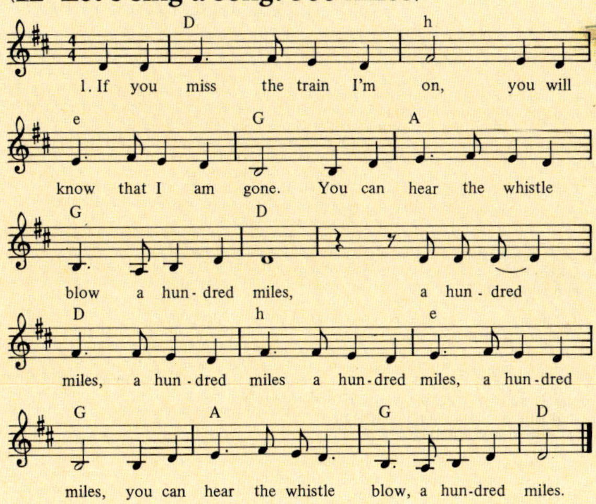

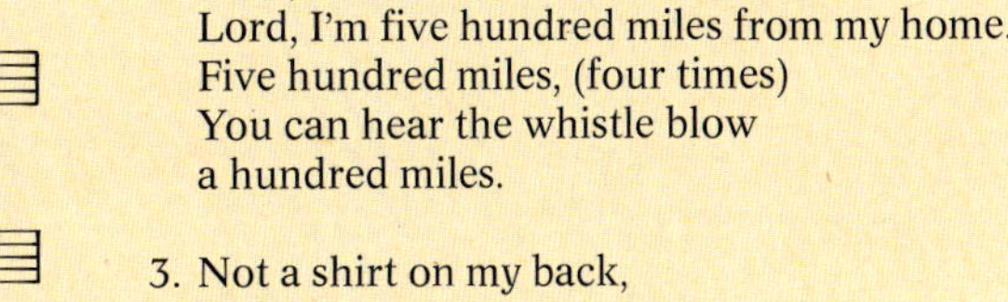

2. Lord, I'm one, Lord, I'm two,
Lord, I'm three, Lord, I'm four,
Lord, I'm five hundred miles from my home.
Five hundred miles, (four times)
You can hear the whistle blow
a hundred miles.

3. Not a shirt on my back,
Not a penny to my name,
Lord, I can't go back home this-a-way.
This-a-way, (four times)
No, I can't go back home this-a-way.

[13 Sorry? What's that?]

Beverly Snyder has got a cold. Today she has even lost her voice. She can only whisper, so Ralph has to help her.

Beverly:	*Ralph:*
a) I haven't done my homework. I had a headache yesterday.	She says (that) she hasn't done her homework. … she had a headache yesterday.
b) Can I shut the window? Is it going to snow today? Did anybody see Old Jeff yesterday?	She asks if she can shut the window. … if it's going to snow today. … if anybody saw Old Jeff yesterday.
c) What did he say about the weather? Why does he always get it wrong?	She asks what he said about the weather. … why he always gets it wrong.
d) Can I go home, please? I'm not feeling well.	She asks if she can go home. She says (that) she's not feeling well.

Now one of you is Beverly and someone else helps her.

1. I don't understand this exercise.
2. Can you write that word on the board, please?
3. What page are we on?
4. I can't find my pencil.
5. Have you finished the exercise, Ben?
6. Why didn't Peggy come to our lemonade stand?
7. I've read this story three times. It's very good.
8. How did Harry do that card trick?
9. I'm not going to study for the next test. I already know everything.
10. When will we get our five dollars from Buddy?

⟨14 Trick no. 729⟩

⟨Authentic America: Ben's pictures⟩

This is my school.

I took this photo of the main street in Enid.

I saw this cowboy on a ranch near Enid.

This tent is in Anadarko, the Indian city, ...

... and so is this – they call it a 'wicki-up'.

Harry and I went to the cinema.

Unit 7

A The raft

Peggy Whitecloud lives on a farm a few miles outside Enid. Near the farm there is a small lake. Last week Peggy invited Ben and Harry to come swimming in the lake.
"You'll like our raft," she said. So the boys cycled out there on Sunday morning. Ben took his camera because he wanted some more photos for his friends in York.
"Let me take the photos," said Harry. "Then you can be in them." "O.K.," said Ben.
When they arrived, Peggy was tying the raft to the jetty. "Hi," she said, "I'm afraid we'll have to repair the raft first." "No problem," said Harry. "You two fetch some tools and another oil-drum and I'll think about what we do next."
So Ben and Peggy fetched the things. And Harry sat and thought hard.

"First we'll have to take off those boards," he said.
So Ben got into the water with Peggy. While they were working, Harry took a photo.
"Now we'll have to tie the new drum on ... Yes, that's O.K. ... tighten it. ... Smile please." Harry took another photo. "And now those boards again ... You'll need some more nails ... The hammer's over there, Ben ... No, that's not straight ... A bit nearer you, Peggy ... Too much! ..." And while they were putting the boards back, Harry took another photo.
"That was hard work," said Harry. "While you're putting the tools away, I'll get a cold drink from your mother, Peggy."

When Harry came back, Ben was holding the camera.
"Get on the raft and I'll take your picture," said Ben.
"Sure," Harry said. But Peggy was hiding under the jetty. When Harry was on the raft, she untied it and pushed it out into the lake.
"Hey! Pull me back!" Harry shouted.
"Swim!" Peggy shouted back.
"My clothes will get wet! Come on you two, pull me back to the jetty!"
And while Harry was dancing about and shouting, Ben called, "Smile please, Harry," and took a photo.

1 What happened while ... ?

1. While Peggy was tying the raft to the jetty, →	a) Ben took a photo of him.
2. While the others were fetching the things,	b) Harry got a cold drink from Peggy's mother.
3. While Ben and Peggy were working,	c) Harry stepped onto the raft.
4. While they were putting the tools away,	→ d) Ben and Harry arrived on their bikes.
5. While Peggy was hiding under the jetty,	e) Harry sat down and thought hard.
6. While Harry was standing on the raft,	f) Harry took a photo of them.
7. While he was dancing about and shouting,	g) Peggy pushed it out into the lake.

2 What were they doing when ... ?

What was everybody doing when Peggy and her friends got back to the house?

Example: 1. When Peggy and her friends got back, Nellie was feeding the hens.

2. Big Paws was ...
3. Mr Whitecloud ...
4. Grandpa ...
5. Spot ...
6. John ...
7. Mrs Whitecloud ...

3 What were they doing? What happened?

Example: 1. While Harry was dancing about, Ben took a photo.
Or: Harry was dancing about when Ben took a photo.

2. While Ben ..., he ...
Ben ... when he ...

B Looking at the farm

In the afternoon Peggy and her little sister Nellie showed the boys around the farm.

Peggy: This is our machine shed.
Ben: Boy, what a lot of machines.
Harry: Hey, there's a tractor. Can we ride on it?
Peggy: We'll have to wait until Dad comes.
Ben: Look over there. A windmill. Do you make your own flour?
Nellie: No, silly. It's for water. It pumps it up from the well.
Harry: Water. That's a good idea. Let's get something to drink. It's hot here.
Peggy: We've got some ice-cold watermelon in the house. But let's wait until we've seen the barn.

In the barn.

Harry: Where are all the animals? I can only see hay and more machines.
Peggy: We haven't got very many. We're wheat farmers.
Ben: Hey, I can see a hen over there.
Peggy: That's Emily. We keep hens so that we don't have to buy any eggs.
Harry: Have you got pigs, too? So that you have lots of bacon?
Ben: And sheep so that you can make pullovers?
Nellie: No, but we've got a bull. Rodney. He won a prize last year.
Ben: What for?
Nellie: Because he's so beautiful. Just wait until you see him. He's over here.
Harry: Oh, hi, Rodney. You *are* a beautiful bull.
Nellie: Hee, hee. You're so funny, Harry.
Harry: Me?
Peggy: Harry, that's not Rodney. That's Elsie, our cow. And we keep her so that we don't have to buy any milk.
Harry: Oh. Can we have that watermelon now?

1 I'm afraid ...

This is what the boys want to do:

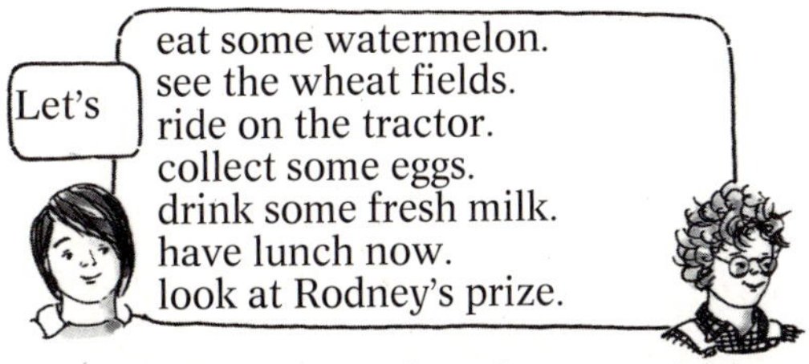

And here are Peggy's answers:

Make dialogues. Work with your neighbour.

2  "What did you do?"

Peggy and Ben are talking about yesterday afternoon. *Put in the verbs. Use the past tense.*

Peggy: Ben, why ... you ... me yesterday? (not phone)
Ben: Er – I ... too busy. (be)
Peggy: What! You ... too busy? (be)
Ben: Well – er – after school I ... my homework, then I ... Mum and Dad in the garden and after that I ... shopping. (do/help/go)
Peggy: Is that all?
Ben: Er – no. Later I ... dinner and then I ..., of course. (cook/wash up) And I ... to bed at seven. (go)
Peggy: Ben, I know you. You ... dinner. (not cook) You ... it. (eat) And I'm sure you ... your homework. (not do) I think you ... records, then you ... ball and after that you ... TV. (listen to/play/watch) And I bet you ... to bed at eleven and ... comics. (go/read)
Ben: I guess you know me too well, Peggy. I ... to phone you but I just .... (want/forget)

3 What were they doing? What did they do?

1. Ben <u>was swimming</u> when a fish <u>touched</u> him. So he <u>ran</u> out of the water.
2. Grandpa was ... *Go on.*

4 Wrong room!

In the afternoon, while Peggy and the boys were riding on the tractor, she told them this story.
But the boys couldn't understand everything because of the noise.
So they asked her a lot of questions.

Grandpa was staying at a hotel. (1)
It was eleven o'clock at night (2)
and Grandpa was lying in bed, (3)
but he couldn't sleep.
Suddenly the door opened (4)
and someone came in.
A man. (5)
It was dark, but Grandpa could
see him.
The man walked over to the bed. (6)
Then he sat down – on Grandpa. (7)
The man was very heavy.
So while he was sitting on him,
Grandpa shouted, "Hey!" (8)
The man jumped up and ran out of
the room. (9)
"Wrong room!" Grandpa shouted
after him and laughed. (10)
And he was still laughing when the
man came back with the owner.
Grandpa was in the wrong room. (11)

5 Ask your neighbour

Did you sleep at your grandparents' last night?

Where did you sleep?

No, I didn't.

I slept at home.

Ask your neighbour if ...

1. ... she (*or* he) slept at her (*or* his) grandparents' last night. (If not, where ... ?)
2. ... she was eating something when the teacher came in. (If not, what was she doing?)
3. ... she came to school by bus. (If not, how ... ?)
4. ... she saw an animal on the way to school. (If she did, what/where ... ?)
5. ... her mother did her homework for her yesterday? (If not, who ... ?)
6. ... she was finishing her homework when the lesson started. (What?)
7. ... she watched TV last night. (What? When?)
8. ... she was talking to her neighbour a moment ago. (What?)

OVER TO YOU *Can you think of more questions?*

C How Rabbit brought fire to the people

In the evening Peggy's Grandpa told the children an old Indian story.

1. At first the earth was cold. There was no fire at all until the Thunderbirds sent their lightning to an old tree. But this fire-tree was on an island where the Weasels lived. So only the Weasels had fire and they did not give it to anyone else.

The people knew that there was fire on the island because they could see the smoke. But they could not go there because the water around the island was very deep.

2. Then the winter came and it was colder than ever, and the people were suffering. So they invited all their animal friends. "We need fire so that we won't freeze," the people said. "You can all swim or fly. Which of you can get us fire?" But the animals were afraid of the Weasels because they ate mice and moles and fish and birds. No one wanted to go until Rabbit stood up and said: "I can swim and run fast. And I can also dance very well. Every night the Weasels make a big fire and dance around it. Tonight I'll swim across and while they're dancing, I'll run away with some fire."

Then Rabbit made a plan. He put some pine tar on his head so that his hair stood up. He waited until it was dark and then he swam across.

3. The Weasels were already dancing around a big fire when Rabbit arrived. "Come and dance with us!" they called to him. "We know you're a good dancer." The Weasels were dancing in a circle – nearer and nearer to the fire. Then they bowed to the fire and danced away from it again. "Yahoo! Here I come!" Rabbit shouted and kicked his legs up into the air, and the Weasels opened their circle for him. "Lead us, Rabbit!" they shouted, and Rabbit danced ahead of them, closer and closer to the fire, and bowed, then back again. "Whahoo!" he shouted and bowed to the fire again, lower this time. And while they were dancing around and around, faster and faster, Rabbit suddenly bowed very low so that the pine tar in his hair caught fire.

4. And with the fire on his head he ran off. "He has stolen our fire! Catch him! Catch him!" the Weasels shouted and rushed after him. It was a wild chase, and they nearly caught him. But Rabbit was faster and jumped into the water and swam across with the fire still in his hair.

The Weasels now called out: "Oh, you great Thunderbirds, send us rain so that the fire on Rabbit's head will go out!" And for days and days it rained and rained until the Weasels were sure that there was no fire anywhere – except in their fire-tree.

5. But while it was raining, Rabbit was with his friends, the people, in a tepee. They were sitting around a warm fire and talking about Rabbit's courage.

1 Comprehension

What belongs together?

– Rabbit stole the fire ----→	**when** the Weasels rushed after him.
– The people were cold in the winter	**if** they ask him.
– Rabbit put pine tar on his head	**until** Rabbit brought them fire.
– The Weasels were happy to see Rabbit	**while** it was raining.
– Rabbit jumped into the water	**because** he was a good dancer.
– Rabbit sat in a tepee	**so that** he could steal the fire.
– Rabbit will help the people again	→ **while** the Weasels were dancing.

⟨2 The fox, the goose and the corn⟩

A farmer had a big problem. He was standing by a river. At his side there was a basket of corn, a fox and a goose – and the farmer had to take all three to the other side. But his raft was only big enough for himself and **one** of his belongings. Now he couldn't take the fox and leave the goose alone with the corn. The goose would eat it. And he couldn't leave the fox and the goose alone because the fox was hungry. What could he do? …
Well, a little later the farmer and all three of his belongings were on the other side of the river.

Can you tell the class how he did it?
First he … Then …

Solution on page 192

3 What they couldn't do

Look at these dialogues.

1. *Peggy:* The hens were too fast for Harry.
   Ben: So he couldn't catch them?
   Peggy: That's right. He couldn't catch them because they were too fast for him.

2. *John:* There was too much fog.
   Harry: You mean – you couldn't see anything?
   John: That's right. We couldn't see anything because there was too much fog.

Can you and your neighbour make more dialogues like these?
Here are some sentences to help you.

3. The homework was too difficult.
4. The film was in French.
5. Our TV broke down yesterday.
6. The bag was too heavy for my little sister.
7. The party was last night, but I had too much work.
8. There were too many people in the water.
9. The book was too expensive for my brother.

4 Going home

Can you put the verbs in the correct form – simple past or past progressive?

It was late when Grandpa finished his story about Rabbit. So the boys … (leave) their bikes at the farm and Mr Whitecloud … (drive) them back to town. While Mr Whitecloud … (drive) them back to town, they … (see) a dog. It … (lie) on the road. Mr Whitecloud … (stop) the car and they … (get out). The dog – a little brown one – … (cry) when they … (come) to it. They … (look at) the little animal. "A car has hit him," Mr Whitecloud … (say). He was angry. "We'll have to take him to a vet," Harry … (add). "Poor doggy. I'm going to call him Freddy," Ben … (say) while they … (put) him in the back of the car. Then Ben and Harry … (get) in the back, too, and Mr Whitecloud … (drive off).

"… you … (hit) him with your car?" Doc Barnes … (ask) while he … (examine) Freddy. "No, I didn't," Mr Whitecloud … (tell) him. "Where … you … (find) him?" Doc Barnes … (want) to know, and the boys … (explain). "Well, it's too late for this little doggy," the doc … (say) at last.

Later, when he … (lie) in his bed, Ben … (cannot) sleep. "What a perfect day," he … (think), "and then we … (find) Freddy." And later still, when his mother … (open) his door, he … (cry).

5 Look, listen and say

[e]	Are you already in bed, Ben? Yes, where ‿else?	[ɜː]	The early bird catches the worm. Have you heard? It's Ernie's third birthday.
[æ]	I had a bad dream: an angry adjective sat in an ash-tray with a mashed apple in its hand.	[aʊ]	How now, brown cow?
		[əʊ]	Rolling home to Oklahoma.
[æ]–[e]	Alice likes Ellis and Ellen likes Alan. Pat's pet had a hat on its head.	[aʊ]–[əʊ]	Open up! It's cold outside in these old trousers.

6 

What have they just done?

a) It is Saturday the 25th.

Can you say what they have (just) done?

Example:
1. Mrs MacDonald has just bought a lamp.
2. Harry … a bath. *Go on.*

b) It is now Monday the 27th.

Can you say what they did <u>*two days ago*</u> *(or: on the 25th, on Saturday, the day before yesterday, last week, last Saturday)?*

Example:
1. Mrs MacDonald bought a lamp two days ago.
2. Harry … *Go on.*

7 Peggy's family

First read this.

1. Grandpa is on the sofa. It is Sunday afternoon and his eyes are closed. Sometimes he drives to town in the afternoons, but not today.

Then ask your neighbour.

a) Ask if Grandpa drives to town.
b) … if he is driving to town.
c) … what he is doing.

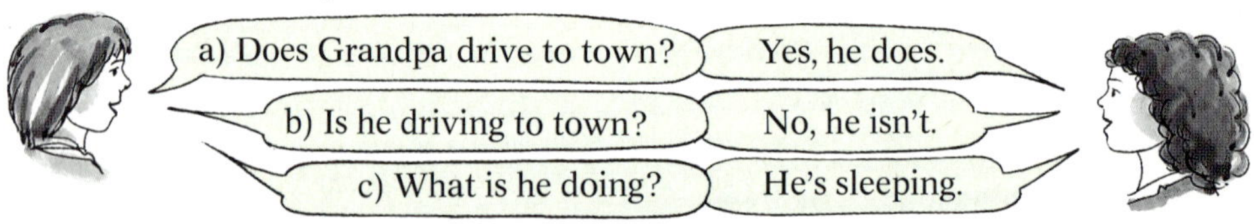

Can you go on?

2. Mr Whitecloud is painting the barn at the moment. "It's hot!" he thinks. "I'd like a nice cold glass of milk."

a) Ask if Mr Whitecloud drinks milk.
b) … if he is drinking milk.
c) … what he is doing.

3. Mrs Whitecloud likes to read books but she doesn't have much time. At the moment she is writing a letter.

a) Ask if Mrs Whitecloud is reading a book.
b) … what she is doing.
c) … if she reads books.

4. John brushes Rodney for a quarter of an hour every afternoon. Then he has a cup of tea. He is still with Rodney.

a) Ask what John is doing.
b) … if John drinks tea.
c) … if he is drinking tea.

5. Nellie is a good swimmer and she often goes to the lake. But this afternoon she is in the house. There is a good film on TV.

a) Ask if Nellie swims in the lake.
b) … if she is swimming in the lake.
c) … what she is doing.

8 

The next morning Ben told his parents about his day with Peggy and Harry.
What did he say? Here are some pictures to help you.

You can start like this:
In the morning Harry and I cycled to Peggy's farm. When we arrived, we ...

9 The homework questionnaire

Ben and Harry have to give a report in school – all about how pupils do their homework. That's why Ben has made this questionnaire for the class. But Harry thinks that they must still put in some words.

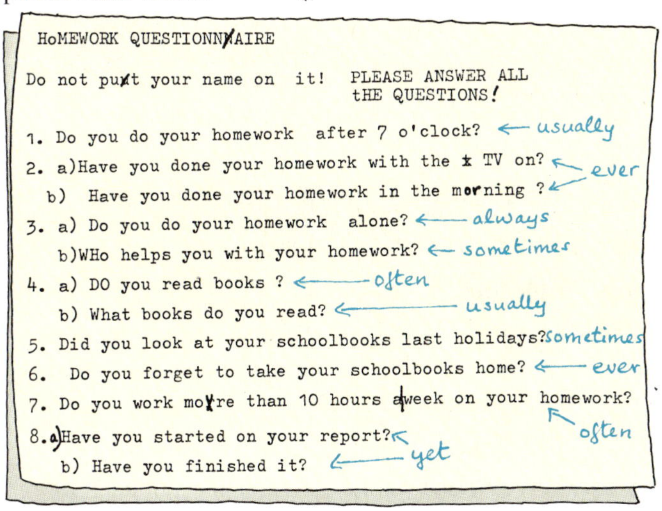
HoMEWORK QUESTIONNAIRE

Do not put your name on it! PLEASE ANSWER ALL tHE QUESTIONS!

1. Do you do your homework after 7 o'clock? ← usually
2. a) Have you done your homework with the TV on? ← ever
   b) Have you done your homework in the morning? ← ever
3. a) Do you do your homework alone? ← always
   b) WHo helps you with your homework? ← sometimes
4. a) DO you read books? ← often
   b) What books do you read? ← usually
5. Did you look at your schoolbooks last holidays? sometimes
6. Do you forget to take your schoolbooks home? ← ever
7. Do you work more than 10 hours a week on your homework? ← often
8. a) Have you started on your report? ← yet
   b) Have you finished it? ← yet

a) *Can you write the questionnaire again with Harry's words?*

b) *Now answer the questions. Use words like*

in your answers.

c) *Did Ben and Harry forget any important questions? Can you think of any?*

Example: 1. Do you usually do your homework after seven o'clock?
– No, I never do my homework after seven. I always do it before we have our meal.
2. Have you ... *Go on.*

⟨10 Let's sing a song: Old MacDonald had a farm⟩

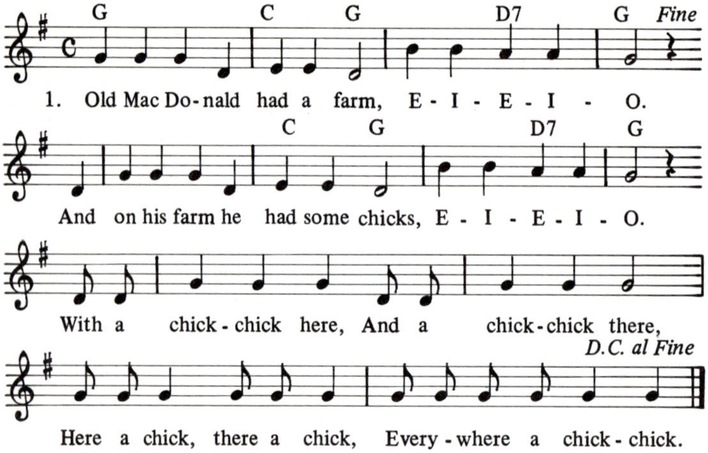

2. ... some ducks (quack-quack)
3. ... some geese (gabble-gabble)
4. ... a pig (oink-oink)
5. ... a cow (moo-moo)

⟨11 Do you know these animals?⟩

a) *Can you give the name of these animals?*

1. This is a big animal. It says "moo" and gives us milk.
2. This animal often lives on a farm. It is a big animal, too, but it does not give us milk. You can ride on it.
3. These are little animals. They do not like cats. They are afraid of them. The most famous one is Mickey ...
4. These animals are often fat. We get bacon from them.
5. This little animal is a bird. It can fly, but it usually lives in a cage.
6. This is a farm animal. It looks like a duck, but it has a long neck.

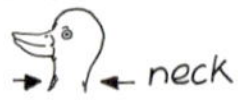

7. This animal barks. It often lives in a house with people.
8. These animals are smaller than foxes. They can run fast and they like to eat hens.

b) *What can you tell the class about these animals? (Where do they live? What do they look like? ... eat? ... "say"? What can they do? ...)*

1. a parrot 2. a fish 3. a hen 4. a rabbit 5. birds 6. a duck 7. cats 8. a deer 9. a cheetah

⟨12 Listening comprehension: Johnny Appleseed⟩

When Old Jeff talks about the weather, Ben and his friends laugh. But they love it when he tells them stories. Here is one of Old Jeff's favourite stories – a true story – from the days of the early settlers. *Listen to it and then answer these questions:*

1. When did John Chapman live?
2. Where was his home when he was a boy?
3. Where did he go when he left home?
4. What was the country in the West like? And who lived there?
5. How did John want to make things better for the white settlers?
6. What did he do when he went back to New England?
7. What happened to all the apple seeds?
8. Why did people call John Chapman 'Johnny Appleseed'?

⟨Photo page: Farming in America⟩

A windmill in the Southwest

A small farm in Oklahoma

Harvesting wheat

In the West, they call this a "cattle drive".

Rounding up the cattle

A farmer and his wheatfield in northern Oklahoma

Unit 8

⟨Authentic America: In town⟩

An American supermarket

Buy your hot pretzels here!

Inside the post office

Firemen at work

"United Skates of America"

A No problem!

Mrs Alassio lives in Ben's neighbourhood.

Mrs Alassio: Ben, could you take this letter to the post office for me? I don't like taking the car into town.

Ben: Yes, of course. I've got something to post, too, and I love cycling into town.

Mrs Alassio: It'll cost 40 ¢. Here's a dollar. The rest is for you.

Ben: Thanks, Mrs Alassio.

Mrs Alassio: Thank *you*, Ben. But please be careful. It's very important. It's a cheque for my mother in Italy. It's her birthday next week. If it goes off today, she'll get it next Tuesday or Wednesday.

At the post office.

Ben: Could you tell me how much this packet will cost? It's some comics for my pen-friend in France.

Clerk: The envelope is still open. Shall I close it?

Ben Yes, please.

Clerk: Do you want to send it by airmail?

Ben: Yes, it'll be faster like that. Pierre enjoys reading American comics.

Clerk: *(closes the envelope)* Good. All right, airmail to France. That'll be $ 2.72.

Ben: O.K. Could you please put on some nice stamps? Pierre collects them.

Clerk: All right. I'll put on four forty-cent stamps, a dollar stamp and a twelve-cent one. And an airmail sticker.

Ben: Great.

That evening.

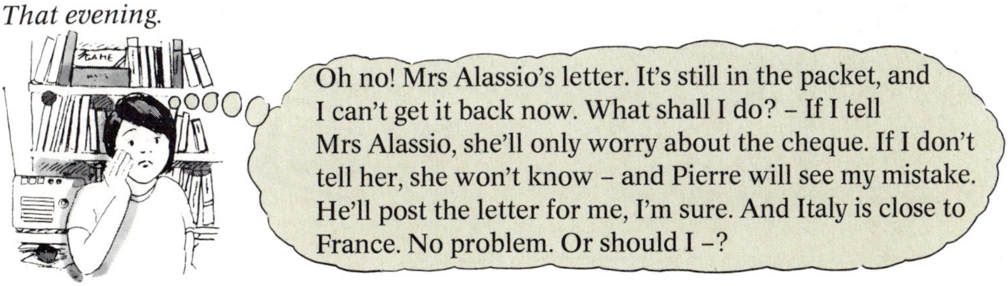

1 Comprehension *Can you finish these sentences?*

1. Mrs Alassio lives …
2. One day she asks Ben to …
3. She does this because …
4. Ben says yes because he …
5. Mrs Alassio gives Ben …
6. She asks him to be careful because …
7. Ben puts the letter into …
8. At the post office the clerk closes …
9. Ben wants to send the letter by airmail because …
10. The clerk puts on …
11. In the evening Ben suddenly remembers Mrs Alassio's letter. "Oh no! It's still … and I …"
12. No problem, he thinks. Pierre will …

2 "What shall I do?"

Make sentences with 'if'. *Examples:* 1. I'll tell Mrs Alassio. She'll know what to do.
→ If I tell Mrs Alassio, she'll know what to do.
2. No – I won't tell her. Then she won't worry.
→ If I don't tell her, she won't worry.

3. I won't say anything. Then there won't be any problems.
4. Pierre will use his brains. He'll send the letter to Italy.
5. Or perhaps he won't understand. Then he'll open the letter or send it back.
6. Perhaps he won't post it to Italy. Then Mrs Alassio's mother won't get it.
7. Mrs Alassio's mother won't get the money on time. Then Mrs Alassio will be angry with me.
8. Perhaps Mrs Alassio can post another cheque. Then her mother will get it next week.
9. She'll phone the bank first. Then there won't be any problems.
10. Yes – I'll tell her. Then everything will be all right.

3 Telling the truth

Later that evening Ben decides to tell Mrs Alassio everything. But what can he say? He could begin like this: "Mrs Alassio, something terrible has happened. You see, when I – er …"

Can you help Ben to find the right words?

4 "What could we do on Saturday?"

Peggy and her friend Sally Kahn are talking about the weekend.

Peggy: We could have a picnic on our farm.
Sally: Great. Could we go swimming in your lake, too?
Peggy: Sure. When could you come? …

Can you make plans, too? Here are some words to help you.

What could we do? When could we … ? Where could we … ? Could we … ? Couldn't we ? …	We could … on … at … Yes, we could. No, we can't (because …). But we could … That's a good idea. Or we could … …

[5 Some people]

a) 

John likes working on the farm,
but he is a **slow** worker.
He works **slowly**.
He is very **careful** with Rodney.
He brushes him **carefully**.

Mrs Alassio likes singing,
but she is a **bad** singer.
She sings **badly**.

Bill Pushy loves driving,
but he is a **dangerous** driver.
He drives **dangerously**.

Pierre likes English.
He thinks it is an **easy** language.
He can read English **easily**.

Peggy is a good swimmer. She can swim well.

She is also a fast runner. She can run fast.

Answer the questions.

1. Is John a fast worker? How does he work?
2. How does he brush Rodney?
3. What can you say about Mrs Alassio's voice?
4. Does Bill Pushy drive carefully?
5. Does Pierre have problems with English?
6. Does Peggy swim badly?
7. Is she a fast runner?
8. What can you say about Rabbit?

b) *Put in the right adverb.*

1. Harry was angry. "Pull me back to the jetty!" he said ... .
2. When the packet arrived, Pierre was excited. He opened it ... .
3. Ben was very nervous. "Er – hello, Mrs Alassio," he said ... .
4. Peggy and Ben did a good job. They repaired the raft very ... .
5. Buddy was happy. He stood under the tree ... and gave the signal.
6. It was a perfect trick. It worked ... .
7. Buddy was too slow. He moved too ... .
8. Ben is a bad tennis-player. He often misses the ball. He plays really ... .

c) *Finish the sentences.*

1. Old Jeff sometimes drives dangerously. But Bill Pushy drives much **more dangerously**.
2. Beverly can run fast. But Peggy can run much **faster**.
3. The Weasels ran quickly. But Rabbit ...
4. Mrs Alassio walks slowly. But Peggy's grandfather ...
5. Peggy can swim fast. But a fish ...
6. Pierre can understand American comics easily. But Ben ...
7. Harry jumped about wildly when Peggy pushed the raft out. But Buddy ... when Pete turned on the water.

B Fire at the Oxford Hotel

Last week Ben's class had to write a tall story. This is what Peggy Whitecloud wrote.

"No, girls, don't visit the fire-station," Mom said to Nellie and me. "Those men can't talk to little kids all day. They have important work to do." But Nellie and I went anyway. And the firemen didn't mind at all. They enjoyed explaining everything to us. They were just showing us a big red fire-engine when the alarm bell rang. So they jumped in and rushed off and left us all alone.

"We'll come back tomorrow when everybody's here," I said to Nellie, but she didn't want to go. "No," she cried. "I like it here. I'm going to stay." Well, I was pulling her out when the alarm bell rang again: a fire at the Oxford Hotel! So I grabbed Nellie, jumped into a fire-engine with her and started off.

"Where are we going?" Nellie asked. She looked worried. "To the fire, of course," I told her. "We have to help." "But you're only 12 and you've never driven a car," she said. She had a lot of nerve: she was only 6. "You're driving on the wrong side of the road," Nellie said. "That's not important. Fire-engines always drive on the wrong side of the road. And please don't worry so much," I said and turned on the siren. We were doing over 150 mph.

When we arrived at the hotel, there were flames everywhere, and everybody was running around and screaming. But I didn't lose my head. I turned on the water. "Is everybody out of the hotel?" I asked. "No," a policeman shouted. "A mother and five children are still on the 21st floor!" I looked up and saw them at the window. "Here," I said and gave Nellie the water hose. "Could you put out the fire while I rescue those people?" Then I raised the ladder and climbed up through the flames.

"Screaming won't help," I told the mother when I arrived at the 21st floor. "Mom hates fires," one of the little kids said, "That's why she's screaming." "Well, I'm going to rescue you now," I said and carried them all down.

Nellie was just putting out the last flames when I put the mother and the kids down. And then I saw a reporter with a camera. He was coming towards us. "Quick," I said to Nellie. "Let's get out of here!" "But I've never had my picture in the newspaper," she said. "Don't be stupid, Nellie. We don't want our picture in the newspaper. If Mom finds out about this, we'll be in trouble," I said and grabbed her, and we hurried home.

1 Tell the story again

Peggy and Nellie were alone at the . All the  were away at a .
Suddenly the  rang: a  at the ! So they jumped into a big  and  off. Peggy turned on the siren. Soon they were doing 150 mph on the wrong side of the . At the  there were  everywhere. But Peggy didn't lose her . She turned on the 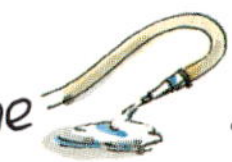. Peggy looked  and saw a  with her  at a  on the 21st floor. She gave Nellie the , raised the  and climbed . When she got  with the  and , a  came towards them with a .
"Let's get out of here," Peggy said. "We don't want our  in the .

2 More plans

When they heard Peggy's tall story, Ben and Harry decided to visit the fire-station. They are making plans right now.

1. *Ben:* I hope I can get our new camera.
   Harry: Yes, we'll take some good photos of those fire-engines with it.
2. *Ben:* But perhaps I won't get it.
   Harry: Then I'll take my old one.
3. *Harry:* Let's go there on Saturday.
   Ben: Good idea. We'll have a lot of time then.
4. *Harry:* And let's go early.
   Ben: But not too early. Or I'll still be half-asleep.
5. *Ben:* I hope it won't rain.
   Harry: Yes. Then we'll take our bikes.
6. *Harry:* But perhaps it will rain.
   Ben: Then I'll ask Dad to take us.
7. *Harry:* I'll do some of my magic tricks for the firemen.
   Ben: Great. They'll show us everything then.
8. *Harry:* My brother has got a book about firemen. We could read that before we go.
   Ben: That's a good idea. Then we'll understand everything better.
9. *Harry:* Perhaps there'll be a fire on Saturday?
   Ben: Well, then we'll go there, too.
10. *Harry:* But let's phone the fire-station first.
    Ben: Of course. Or the firemen won't be ready for us.
11. *Ben:* Let's ask the others. Perhaps they'll come, too.
    Harry: Sure. It'll be more fun then.

Can you make sentences with 'if'?

1. If Ben can get the new camera, they will take some good photos of the fire-engines with it.
2. If he doesn't get it, Harry … *Go on.*

3 

Mickey, come back!

Here is Ben's story about something that happened in his neighbourhood.
Can you put the verbs in the correct form?

1 It happened two weeks ago, but nobody has forgotten it.
And I don't think anybody in our neighbourhood will forget it for a long time.
You see, Mickey ran away from home, or flew away, I should say. Mickey is a budgie.
He is Old Jeff's budgie.

2 Well, two weeks ago Old Jeff … (open) a window while Mickey … (fly) around in the house. And Mickey … (fly) out and … (land) in a big tree in front of the house. Old Jeff … (run) out after him, of course. And while he … (call) his "Mickeybird", everybody in our neighbourhood … (come) out to see what … (happen).

3 "That poor man. Now he … (lose) his best friend," Mrs Hopper said. "Not yet," Harry said. "I … (call) the fire department now. I'm sure they … (rescue) that bird in a few minutes."

4 When the fire-engine … (arrive), everybody … (stand) out in the street. Mickey … (be) still up in the tree and Old Jeff … still … (call) him. "I … (not let) that bird out of his cage again when he … (come) back," Old Jeff said. "Not for three days at least."

5 "Look. What … those firemen … (do) over there?" little Jimmy asked. "They … (raise) a ladder up into that tree. They … (fetch) Mickey," Mum told him. "Don't worry. We … (have) him in a minute!" a fireman … (shout) down while he … (climb) up the ladder.

6 But it … (not happen) like that. You see, he … (fall) down – the fireman, I mean. "Oh no! Fred … (break) his arm," a fireman said. There … (be) a lot of shouting and running around then, and Mickey … (fly) to another tree. After that we … (cannot) see him any more.

7 "This is exciting. I … (never see) anything like this before," Jimmy said. "What … they … (do) next?" "They … (take) that fireman to hospital," I said. "And Mickey?" he asked.

8 "I … (be) sorry," one of the firemen said to Old Jeff. "Perhaps your bird … (come) back later." "Yes, sometimes they … (come) back," another one added. And then they … (leave) in their fire-engine.

9 Old Jeff was very unhappy. For a long time he just stood there and looked up into the tree. Then he turned and started to walk back to his house – and then, suddenly, there was a noise and something green landed on his head. Mickey! Well, I have never seen anyone as happy as Old Jeff and Mickey when they went home together.

[4 Who are they?]

a) *Can you say who they are?*

Start like this: I think number one is ... because ... likes riding and helping on the farm.
I think number two is ... because ... *Go on.*

b) Here are some more facts. *Which gerund goes where?*

1. Buddy can't stop **playing** tricks on people.
2. Beverly doesn't like ... .
3. Ben likes ... his bike.
4. Ralph has always hated ... in front of the class.
5. Peggy and her friends enjoy ... in the lake.
6. Nellie loved ... her teddy when she was a baby.
7. Harry loves ... chocolate pudding.

washing up, ~~playing~~, riding, swimming, eating, holding, singing

c) And here is what they say about them.

Can you put in the right words?

1. *Buddy:* Playing tricks on people is a lot of fun. It's my hobby.
2. *Beverly:* ... is hard work. Eating is better.
3. *Ben:* ... is good for you and it's fun, too.
4. *Ralph:* ... makes me nervous.
5. *Peggy:* ... keeps us cool on hot days.
6. *Nellie:* ... was always very nice.
7. *Harry:* ... is good for magicians.

d) OVER TO YOU What do you like doing?

- Tell the class what you like (or don't like)/love/enjoy/hate doing. What about your family/friends/pets?
- What is a lot of fun/interesting/boring/difficult/...? *Use gerunds.*

[5 What do they do?]

Example: 1. The man you can see on the tractor is a farmer.
2. The woman you ... *Go on.*

[6 Peggy's tall story]

The fire-station	Peggy drove	were on the 21st floor.
The firemen	she rescued from the fire	had a very loud siren.
The things	Peggy and Nellie visited	were very nice people.
The fire-engine	the firemen explained	was in Enid.
The people	Peggy wrote	wasn't a true story.
The ladder	they met there	were very interesting.
The story	she raised	was just long enough.

[7 What was the name of ...?]

There were a lot of new names in this book. *Ask your neighbours about them.*

Example: 1. David bought a *pet.*

2. Nick, Barbara and Elke visited a *castle.* – What was the name of the ...?
3. The girls at Fulford play a *game.* – What is the name of the ...?
4. Kate helped a *pony.* – What was the name ...?
5. Ben, Harry and Mr Whitecloud found a *dog* on the road. – What was ...?
6. You can see a famous *statue* in Nottingham. – ...?
7. The Saxon people didn't like *him.* – ...?

[8 Oh no! Not again!]

a) Somebody has moved everything in the classroom again.

Can you put in the correct words?

2. *Ben:* Hey, girls are these books … ?
Peggy: No, … are much nicer than that.
3. *Harry:* This isn't my ruler. … is longer than that.
Beverly: I think it's Ben's. … looks like that.
4. *Ben:* Whose pencil cases are these?
Harry: They belong to Peggy and Suzy.
Ralph: No, they don't. … are under my desk.
5. *Beverly:* Is this sandwich …, Peggy?
Peggy: No, it isn't. Where's Sally? I'm sure it's …
6. *Harry:* What a mess. This old paper must be …, girls.
Beverly: … ?! Very funny. It's … . You just don't want to throw it away.

whose?	
mine	– ours
yours	– yours
his	
hers	– theirs

b) OVER TO YOU Now one of you can walk through the classroom. He must pick up things (pens, biros, pencil cases, schoolbags, …) and ask questions: Is this your … ? …

⟨9 Let's sing a song: This land is your land⟩

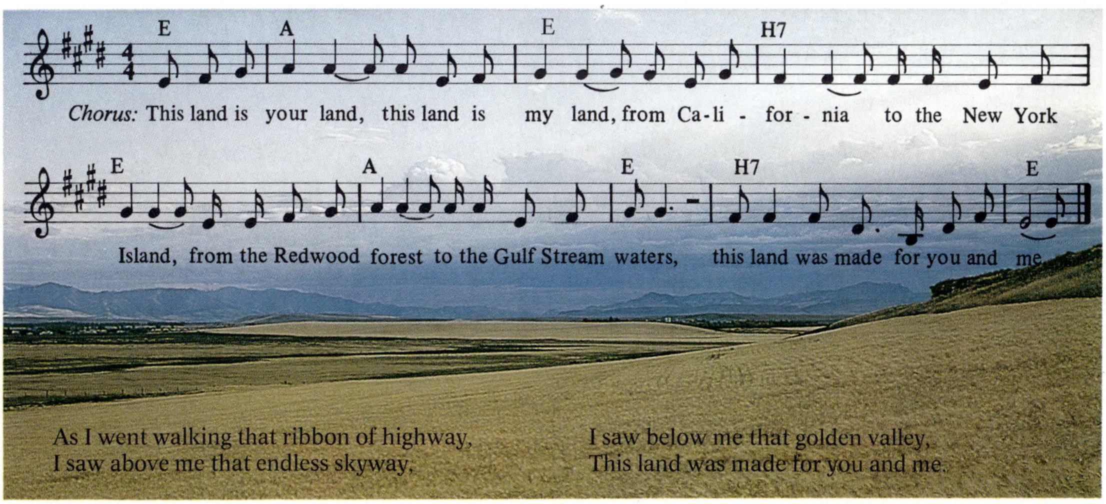

⟨Photo page: American cities⟩

The skyline of Chicago

Fifth Avenue in New York

A cable car in San Francisco

A telephone call in New York!

The centre of Oklahoma City

New Orleans: The old French Quarter

⟨Reading corner⟩

1 All change! – A party game

Perhaps you can play this game at your next party. It's a good game for a group of twenty people or more, but you can play it with only five or six, too.
You need: chairs for all **except one.**
First put the chairs in a circle. You stand in the middle of the circle, and everybody else sits down.
Then you say, for example: "Change places if … you're wearing white socks!" As soon as you say this, **all** the people with white socks on **must** get up and go to another chair. They aren't allowed to go back to their old chair.
When they all get up, **you** go to one of the empty chairs and sit on it. This means that one person will not find a seat, so he or she now stands in the middle, and it's his or her turn to think of something new.
Some examples: "Change places if … you had an egg for breakfast this morning!"
… you've got brown eyes!"
… you go to school by bus!"
… you like chocolate!"
The game goes on until you've had enough of it.

circle ['sɜ:kl] – *Kreis*

to change places ['tʃeɪndʒ ˌpleɪsɪz] – *Plätze tauschen*
As soon as … – *Sobald …*

2 Coleslaw[1] – An American recipe[2]

You will need: half a kilo of white cabbage[3] / 2 tablespoons[4] of vinegar[5] / 1 tablespoon of sugar / salt and pepper[6] / 1 small onion[7] / 3 tablespoons of mayonnaise[8] / 50 ml of sour cream[9].

1. Shred[10] the cabbage, then put it in cold water for 20 to 30 minutes.
2. Throw away the water (the cabbage must be dry).
3. Mix[11] the vinegar, sugar, salt and pepper in a salad bowl. Add the cabbage and mix everything well. Leave it for another 20 to 30 minutes.
4. Cut an onion into small pieces. Then add it.
5. Mix the mayonnaise with the sour cream, then add them to the cabbage and mix well.
6. Taste the salad. Perhaps you will need a little more salt and pepper.

This salad is good with cold meat[12], or you can try it with pizza[13].
There are a lot of different recipes for coleslaw. You can add carrots or apples (shred them first).

(This recipe is enough for 4 people.)

---

1 coleslaw ['kəʊlslɔ:] – *Krautsalat* 2 recipe ['resɪpɪ] – *Rezept* 3 cabbage ['kæbɪdʒ] – *Kohl* 4 tablespoon ['teɪblspu:n] – *Eßlöffel* 5 vinegar ['vɪnɪgə] – *Essig* 6 pepper ['pepə] – *Pfeffer* 7 onion ['ʌnjən] – *Zwiebel* 8 mayonnaise [ˌmeɪə'neɪz] – 9 sour cream [ˌsaʊə 'kri:m] – *saure Sahne* 10 to shred [ʃred] – *hobeln* 11 to mix [mɪks] – *(ver)mischen* 12 meat [mi:t] – *Fleisch* 13 pizza ['pi:tsə]

3 A poem[1]: Mice[2]

I think mice
Are rather[3] nice.

Their tails are long,
Their faces small,
They haven't any
Chins[4] at all.
Their ears are pink[5],
Their teeth[6] are white,
They run about
The house at night.
They nibble[7] things
They shouldn't touch
And no one seems[8]
To like them much.

But I think mice
Are nice.

Rose Fyleman (1877–1957)

4 Just for fun

First man: Have you seen a policeman anywhere near here?
Second man: No, I haven't.
First man: Do you know where the nearest police station is?
Second man: Sorry, I don't.
First man: All right then. Hands up!

What four letters are thieves afraid of?
O I C U

Why do birds fly south in the winter?
Because it's too far to walk.

A girl in a sweet shop is one metre fifty tall, and she wears size 4 shoes. What does she weigh?
Sweets.

5 Think about it!

1. The two trains

Two trains – a fast one and a slow one – run between Oklahoma City and Kansas City. The fast train leaves Oklahoma City at nine o'clock in the morning. The slow one leaves Kansas City at the same time. The fast train travels[9] at a hundred miles per hour; the slow one at fifty miles per hour.
Now, which train is further from[10] Oklahoma City when they meet? It is 400 miles from Oklahoma City to Kansas City.

2. The four brothers

Four brothers live in the same town. The brothers' names are John, David, Paul and William. They all have different jobs. One of them is a butcher, one is a taxi driver, one is a farmer, and one is a policeman. But which man does which job?
These facts will tell you:

- The taxi driver often visits John at the weekends.
- William often goes to the cinema with the policeman.
- David and William sometimes play cards with the taxi driver and the farmer.

3. The snail[11]

Sam, the snail, is at the bottom of a garden wall, ten metres high. He wants to see what it is like at the top of the wall, so he begins to climb up. Every day he climbs up three metres, but he slips back[12] two metres every night.
The question is, after how many days does Sam get to the top of the wall?

---

1 poem ['pəʊɪm] – *Gedicht* 2 mice [maɪs] – *Mäuse* 3 rather ['rɑːðə] – *ziemlich* 4 chin [tʃɪn] – *Kinn*
5 pink [pɪŋk] – *rosa* 6 teeth [tiːθ] – *Zähne* 7 to nibble ['nɪbl] – *anknabbern* 8 to seem [siːm] – *scheinen*
9 to travel ['trævl] – *fahren, reisen* 10 further from ['fɜːðə] – *weiter entfernt von* 11 snail [sneɪl] – *Schnecke*
12 to slip back [slɪp] – *zurückrutschen*

6 Joy's pearls[1]: A one-act play[2]

Characters[3]*:*

Joy Newman, an actress[4]
Greg Newman, her husband
Connie, their maid[5]
Lieutenant[6] Donahue[7]
Sergeant[8] Oleson[9]

Mary Fabiani
Paul Fabiani
Nancy Parker
Stan Parker
Norman Cole
Dolly, his girl-friend
} guests[10]

Scene I

The Newmans' dining-room. Joy and Greg Newman are sitting at the breakfast table. Greg is reading a newspaper. There is a telephone on a small side-table.

Joy: I forgot to tell you, Greg, there'll be eight at the party.
Greg: What, dear? What did you say?
Joy: Oh Greg, you know we wanted to have a little party. On Friday evening. Don't look at me like that! It won't be so expensive.
Greg: Hm. – Well, have you invited Stan and Nancy?
Joy: Yes, I have. And Mary and Paul Fabiani. And Norman Cole and his new girl-friend. What's her name – Dolly.

The door opens and Connie, the maid, comes in with some letters.

Connie: Excuse me, Mrs Newman. These letters have just arrived.
Joy: Thank you, Connie.

Connie puts the letters on the table and goes out of the room.
Joy looks at the letters. She gives one to Greg.

Joy: For you, dear.

Greg (takes the letter and opens it): Another bill[11]! Five hundred dollars for a dress? Last week it was a coat. And we couldn't pay for that either[12]. Joy, when will you understand? We haven't got the money for all this!
Joy: Don't worry, Greg. When I get my next role –
Greg (laughs): Your next role? When will that be? Your last film was three years ago.

Joy looks away. She opens one of her letters, reads it – and laughs.

Joy: Greg! Look at this. An anonymous[13] letter! Did you ever hear of anything so crazy?

She shows Greg the letter. He reads it.

Greg: "Dear Mrs Newman. I want a hundred thousand dollars. Be at the end of Greenfield Road – alone – at 11.30 p.m. on Thursday with the money. I mean business[14].

---

1 pearl [pɜ:l] – *Perle* 2 one-act play – *Einakter* 3 characters ['kærəktəz] – *Charaktere, Personen* 4 actress ['æktrıs] – *Schauspielerin* 5 maid [meıd] – *Haus-, Dienstmädchen* 6 Lieutenant [lu:'tenənt] – *Kriminalinspektor (U.S.)* 7 Donahue ['dɒnəˌhju:] – 8 Sergeant ['sɑ:dʒənt] – *Wachtmeister* 9 Oleson ['əʊlsən] – 10 guest [gest] – *Gast* 11 bill [bıl] – *Rechnung* 12 not … either ['aıðə/'i:ðə] – *auch nicht* 13 anonymous [ə'nɒnıməs] – *anonym (ohne Absender)* 14 I mean business ['bıznəs] – *Ich meine es ernst*

If you don't hand over[1] the money, you'll be sorry." *(Joy laughs again.)* Hey, don't laugh like that, Joy. Maybe[2] it's serious[3].

Joy: Serious? Some crazy idiot, that's all! Anyway, we haven't got a hundred thousand dollars.

Greg: But wait – what about your pearls? They're worth[4] over a hundred thousand!

Joy: My pearls? I'm not going to sell my family pearls! Just because I get this crazy letter? *(She laughs again.)* The letter's a silly joke[5], Greg. *(She tears the letter to pieces[6].)*

Greg: Maybe it is. I hope you're right. *(He gets up from the table.)* Well – I must go to the office now. Bye. *(He kisses[7] her and leaves the room.)*

Scene II

Later. Connie is taking the breakfast things to the kitchen. The telephone rings and Connie answers it.

Connie: Hello? ... Yes. ... I'll call her. *(She laughs to herself.)* – Mrs Newman! Telephone!

Joy comes in and goes to the phone. Connie goes out with some plates.

Joy: Hello? Who's speaking? ... What? ... Are you crazy?

She listens for a few moments, then puts the receiver[8] back. Then she picks it up again and dials[9].

Joy: Hello? Greg? Listen. Somebody has just phoned me. About the money. That idiot again. ... Yes, it was a man's voice. ... He said, "Thursday, don't forget." And "no police". And then he said, "If you don't bring the money then, you'll be sorry."

Scene III

Friday. The Newmans' sitting-room. A big window at the side of the room. On the other side of the room, a door into the hall. Joy's six guests have arrived and they have got drinks. There are some bottles on a side-table. The tonic water[10] bottle is nearly empty. It is dark outside, and the lights are on in the room. Joy Newman is wearing an expensive dress, and her pearls.

Norman: How's the business[11], Stan?

Stan: Not too good, I'm afraid, Norman. *(He looks nervous, but laughs.)* Maybe next year things will be better ...

Greg: Does anyone mind if I open the window? It's so warm this evening.

Paul: That's O.K., Greg.

Greg goes to the window and opens it. Then he sits down.

Dolly: Ah! That's better.

Nancy: Joy! Your pearls! They're **so** beautiful! Did you say they belonged to your grandmother?

---

1 to hand over – *überreichen* 2 maybe ['meɪbi:] – *vielleicht* 3 serious ['sɪərɪəs] – *ernst* 4 to be worth [wɜ:θ] – *wert sein* 5 joke [dʒəʊk] – *Scherz* 6 to tear to pieces [teə] – *in Stücke reißen* 7 to kiss [kɪs] – *küssen* 8 receiver [rɪ'si:və] – *Hörer* 9 to dial ['daɪəl] – *wählen* 10 tonic water ['tɒnɪk] – *chininhaltiges Erfrischungsgetränk* 11 business ['bɪznəs] – *Geschäft*

Joy: That's right.
Mary: But what did you do about that anonymous letter, Joy? Did anything happen?
Paul: You didn't go there last night, I hope?
Joy: Of course not! I'm not crazy.
Nancy: It was some stupid joke, I guess.
Dolly: Or are you afraid something will still happen?
Joy (laughs): No, not at all. But Greg was a little worried at first.

Greg gets up and fills the guests' glasses. When the tonic water bottle is empty, he rings a small bell on the side-table. A moment later Connie comes in.

Connie: Yes?
Greg: Bring another bottle of tonic water, please, Connie.

Connie goes out. Greg goes to the window and looks out.

Norman: What's the matter, Greg?
Greg: I heard something. Outside.
Mary: Out in the garden? I didn't hear anything.
Dolly: No, I didn't hear anything either.
Joy (gets up): Well … let's shut the window.

Suddenly all the lights go out. There are gasps[1] of surprise.

Dolly: Ooh! Isn't it dark!
Norman: What's happened? Is it a fuse[2]?
Joy (screams): Aah! What was that? My pearls! – My pearls are gone!
Greg: What?! Just a minute. I'll see if it's a fuse.

There are noises while Greg goes to the door. The door bangs. A few moments later, the lights come on. Greg is at the door. Joy is in a panic[3], her hands at her neck[4].

Greg: Yes, it was only a fuse.
Joy: But Greg! My pearls! Someone's stolen them! A thief! A burglar!
Nancy: That anonymous letter was serious after all!
Stan: The open window! Why didn't we shut it?
Mary: So there *was* someone outside. *(The men run to the window.)*

Greg: I'll try to catch him! Paul, phone the police!

Greg climbs through the open window and Paul goes to the phone and dials.

Scene IV

The sitting-room again. The guests are still there, with Joy and Greg. Lieutenant Donahue is in the middle of the room. He is examining Mary Fabiani's handbag. Sergeant Oleson is looking in Stan Parker's pockets[5]. He takes out a box of matches[6].

Stan (angry): Finished, Sergeant? *(He laughs.)* Go on – look in the matchbox[7], too. Perhaps the pearls are in there!

---

1 gasp (of surprise) [gɑ:sp] – *erschreckter Aufschrei* 2 fuse [fju:z] – *(durchgebrannte) Sicherung*
3 in a panic ['pænɪk] – *in Panik* 4 neck [nek] – *Hals* 5 pocket ['pɒkɪt] – *Tasche* 6 match [mætʃ] – *Streichholz* 7 matchbox ['mætʃbɒks] – *Streichholzschachtel*

Paul: Lieutenant Donahue! You don't really believe that one of us has taken Mrs Newman's pearls? This is too much!

Mary (in a cold voice): Thank you, Lieutenant. *(She takes her handbag from him.)*

Norman: Well, now that you know nobody in this room has got the pearls – where's the real[1] thief? He got in through the open window. We can be sure about that.

Donahue: Can we? Climb out of the window, Oleson. Any footprints[2] out there?

Oleson goes to the window and climbs out. He calls back.

Oleson: Yes, sir. There are a few footprints under the window. All from the same shoes.

Donahue: Now, Mr Newman. You climbed out of the window when you tried to run after the thief. Please give Sergeant Oleson one of your shoes.

Greg takes off one of his shoes and hands it through the window.

Oleson: Yes, sir. These must be the shoes. There are no other prints.

Donahue: All right, Oleson. Come back in.

Oleson comes back through the window, shuts it, and Greg puts his shoe on again.

Donahue: So the thief didn't come in through the window. But the pearls are not in this room. – Did anyone leave the room before I arrived, Mrs Newman?

Joy: No, Lieutenant.

Oleson: Is there anyone else in the house?

Joy: Only Connie. My maid.

Donahue: Bring her in, Oleson. *(Oleson goes out and comes back with Connie.)*

Oleson: Right. Everyone is here, sir.

Donahue: When the lights went out, someone took Mrs Newman's pearls. But **why** did the lights go out? There wasn't a power failure[3].

Stan: No, it was a fuse.

Oleson: A fuse? Were you using a lot of electricity[4] in the house?

Joy: Well, the lights were on, and the stove[5] and fridge[6] in the kitchen. That's all.

Oleson: That's not enough to blow a fuse[7].

Donahue: Were you all in this room when the lights went out?

Greg: Yes.

Donahue: What about you, Connie? Where were you?

Greg: She was in the kitchen.

Donahue: I asked Connie, not you, Mr Newman. – Now, what happened just **before** the lights went out?

Nancy: Greg rang the bell – and sent Connie out for a bottle of tonic water.

Oleson: Ah! So when **Connie** left the room, the lights went out?

Connie (shouts): I didn't switch them off!

Oleson: Well, maybe you went to the fuse-box – and switched off the fuse?

Connie: No! I –

Donahue: Quiet! And **you**, Mr Newman, **you** stole your wife's pearls when the lights went out. You took them into the hall when you went to the fuse-box. Oleson, look for the pearls in the hall – and in the kitchen. *Oleson goes out.*

---

1 real [rɪəl] – *echt, wirklich* 2 footprint [ˈfʊtprɪnt] – *Fußabdruck* 3 power failure [ˈpaʊə ˌfeɪljə] – *Stromausfall* 4 electricity [ˌɪlekˈtrɪsətɪ] – *Elektrizität, Strom* 5 stove [stəʊv] – *Herd* 6 fridge [frɪdʒ] – *Kühlschrank* 7 to blow a fuse [ˌbləʊ əˈfjuːz] – *eine Sicherung durchbrennen*

Greg: Are you crazy, Lieutenant? You think **I** stole my own wife's pearls? I never heard anything so –

Donahue: Yes, you stole them. You were short of money[1]. You often asked your wife to sell her pearls. But she didn't sell them. So you tried a trick. Your wife told me about the anonymous letter. **That** was from you. **And** the phone call. You put something over the receiver, so she didn't know your voice. Easy.

Joy: Oh Greg! What a cruel trick!

Donahue: So when the pearls disappeared[2], everyone thought of the letter. But nobody thought of **you**!

Greg: I never wrote that letter! I –

Donahue: Then perhaps Connie did it for you?

Oleson comes back with the pearls in his hand.

Oleson: Here they are, sir. Nice and fresh! I found them in the fridge – in a box of peas. *(He gives the Lieutenant the pearls.)*

Donahue: Thank you, Oleson.

Connie sits down. She is crying now.

Greg: Stop it, you stupid girl!

Connie: Oh! How can you be so cruel? *(To Lieutenant Donahue)* I know it was wrong! But he was so sure about it all. He wanted to sell the pearls. He – he wanted to take me with him to Mexico. He wanted –

Donahue: Arrest them, Oleson.

1 short of money – *knapp bei Kasse* 2 to disappear [ˌdɪsəˈpɪə] – *verschwinden*

7 Fun with words Do you know these games? You can play them all in the classroom.

1. Add-a-letter

The first player goes to the board and writes one letter on it – the first letter of a word. Then the next player writes another letter after it, the third player another one, and so on until there is a word. Try to make your words as long as possible. Here is an example: – W - A - T are the first three letters. If the next player adds an 'E', you will get 'WATER' – or even 'WATER-PISTOL'. But if he or she adds a 'C', you will get 'WATCH' (or you can make 'WATCHES', 'WATCHED' or 'WATCHING'.

You are 'out' if you can't add a letter, or if 'your' letter can't help to make a word.

Of course, you are not 'out' if you finish a word.

2. Add-a-word

In this game, you try to tell a 'story'. You all take turns. But each player can only add **one** word at a time. You will see how it works if you look at this example: –

8 Little House in the Big Woods[1]

When Laura Ingalls[2] was a little girl – over a hundred years ago now – she and her family lived in the forests of Wisconsin[3]. Around their house, there was nothing but[4] trees. As far as a man could go to the north in a day, or a week, or even a month, there was nothing but woods. No other houses. No roads. No people. Only trees and wild animals. To the east, and to the west, there were miles of trees, and only a few log houses[5] here and there. As far as Laura could see, there was only the one little house where she lived with her father and mother and her two sisters.

In her books for children, Laura tells us of her family's adventures, and of their life together – first in Wisconsin, and later in many other parts of America. This story comes from her first book, which is called 'Little House in the Big Woods'.

All alone in the wild big woods, and the snow, and the cold, the little log house was warm and cosy[6]. Pa and Ma and Mary and Laura and Baby Carrie were comfortable[7] and happy there, especially at night.

Then the fire was shining, the cold and the dark and the wild animals were all shut out, and Jack the dog and Black Susan the cat were close to the fire.

Ma sat near the lamp and sewed[8]. It was a lovely little lamp, and Laura loved to look at it. She loved to look at the fire, too. The flames were yellow and red, and sometimes green and blue. And then Pa told stories.

One night Pa looked at Black Susan, as she sat close to the fire, and he said:
"Do you know that a panther[9] is a cat – a great big, wild cat?"
"No," said Laura.
"Well, it is," said Pa. "Just think of Black Susan – but bigger and fiercer[10] than Jack. Then she would be just like a panther. – Now I'll tell you about Grandpa and the panther."
"Your grandpa?" Laura asked.
"No, Laura, your grandpa. My father."
"Oh," said Laura. She knew her grandpa. He lived far away in the Big Woods, in a big log house.
Pa began:

"Your grandpa went to town one day and it was late when he started home. It was dark when he was riding his horse through the Big Woods, so dark that he could hardly see the road, and when he heard a panther scream, he was afraid, because he had no gun[11]."

"How does a panther scream?" Laura asked.
"Like this," said Pa. Then he screamed so that Laura and Mary shivered[12].

"The horse, with Grandpa on it, ran fast, because it was afraid, too. But it could not get away from the panther. The panther followed them through the dark woods. It was a hungry panther, and it came as fast as the horse could run. It screamed now on this side of the road,

---

1 wood [wʊd] – *Wald* 2 Laura Ingalls [ˌlɔːrə ˈɪŋgɔːlz] 3 Wisconsin [wɪsˈkɒnsɪn] – *amerikanischer Bundesstaat* 4 nothing but … – *nichts als* 5 log house [lɒg] – *Blockhaus* 6 cosy [ˈkəʊzɪ] – *gemütlich, behaglich* 7 comfortable [ˈkʌmfətəbl] – *bequem, gemütlich* 8 to sew [səʊ], sewed, sewn – *nähen* 9 panther [ˈpænθə] – *Panther* 10 fierce [fɪəs] – *wild, scharf* 11 gun [gʌn] – *Gewehr* 12 to shiver [ˈʃɪvə] – *zittern*

now on the other side, and it was always close behind. Then Grandpa saw it for a moment, as it jumped from treetop to treetop.
It was a big panther, and it jumped through the air like Black Susan when she jumps on a mouse. It was many, many times bigger than Black Susan. It was so big that if it jumped on Grandpa it could kill him with its big claws[1] and its long, sharp[2] teeth[3].
Grandpa, on his horse, was running away from it just as a mouse runs from a cat.
He could feel that the panther was getting closer all the time. It did not scream any more. Grandpa could not see it any more. But he knew that it was coming. He knew that it was jumping after him in the dark woods behind him. The horse ran and ran.
At last the horse ran up to Grandpa's house. Grandpa saw the panther, and he jumped off the horse. He rushed through the door and banged it behind him. The panther landed on the horse's back[4].
The horse screamed, and ran. It was running away into the Big Woods, with the panther on its back. The panther was tearing[5] the horse's back with its claws. But Grandpa grabbed his gun from the wall and ran to the window, just in time to shoot the panther dead[6]."

When Pa told this story, Laura and Mary shivered. But they were safe[7] and cosy, with Pa's strong arms around them.
They liked to be there, in front of the warm fire, with Black Susan and Jack the dog. When they heard a wolf[8] outside, Jack's hairs[9] went up on his back. But Laura and Mary listened to the sound[10] of the wolf in the dark and the cold of the Big Woods, and they were not afraid.
They were cosy and comfortable in their little log house with the snow around it and the wind outside.

9 Let's sing a song: I love the mountains

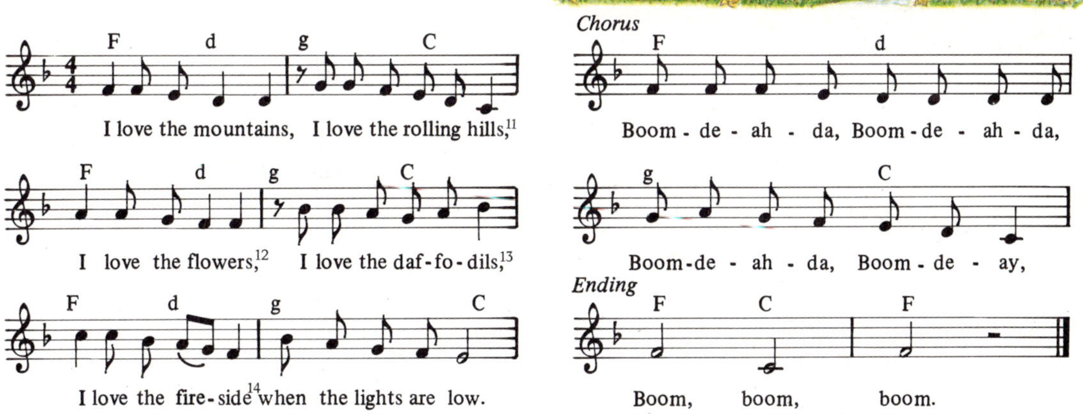

1 claw [klɔː] – *Klaue, Kralle* 2 sharp [ʃɑːp] – *scharf* 3 teeth [tiːθ] – *Zähne* 4 back [bæk] – *Rücken* 5 to tear [teə] – *zer-, aufreißen* 6 dead [ded] – *tot* 7 safe [seɪf] – *sicher, geschützt* 8 wolf [wʊlf] – *Wolf* 9 hair [heə] – *Haar* 10 sound [saʊnd] – *hier: Heulen, Stimme* 11 rolling hills [ˈrəʊlɪŋ ˈhɪlz] – *wellige Hügelketten* 12 flower [ˈflaʊə] – *Blume* 13 daffodil [ˈdæfədɪl] – *Narzisse* 14 fireside [ˈfaɪəsaɪd] – *Platz am Kamin*

(Translation practice)

1 Barbara hilft

Unit 1 Step B

Kates Brieffreundin Bettina schreibt in ihrem Brief an Kate die erste Seite auf englisch, die zweite auf deutsch. Kate kann nur wenig Deutsch und Barbara hilft ihr.

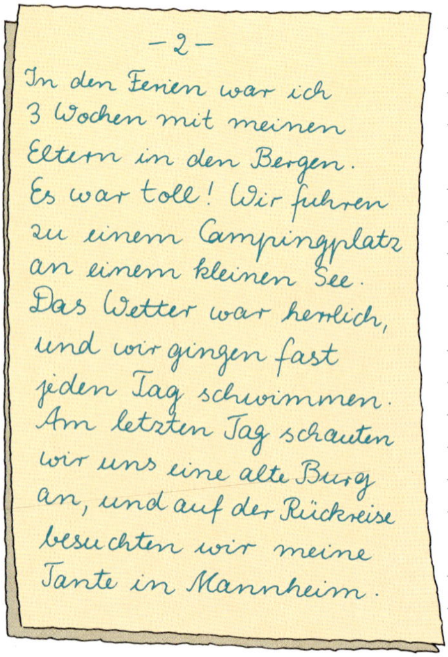

– 2 –
In den Ferien war ich
3 Wochen mit meinen
Eltern in den Bergen.
Es war toll! Wir fuhren
zu einem Campingplatz
an einem kleinen See.
Das Wetter war herrlich,
und wir gingen fast
jeden Tag schwimmen.
Am letzten Tag schauten
wir uns eine alte Burg
an, und auf der Rückreise
besuchten wir meine
Tante in Mannheim.

Kate: I know '3 Wochen' means three weeks. But what does 'Ferien' mean? And what's 'Eltern'?
Barbara: …
Kate: So she wants to tell me about her holidays. With her parents! Where did they go?
Barbara: …
Kate: 'Es war toll!' What does that mean?
Barbara: …
Kate: Oh! I understand 'Campingplatz'. But then she says something about 'See'. Is that the sea?
Barbara: … .
Kate: I see. Did they go swimming at all?
Barbara: …
Kate: Does she say what else they did there?
Barbara: …
Kate: And what does she say about Mannheim? Did they go there, too?
Barbara: …
Kate: Thanks, Barbara! But I must tell Bettina to write more in English next time.

2 Besichtigung auf Carisbrooke Castle

Unit 1 Step D

Auf Carisbrooke Castle sah Elke zwei deutsche Touristen. Deren Englisch war nicht so gut und der Fremdenführer konnte kein Deutsch. Elke hat ihnen geholfen. Was hat sie gesagt?

Elke: Ich spreche deutsch. Kann ich Ihnen helfen?
1st tourist: Prima! – Also, wie alt ist die Burg?
Elke: How …?
Guide: The oldest parts are more than eight hundred years old.
Elke: …
2nd tourist: Hier ist ein Bild von Charles dem Ersten. Wohnte er in Carisbrooke?
Elke: …
Guide: No, he didn't. He lived in London. But he was a prisoner here before his execution.
Elke: …
2nd tourist: Ach, das wußte ich nicht! Und wann war das?
Elke: …
Guide: That was more than three hundred years ago. His execution was in 1649.
Elke: …
1st tourist: Als wir reinkamen, sahen wir zwei alte Türme am Eingang. Können wir sie besichtigen?
Elke: …
Guide: Yes, of course. But don't go there just now. It's raining.
Elke: …
1st tourist: Stimmt! Schauen wir uns die Sachen hier im Museum an, bis der Regen aufhört.
Elke: …
Guide: Have a good time.
Elke: …
2nd tourist: Vielen Dank! Auf Wiedersehen.

3 Beim Einkauf

Unit 2 Step C

Thomas Müller ist zu Besuch bei seinem Cousin Peter in Nottingham, der schon zwei Jahre dort lebt. Bevor Thomas zurückfährt, möchte er für seine Schwester ein Geschenk kaufen. Also geht er mit Peter in ein Einkaufszentrum. Thomas kann noch nicht so gut Englisch, und Peter hilft ihm.

Assistant: Yes, please? Can I help you?
Thomas: Ich will etwas für meine Schwester kaufen.
Peter: …
Assistant: We've got some nice things over here. What about this little purse?
Peter: …
Thomas: O nein, danke. Sie hat schon zwei Geldbeutel. Haben Sie Kassetten oder Schallplatten?
Peter: …
Assistant: I'm afraid we haven't got any cassettes or records. But we've got some children's books. This book is good – "Somewhere in Sherwood Forest".
Peter: …
Thomas: Ja, aber meine Schwester kann kein Englisch lesen. Sie ist erst acht.
Peter: …
Assistant: Oh, I see! Well, what about a doll[1]?
We've got some lovely little dolls, look.
Peter: …
Thomas: Ja, sie sind schön. Aber ich kann nichts Teures kaufen. Ich habe nicht sehr viel Geld.
Peter: …
Assistant: This doll isn't expensive. It's only two pounds.
Peter: …
Thomas: O prima! Jetzt habe ich etwas für sie! Vielen Dank.
Peter: …
Assistant: Thank you! Goodbye!

1 doll [dɒl] – *Puppe*

4 Ein neuer Brief von Bettina

Unit 2 Step C

Kates Brieffreundin Bettina hat einen neuen Brief geschrieben. Hier ist ein Teil davon. Der Brief ist noch ein bißchen zu schwierig für Kate, deshalb übersetzt Barbara.

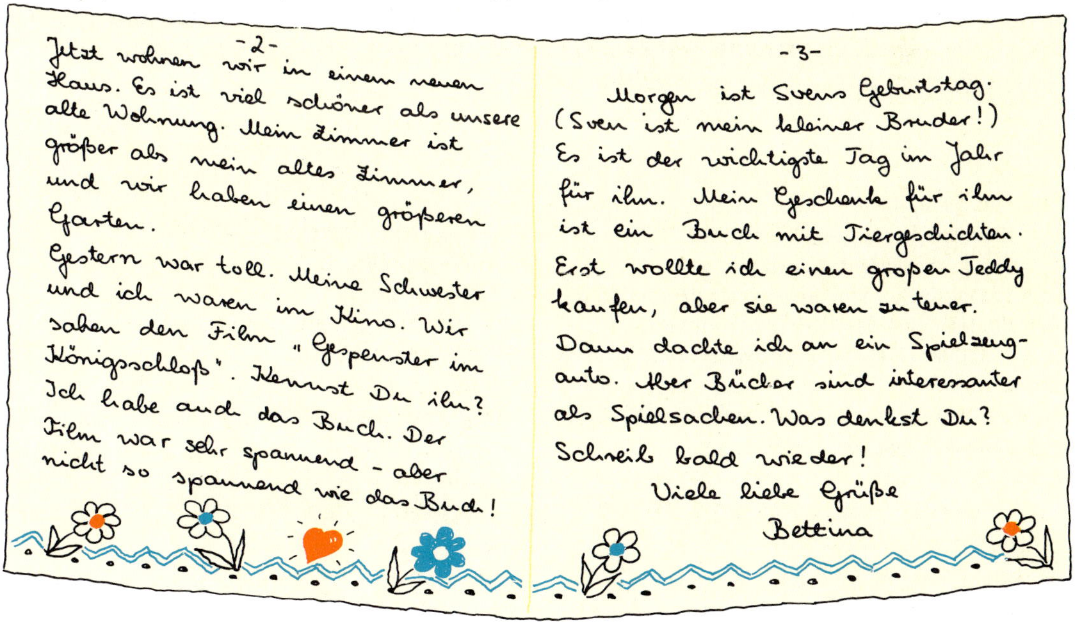

-2-

Jetzt wohnen wir in einem neuen Haus. Es ist viel schöner als unsere alte Wohnung. Mein Zimmer ist größer als mein altes Zimmer, und wir haben einen größeren Garten.

Gestern war toll. Meine Schwester und ich waren im Kino. Wir sahen den Film „Gespenster im Königsschloß". Kennst Du ihn? Ich habe auch das Buch. Der Film war sehr spannend – aber nicht so spannend wie das Buch!

-3-

Morgen ist Svens Geburtstag. (Sven ist mein kleiner Bruder!) Es ist der wichtigste Tag im Jahr für ihn. Mein Geschenk für ihn ist ein Buch mit Tiergeschichten. Erst wollte ich einen großen Teddy kaufen, aber sie waren zu teuer. Dann dachte ich an ein Spielzeugauto. Aber Bücher sind interessanter als Spielsachen. Was denkst Du?

Schreib bald wieder!

Viele liebe Grüße

Bettina

5 Beim Arzt

Unit 3 Step C

Tony, aus Leeds, wohnt bei einer Familie in Büren. Er hat Schmerzen am Fuß und muß zum Arzt. Sein deutscher Freund Bernd geht mit ihm. Er dolmetscht für Tony.

Arzt: Hallo, dich kenne ich nicht. Wie heißt du? Wo kommst du her?
Bernd: …
Tony: I come from Leeds in England. My name is Tony Clark.
Bernd: …
Arzt: Nun, du bist weit weg[1] von zu Hause. Bist du mit deinen Eltern hier?
Bernd: …
Tony: No, I'm visiting the Nowak family here in Büren.
Bernd: …
Arzt: Ich verstehe. Nun, was fehlt dir?
Bernd: …
Tony: My foot is swollen, and it hurts.
Bernd: …
Arzt: Schauen wir ihn an. Was ist passiert?
Bernd: …
Tony: Somebody dropped a bag on my foot in the train.
Bernd: …
Arzt: Tut es die ganze Zeit weh?
Bernd: …
Tony: No, it only hurts when I walk. Is it broken?
Bernd: …
Arzt: Nein, aber du mußt einige Tage lang vorsichtig sein.
Bernd: …
Tony: Bernd's class is going to visit a castle on Saturday. Can I go with them?
Bernd: …
Arzt: Na gut. Aber du darfst nicht zu viel laufen. Vielleicht kannst du im Bus bleiben, wenn die anderen in der Burg sind. Oder du kannst dich irgendwo hinsetzen.
Bernd: …
Tony: That's a good idea. Thanks a lot.
Bernd: …
Arzt: Auf Wiedersehen.

[1] a long way

6 Das Buch aus Deutschland

Unit 3 Step C

Barbara hat aus Deutschland ein Buch über Haustiere bekommen. Die vier Freunde wollen wissen, was drin steht. Barbara liest den Abschnitt über Kaninchen vor. Hier sind die Regeln. Barbara übersetzt sie ins Englische. Kannst du es auch?

1. Du mußt das Kaninchen in einem Stall[2] halten. Der Stall darf nicht zu klein sein.
2. Im Sommer und im Winter[3] kannst du dein Kaninchen draußen halten. Es hat ein warmes Fell[4].
3. Gib deinem Kaninchen jeden Tag frisches Gras und Möhren.
4. Du brauchst deinem Tier kein Wasser zu geben. Im Gras ist genug Wasser.
5. Du darfst deinem Kaninchen keine Kekse und keine Süßigkeiten geben.
6. Du mußt den Stall zwei- oder dreimal in der Woche saubermachen.
7. Du brauchst dein Kaninchen nicht zu waschen. Es kann sich selbst waschen.
8. Laß dein Kaninchen in einem Garten herumlaufen, aber nicht in der Wohnung. In einer Wohnung frißt es alles – auch gefährliche Gegenstände.
9. Ein Kaninchen ist kein Spielzeug. Sei also immer vorsichtig, wenn du es trägst oder wenn du mit ihm spielst.
10. Wenn dein Tier krank ist oder krank aussieht, bring es zum Tierarzt.

[2] hutch [hʌtʃ] [3] winter [4] coat

7 Das alte Fahrrad — Unit 4 Step C

Pam, eine junge Engländerin, ist bei der Familie König in Traunstein zu Besuch. Ute, die Tochter der Königs, und Pam basteln an einem älteren Fahrrad, so daß sie gemeinsam eine Fahrradtour unternehmen können. Herr König schaut aus dem Wohnungsfenster, um festzustellen, wie weit sie mit der Arbeit sind.
Pam versteht nicht viel Deutsch, deshalb dolmetscht Ute für sie.

Herr König: Ach, ihr habt das Fahrrad geputzt. Jetzt sieht es viel schöner aus.
Ute: ...
Pam: I've repaired the brakes, too. They're O.K. now.
Ute: ...
Herr König: Ich sehe, ihr habt den Sattel ausgewechselt. Der neue Sattel ist viel besser.
Ute: ...
Pam: And I've put on new mudguards.
Ute: ...
Herr König: Aber das Rad sieht immer noch arg zerkratzt aus. Wollt ihr es nicht lackieren?
Ute: ...
Pam: That's a good idea, but not today. We want to cycle to the river this afternoon.
Ute: ...
Herr König: Ach ja, Schlegels haben gerade angerufen. Am Wochenende wollen sie mit ihrem großen Wohnwagen zum See fahren. Sie haben noch Platz für zwei. Wollt ihr mit ihnen fahren?
Ute: ...
Pam: Great, but how far is it to the lake? Can we cycle there?
Ute: ...
Herr König: Etwa 20 Minuten mit dem Auto. Ute ist noch nie mit dem Fahrrad dorthin gefahren.
Ute: ...
Pam: But that doesn't sound very far, Mr König. Ute has got a good bike and my bike is O.K. now.
Ute: ...
Herr König: O.K. Ihr könnt zusammen fahren.
Ute: ... und danke, Paps!

8 Deutsch mit Timmy — Unit 4 Step C

Ronny hat heute eine deutsche Hausaufgabe, aber er kommt nicht dazu, weil Timmy ihn nicht in Ruhe lassen will. Timmy will wissen, was im Text steht. Schließlich gibt Ronny nach und übersetzt den Text für Timmy. Kannst du es auch?

1. Gisela, Rolf und Rudi haben angefangen, das Auto von Herrn Zeller zu waschen.
2. Rolf hat einen Eimer mit frischem Wasser gebracht.
3. Rudi hat die Fenster gereinigt, aber sie sind noch schmutzig. Er wäscht sie noch einmal.
4. Gisela hat das Chrom poliert, aber es sieht nicht neu aus, weil das Auto zu alt ist.
5. Herr Zeller hat nicht vergessen, das Öl zu überprüfen.
6. Herr Zeller hat auch neue Zündkerzen gekauft. Er hat die alten Zündkerzen noch nicht ausgewechselt.
7. Rudi und Gisela haben versucht, die alten Kerzen herauszunehmen, aber es ist zu schwierig.
8. Herr Zeller beabsichtigt, das Auto zu verkaufen. Er will einen neuen Wagen kaufen.
9. Er will den Kindern DM 10,– geben, wenn sie die Arbeit fertiggemacht haben.

9 Was bedeutet das? — Unit 5 Step A

Stell dir vor, du bist mit englischen Freunden in einem deutschen Museum. Sie verstehen die Hinweisschilder nicht und bitten dich, sie zu übersetzen. Da man nicht Wort für Wort übersetzen kann, mußt du erklären, was die einzelnen Schilder bedeuten. Was würdest du sagen?

Beispiel: ‚Schulkinder und Gruppen erhalten Ermäßigung'. That means: School children and groups don't have to pay as much as everybody else.

10 Die Kamera — Unit 5 Step D

Frau Stoll macht Urlaub in York, und nun hat sie ihre Kamera verloren. Da sie nicht sehr viel Englisch kann, ist Barbara mit ihr zum Polizeirevier gegangen und dolmetscht.

Policeman: Yes please? What can I do for you?
Frau Stoll: Ich habe meinen Fotoapparat verloren.
Barbara: …
Policeman: I see. Where did you lose it?
Barbara: …
Frau Stoll: Gestern waren wir in Whitby. Wir sind mit dem Reisebus gefahren.
Barbara: …
Policeman: And you left your camera in the coach? Is that right?
Barbara: …
Frau Stoll: Ja. Ich hab's gemerkt, als wir wieder im Hotel waren.
Barbara: …
Policeman: Have you asked about it at the bus company?
Barbara: …
Frau Stoll: Ja, wir sind gerade eben da gewesen. Wir haben vor einer halben Stunde mit dem Busfahrer gesprochen, aber er konnte uns nicht helfen.
Barbara: …
Policeman: Well, perhaps someone saw the camera on the seat and stole it. Were there a lot of people in the coach?
Barbara: …
Frau Stoll: Ja, der Bus war voll. Wir saßen vorne und sind vor den anderen ausgestiegen.
Barbara: …
Policeman: Hm. Was the camera an expensive one?
Barbara: …
Frau Stoll: Ja, und neu auch! Ich habe ihn vor zwei Monaten gekauft. Schauen Sie – hier sind die Bedienungsanleitungen[2].
Barbara: …
Policeman: Right. I've written down the name of the camera. Now give me your name and the address of your hotel.
Barbara: …
Frau Stoll: Gut. Dann können Sie mich anrufen, wenn Sie den Fotoapparat finden.
Barbara: …
Policeman: That's right. But I don't think there's much chance.
Barbara: …
Frau Stoll: Vielen Dank. Auf Wiedersehen.
Barbara: …

---
[1] to smoke [2] instructions [ɪnˈstrʌkʃnz]

11 Das Wetter

Unit 6 Step C

Uschi (11) und Bernd (12) Holzer aus München verbringen ihre Sommerferien in Enid, Oklahoma, bei ihrer Tante Trude. Sie möchten sehr gerne an einen See fahren, aber es regnet. Wie lange noch? Uschi schlägt vor, Jim Doyle anzurufen. Bernd findet das gut, meint aber, sie sollten sich vorher alle möglichen Fragen auf englisch aufschreiben. „Ja, besser ist besser", sagt Uschi und macht Vorschläge auf deutsch, und Bernd versucht, sie auf englisch aufzuschreiben. Uschis Vorschläge:

1. Wird es das ganze Wochenende regnen?
2. Wann hört's denn wieder auf?
3. Wann wird das Wetter wieder besser?
4. Und nächste Woche? Wie ist das Wetter dann?
5. Wo regnet es in Oklahoma dieses Wochenende nicht?
6. Ist es morgen im Nordwesten trocken/naß/heiß/schön?
7. Ist es am Sonntag windig?
8. Brauchen wir dann warme Kleider?
9. Wo ist das Wetter denn schön dieses Wochenende?
10. Wie warm wird's denn morgen? – Ich glaube, da mußt du was über die Temperatur fragen.

Bernd übersetzt:
1. Will it rain all weekend? 2. When will ... *Kannst du ihm weiterhelfen?*

12 Nächste Woche in Quark

Unit 6 Step D

Ben – I found this in a German magazine. Shall I send you the article? Perhaps I'll win a free flight to the US like you. Then I'll visit you ... Barbara

IN QUARK – EIN BERICHT ÜBER OKLAHOMA

Dr. Werner Ruhmfarer erzählt Euch alles über Oklahoma. Ihr lernt alles über das Land, das Wetter und die Leute. Es gibt Bilder von Weizenfeldern, von Indianern, von einem Rodeo – und eine aufregende Geschichte über einen Cowboy im Regen. Und auf der letzten Seite ist ein neuer großartiger Zaubertrick.
Und nicht vergessen – wir stellen wieder drei einfache Fragen ... Vielleicht gewinnst DU diesmal eine kostenlose Flugreise in die Vereinigten Staaten für DICH und DEINE Eltern. Ein heißer Sommer in Oklahoma! Wow! Wir sind sicher, es wird Euch gefallen.
Kauft QUARK nächste Woche! Ihr werdet es nicht bereuen![1]

Ben zeigte dies seinen amerikanischen Freunden. Er versuchte, den Text vom Deutschen ins Englische zu übersetzen, aber es war nicht leicht.

Er fing so an: There will be a report on Oklahoma in this magazine next week. Dr. Werner Ruhmfarer will ... *Kannst du weitermachen?*

[1] to be sorry

13 Eine Foto-Safari in den Zoo — Unit 7 Step B

Uschi will ihrem Onkel erzählen, was ihr im Zoo passiert ist. Und da Onkel Dave kein Deutsch kann und Tante Trude nicht da ist, muß Bernd übersetzen. Hier ist Uschis Geschichte:

Letztes Jahr hat meine Klasse eine Foto-Safari[1] in den Zoo[2] gemacht. „Erst fotografieren wir die wilden Tiere, Kinder," sagte Frau Weber. „Wir hängen[3] die besten Bilder im Klassenzimmer auf." Und als wir dann Aufnahmen von den Elefanten[4] machten, sagte sie: „Auf zum ‚Bauernhof'!" Da gab's nämlich eine Scheune mit Kühen und Bullen, Pferden und Hühnern und Hasen. Und Schafe. Und ein kleiner See mit Enten. Und auch ein paar Schweine. Man konnte reingehen und die Tiere streicheln[5]. Ganz toll. Karola, meine Freundin, versuchte ein großes schwarzes Schwein zu streicheln, während Frau Weber und ich die Enten fütterten. Aber dem Schwein hat das nicht gefallen und es lief weg – und gegen Frau Webers Beine, und sie fiel in den See. Nun, dann sind alle gekommen und haben sie angeguckt, als sie im Wasser saß. Und Fotos von ihr haben wir auch gemacht. Zuerst fand das Frau Weber nicht sehr lustig. Aber dann hat sie auch gelacht. Sie war naß, aber es war ein sehr warmer Tag. Und die Bilder von ihr waren sehr gut.

So fing Bernd an: Last year my class went on a photo-safari to the zoo. …
Kannst du weitermachen?

14 Auf, ins Autokino! — Unit 7 Step C

Harry hat Bernd und Uschi eingeladen, am Wochenende mit ihm und seinem Bruder ins Autokino (drive-in theatre[6]) mitzukommen. Bernd findet das gut. Aber Uschi hat Harry nicht genau verstanden. Also muß Bernd für sie und Harry dolmetschen. Kannst du ihm helfen?

Uschi:	*Bernd:*	*Harry:*
Sagt man „drive-in", weil man da mit seinem Auto reinfährt?	Do you … Ja, … Parkplatz.	Yes, you drive in with your car. It's like a big parking lot.
Müssen wir dann warten, bis es dunkel ist?	… …	Yes, of course.
Bleibt man im Auto, während man den Film sieht?	… … Lautsprecher …	Yes, you do. But you can sit outside, too. If you stay in the car, you must put in a loudspeaker.
Dann kann man alles gut hören.	… …	That's right.
Und wenn's regnet?	… …	Let's hope it won't. It rained the last time we went.
Was habt ihr gemacht, als es anfing?	… …	We closed the windows.
Ich meine, während es regnete.	I mean … …	Well, we couldn't see the film very well. But it wasn't too bad. We had a lot of food in the car and we ate everything.
Das hat bestimmt Spaß gemacht. Aber wir müssen warten, bis wir mit Onkel Dave und Tante Trude gesprochen haben – damit sie nicht böse werden.	I'm sure … …	O.K., but phone me later and tell me if you can go.

[1] safari [sə'fɑ:rɪ] [2] zoo [zu:] [3] to hang up
[4] elephant ['elɪfənt] [5] to pet [6] ['θɪətə]

15 Ein Geist auf dem Dach

Unit 8 Step B

Gestern nacht kurz nach eins wurde Frau Henchel wach. Sie sah einen „Geist" auf dem Dach des Nachbarhauses. Also rief sie die Polizei. Kurz darauf kamen zwei Polizisten und entdeckten ein elfjähriges Mädchen auf dem Dach. Es war Uschi Holzer – im Nachthemd. Dies ist Uschis Erklärung. Kannst du sie für die Polizei übersetzen?

1. Ich bin um ein Uhr wach geworden, weil der Hund von den Nachbarn bellte. Ich machte das Fenster auf und rief: „Sei ruhig, Fido[1]. Ich will schlafen." Aber Fido hat nicht aufgehört.
2. „Was soll ich machen?" dachte ich. „Warte – vielleicht sieht Onkel Dave noch fern", – er bleibt oft sehr lange auf – „dann kann er was tun."
3. Aber Onkel Dave war nicht unten. Er war schon im Bett, und Tante Trude auch. Ich schaute in ihr Schlafzimmer, und sie schliefen.
4. Ich wollte sie nicht wecken. Aber der blöde Hund bellte immer noch. „Der bellt wie ein verrückter Hund. Mit diesem Lärm kann ich nicht schlafen. Aber vielleicht kann mein Bruder … – nein, der lacht[2] mich nur aus."
5. Also entschied ich mich, alleine rauszugehen. „Ich werde das blöde Tier mal anschreien", sagte ich und ging raus. Im Nachthemd[3].
6. Als ich draußen war, fiel mir was ein[4]: „O nein. Wie blöd! Ich habe die Tür zugemacht. Jetzt kann ich nicht wieder rein." Ich habe nicht mehr an Fido gedacht. Ich mußte wieder ins Haus kommen.
7. Dann hatte ich eine Idee: „Ich werde durchs Fenster reinklettern. Erst klettere ich auf diesen Baum und dann …"
8. Nun, während ich raufkletterte, bellte Fido mehr als je. Also wachte Frau Henchel auf, schaute zum Fenster raus und sah einen Geist – mich. Und dann hat sie die Polizei gerufen. Das ist alles.

16 Brieffreunde

Unit 8 Step B

Bernd Holzer füllt gerade einen Fragebogen aus, weil er überall in Amerika Brieffreunde haben möchte. Und weil er keine Fehler machen will, hat er erst alles auf deutsch vorgeschrieben. Nun soll ihm Tante Trude helfen, es ins Englische zu übersetzen.

Was muß Bernd schreiben?

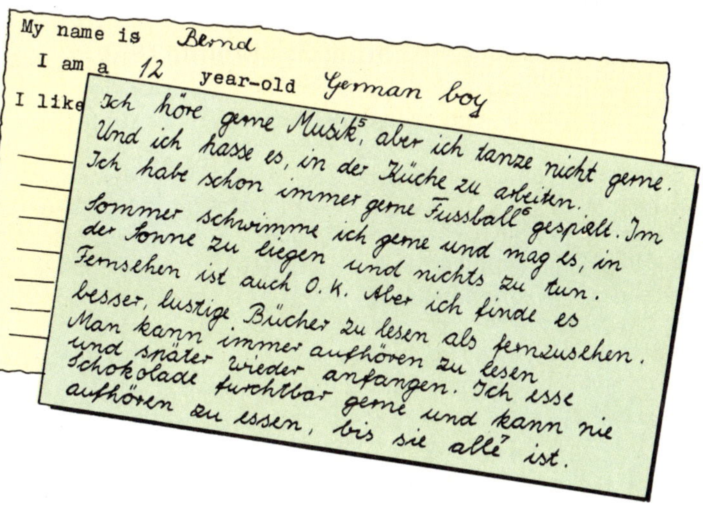

[1] ['faɪdəʊ] [2] to laugh at s.o. [3] night gown ['naɪt gaʊn] [4] to remember [5] music ['mju:zɪk] [6] soccer ['sɒkə] [7] all gone

Grammar

Unit 1

§ 1 Das Simple Past: regelmäßige Formen

The simple past: regular forms

Das *simple past* drückt Ereignisse oder Handlungen aus, die in der Vergangenheit liegen und abgeschlossen sind. Deshalb benutzt man es, z. B. um Geschichten zu erzählen oder über Ferienerlebnisse zu berichten.

All this happened		in the holidays:
I	**climbed**	Great Gable.
You	**sailed**	round the Isle of Wight.
Ben	**dropped**	his ice-cream into Helen's beach bag.
Barbara	**stayed**	at her aunt's house.
It	**rained**	nearly every day.

We	**looked**	at interesting old houses.
You	**walked**	round some lakes.
They	**visited**	York Minster.

- Das *simple past* (die einfache Vergangenheit) von regelmäßigen Verben wird dadurch gebildet, daß man die Endung **-ed** an die Stammform des Verbs (Infinitiv ohne *to*) anhängt: Stammform: walk; *simple past:* walk**ed**
- Die Form des *simple past* ist für alle Personen gleich.

⚠ Im Deutschen kann man das *simple past* sowohl durch das Präteritum wie auch durch das Perfekt wiedergeben:

It rained nearly every day. Es regnete fast jeden Tag. (Präteritum)
Es hat fast jeden Tag geregnet. (Perfekt)

§ 2 Aussprache und Schreibung des Simple Past (regelmäßige Formen)

Bei der Aussprache und beim Schreiben muß man auf folgende Besonderheiten achten:

Beim Sprechen	
stay**ed** [eɪd] sail**ed** [ld] clos**ed** [zd]	Nach Vokalen und nach stimmhaften Konsonanten spricht man [d].
laugh**ed** [ft] look**ed** [kt] fetch**ed** [tʃt]	Nach stimmlosen Konsonanten spricht man [t].
end**ed** [dɪd] visit**ed** [tɪd]	Nach [d] oder [t] spricht man [ɪd].

Beim Schreiben	
to cycl**e** – cycl**ed** to chang**e** – chang**ed** to hop**e** – hop**ed**	Das stumme End -e fällt weg.
to car**ry** – car**ried** to c**ry** – c**ried**	Verben, die auf Konsonant + **y** enden, erhalten die Endung **-ied**.
to dr**op** – dr**opped** to st**op** – st**opped**	Nach kurzem, betontem Vokal wird ein einfacher Endkonsonant verdoppelt.

§ 3 Das Simple Past: unregelmäßige Formen
The simple past: irregular forms

Im Englischen gibt es, wie auch im Deutschen, regelmäßige und unregelmäßige Verben.

to have	had	Helen and her parents **had** a lovely time in Cornwall.
to do	did	They **did** a lot of interesting things.
to go	went	They **went** to the beach nearly every day.
to see	saw	One day they **saw** Ben MacDonald.
to come	came [keɪm]	He **came** and talked to them.
to say	said [sed]	Ann **said:** "Please Ben, don't drop anything on me."

- Während die regelmäßigen Verben im *simple past* alle auf *-ed* enden, gibt es für die unregelmäßigen Verben keine Bildungsregeln. Die einzelnen Formen müssen gelernt werden.
- Aber auch bei den unregelmäßigen Verben sind die Formen des *Simple Past* für alle Personen gleich. (Die einzige Ausnahme ist *to be* – s. § 4).

⚠ Auf Seite 191 findet sich ein Verzeichnis aller unregelmäßigen Verben, die in **Green Line 1** und **2** vorkommen. Alle anderen Verben in **Green Line 1** und **2** sind regelmäßig.

§ 4 Das Simple Past von ‚to be' The simple past of 'to be'

In the holidays	**I was**	in Scotland.
Kate,	**you were**	in Scotland, too.
What about Ben?	**He was**	in Cornwall.
And Barbara?	**She was**	in Hampshire.
What about the weather, Barbara?	**It was**	lovely.
	We were	on the beach a lot.
And you, Kevin and Kate –	**you were**	on a farm.
What about Mr and Mrs Pearson?	**They were**	at home.

- Es gibt zwei verschiedene Formen des *simple past* von *to be:*
was (in Verbindung mit *I, he, she, it*)
were (in Verbindung mit *you, we, they*)

§ 5 Die Verneinung im Simple Past mit ‚didn't' **Unit 1 Step B**
Negative sentences with 'didn't'

Im *simple present* verneint man mit *don't* oder *doesn't* (+ Infinitiv des Vollverbs):
z. B. She **doesn't like** football.

- Im *simple past* verneint man mit *didn't* (*did not*) (+ Infinitiv des Vollverbs):
  Two years ago it **rained** a lot in the holidays. (bejaht)
  But last year it **didn't rain** at all. (verneint)

subject	*didn't*	infinitive	object/adverbial
I	didn't	go away	in the holidays.
Christine	didn't	cycle	all the way to the Lake District.
We	didn't	stay	at a caravan site this year.
They	didn't	like	it at that hotel.

- Die Form *didn't* ist bei allen Personen gleich.

⚠ Nach *didn't* steht der Infinitiv. Keinesfalls darf auf *didn't* eine Form des *simple past* folgen!

§ 6 Entscheidungsfragen mit ‚did' Yes/no questions with 'did'

- Entscheidungsfragen werden im *simple present* mit *do* oder *does* gebildet. Im *simple past* werden sie mit *did* gebildet.

auxiliary (did)	subject	verb (infinitive)	object/adverbial	short answers
Did	you	tour	the Lake District in the holidays?	Yes, I did.
Did	Kevin	go	to Scotland in August?	Yes, he did.
Did	Linda	go away	this year?	No, she didn't.
Did	it	rain	a lot last week?	Yes, it did.
Did	the girls	go swimming	in the sea yesterday?	No, they didn't.

§ 7 Fragen mit Fragewörtern und ‚did' Questions with question words and 'did'

- Fragen mit *what, when, where, why, how* usw. werden im *simple present* mit *do* und *does* gebildet. Im *simple past* werden sie mit *did* gebildet.

question word	auxiliary (did)	subject	verb (infinitive)	object/adverbial	
What	did	you	do	in the holidays?	We toured the Lake District.
Where	did	Linda	go?		She didn't go away.
When	did	the Kleins	arrive	at Barton-on-Sea?	In the afternoon.

§ 8 Die Steigerung von Adjektiven mit ‚-er' und ‚-est' The comparison of adjectives with '-er' and '-est'

Unit 1 Step C

Die beiden Steigerungsformen des Adjektivs werden verwendet, um Vergleiche zu machen:

Ben Nevis is a	**high**	mountain.
The Matterhorn is	**higher.**	
But Mount Everest is the	**highest**	mountain in the world.

- Die erste Steigerungsform *(comparative)* wird gebildet, indem man *-er* an die Grundform des Adjektivs *(positive)* anhängt: *high + er → higher*
- Die zweite Steigerungsform, den Superlativ *(superlative)*, bildet man durch das Anhängen von *-est: high + est → highest.*
- Mit *-er* und *-est* werden gesteigert:
  alle einsilbigen Adjektive (*high, long, new, old, big* usw.)
  zweisilbige Adjektive, die auf *-y* enden (*dirty, early, funny, heavy* usw.)

⚠ Dabei muß man auf folgende Besonderheiten achten:

Beim Schreiben

big bigger (the) biggest Ebenso z. B.: *wet*	Nach kurzem, betontem Vokal wird der Endkonsonant verdoppelt.	fine finer (the) fin**est** Ebenso z. B.: *strange*	Das stumme End *-e* entfällt.	funn**y** funn**ier** (the) funn**iest** Ebenso z. B.: *angry, dirty, heavy.*	Bei Adjektiven, die auf *-y* enden, wird das *y* durch *i* ersetzt

Bei der Aussprache

strong [strɒŋ] stronger ['strɒŋgə] (the) strongest ['strɒŋgɪst]	Bei Adjektiven, die auf *-ng* enden, wird in der ersten und zweiten Steigerungsform ein [g] gesprochen. Ebenso z. B.: *long, young.*

§ 9 Der Vergleich im Satz (I) Sentences with comparisons

London is	**bigger than**	Leeds.	… größer als …
Ben Nevis is	**higher than**	Great Gable.	… höher als …
The Thames is	**longer than**	the Humber.	… länger als …

- Durch die erste Steigerungsform *(comparative)* + *than* kann man ausdrücken, daß zwei Dinge ungleich sind.

Unit 2

10 Die Steigerung von Adjektiven mit ‚more' und ‚most' — Unit 2 Step A

The comparison of adjectives with 'more' and 'most'

Today the Sheriff of Nottingham is not very		**powerful.**		… mächtig
In Robin Hood's time the Sheriff was	**more**	**powerful.**		… mächtiger
In those days the King was	**the most**	**powerful**	man in England.	… der mächtigste …

Nottingham is a **famous** city.	… berühmt(e) …
York is **more famous.**	… berühmter
But, of course, London is **the most famous** city in Britain.	… die berühmteste …

- Alle Adjektive, die mehr als zwei Silben haben, werden mit *more* und *most* gesteigert: *powerful (positive) – more powerful (comparative) – the most powerful (superlative)*. Ebenso z. B.: *dangerous, difficult, exciting, expensive, important, interesting, terrible, wonderful.*
- Auch die meisten zweisilbigen Adjektive, die nicht auf *-y* enden, werden mit *more* und *most* gesteigert; z. B.: *afraid, careful, famous, modern, surprised, useful.*

§ 11 Der Vergleich im Satz (II) Sentences with comparisons (II)

Es gibt zwei Arten, Dinge miteinander zu vergleichen:

Gleichheit

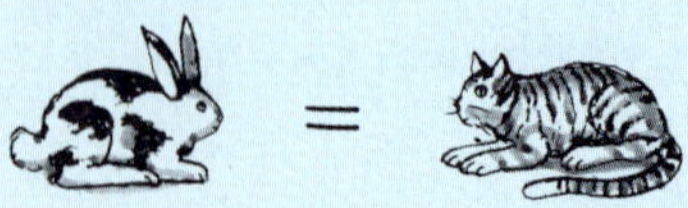

A rabbit is **as big as** a cat.	… so groß wie …
Is it **as interesting as** a cat?	… so interessant wie …

Ungleichheit

A cat is **not as big as** a cheetah.	… nicht so groß wie …
And it is **not as dangerous as** a cheetah.	… nicht so gefährlich wie …
A horse is **bigger than** a pony.	… größer als …
It is **more powerful than** a pony, too.	… stärker als …

⚠ **than** nicht verwechseln mit **then** (= dann)!

§ 12 ‚Some' und ‚any' und ihre Zusammensetzungen 'Some' and 'any' and their compounds

Unit 2 Step B

Im Englischen wird eine unbestimmte Menge oder Anzahl (im Sinne von ‚etwas' oder ‚einige') mit *some* oder *any* ausgedrückt.

a) **,some' und ,any'**

Fragen (questions)	Verneinte Aussagen (negative statements)	Bejahte Aussagen (affirmative statements)
Have we got **any** crisps? Haben wir (noch) Chips?	No, we haven't got **any** (crisps). Nein, wir haben keine (Chips).	We must buy **some** (crisps). Wir müssen welche kaufen. (Wir müssen Chips kaufen).
And is there **any** lemonade? Und ist (noch) Limonade da?	No, there isn't **any** (lemonade). Nein, es ist keine (Limonade) da.	Let's get **some** (lemonade). Kaufen wir welche. (Kaufen wir Limonade.)

- In Fragen und verneinten Sätzen wird meistens *any* gebraucht, in bejahten Sätzen *some*.
- *some* und *any* bleiben oft unübersetzt:

  Have you got any cassettes about Robin Hood?
  Haben Sie Kassetten über Robin Hood?

b) **'something/anything' 'somebody/anybody' ('someone/anyone') 'somewhere/anywhere'**

Wie *some* und *any* selbst werden auch ihre Zusammensetzungen gebraucht:
- In Fragen und verneinten Sätzen verwendet man Zusammensetzungen mit *any*.
- In bejahten Sätzen verwendet man Zusammensetzungen mit *some*.

Fragen (questions)	Verneinte Aussagen (negative statements)	Bejahte Aussagen (affirmative statements)
Must we buy **anything** else? Müssen wir sonst noch etwas kaufen?	I can't think of **anything**. Mir fällt nichts anderes ein.	But wait, there was **something**. Aber warte mal, da war etwas.
Is there **anyone** at the door? Ist da jemand an der Tür?	No, there isn't **anyone**. Nein, da ist niemand.	I'm sure I heard **someone**. Ich bin sicher, ich habe jemand gehört.
Are the oranges **anywhere** in the kitchen? Sind die Apfelsinen irgendwo in der Küche?	I can't see them **anywhere**. Ich kann sie nirgends sehen.	But they must be **somewhere**. Aber sie müssen irgendwo sein.

13 Die Grundzahlen The cardinal numbers

1	one	11	eleven	21	twenty-one	100	a/one hundred
2	two	12	twelve	22	twenty-two	101	a/one hundred and one
3	three	13	thirteen	23	twenty-three	102	a/one hundred and two
4	four	14	fourteen	30	thirty	200	two hundred
5	five	15	fifteen	40	forty	360	three hundred and sixty
6	six	16	sixteen	50	fifty	999	nine hundred and ninety-nine
7	seven	17	seventeen	60	sixty	1000	a/one thousand
8	eight	18	eighteen	70	seventy	1001	a/one thousand and one
9	nine	19	nineteen	80	eighty	1500	one thousand five hundred
10	ten	20	twenty	90	ninety	1810	one thousand eight hundred and ten

⚠ Jahreszahlen werden aber so gesprochen:

1066	ten sixty-six	1900	nineteen hundred
1215	twelve fifteen	1901	nineteen oh-one
1649	sixteen forty-nine	1945	nineteen forty-five

Unit 3

§ 14 'Going to' — Unit 3 Step A

Um auszudrücken, daß etwas geplant oder beabsichtigt ist, wird *going to* verwendet. Man erwartet, daß der Plan oder die Absicht in der Zukunft verwirklicht wird.

Mrs Bennett **is going to stay** in hospital for a few days.	Frau Bennett wird für ein paar Tage im Krankenhaus bleiben.
Who **is going to cook** the meals?	Wer wird das Essen kochen?
Mr Bennett and Ronny **are going to cook** every day.	Herr Bennett und Ronny haben vor, jeden Tag zu kochen.
And who **is going to look** after Timmy?	Und wer paßt auf Timmy auf?
The neighbours **are going to do** that.	Die Nachbarn wollen das tun.
"And you, Timmy, **are you going to do** the shopping?"	„Und du, Timmy, wirst du das Einkaufen übernehmen?"
"No, I **'m not.**"	„Nein."
"I **'m going to take** everybody's temperature."	„Ich habe vor, bei allen Leuten Fieber zu messen."
"But I **'m not going to send** anyone to hospital."	„Aber ich habe nicht vor, irgend jemand ins Krankenhaus zu schicken."

- Auf *am/are/is + going to* folgt ein Infinitiv.

⚠ *Going to* darf man nicht mit der Verlaufsform der Gegenwart verwechseln:
Verlaufsform der Gegenwart: "I'm going home." „Ich gehe (gerade) nach Hause"
Going to: "I'm *going to* go home." „Ich habe vor, nach Hause zu gehen."

§ 15 May/may not/mustn't — Unit 3 Step B

May I play with Nelson, Mum?	Yes, of course, you **may.**
May I cycle with him into York?	No, you **may not.** It's too dangerous.
May I give him these sweets?	No, you **mustn't.** Sweets are not good for dogs.

- *May* kann man gebrauchen, um höflich um Erlaubnis zu bitten.
- Ein Verbot kann durch *may not* oder *mustn't* ausgedrückt werden (auf deutsch: nicht dürfen). *Mustn't* wird häufiger verwendet als *may not.*
- Die Formen *may, may not* und *mustn't* sind bei allen Personen gleich.

16 Must/needn't

Must David look after Nelson?	Yes, he **must.** Nelson is his dog.
Must he wash him every week?	No, he **needn't.** He must only wash him when he's very dirty.

- Während man mit *must* eine Notwendigkeit oder Verpflichtung ausdrückt, verwendet man *needn't* um auszudrücken, daß man etwas nicht zu tun braucht.
- Die Form *needn't* ist für alle Personen gleich.
- Die Hilfsverben *may, must* und *needn't* können nur im *present tense* gebraucht werden.

⚠ *Mustn't* nicht verwechseln mit *needn't!*

You **must** give Nelson his food every day.	Du **mußt** Nelson jeden Tag sein Futter geben.
You **mustn't** forget that!	Du **darfst** das **nicht** vergessen!
But you **needn't** pay for the food.	Aber du **mußt** das Futter **nicht** bezahlen. (Aber du brauchst das Futter nicht zu bezahlen.)

Unit 4

17 Das Present Perfect: regelmäßige Formen — Unit 4 Step A

The present perfect: regular forms

Mit dem *present perfect* drückt man aus, daß eine Handlung, die in der Vergangenheit stattgefunden hat, in der Gegenwart von Bedeutung ist.
Zum Beispiel: *I have washed my hands.* ⟶ *They're clean now.*
Die Handlung selbst (das Händewaschen) ist zwar vorbei, aber das Ergebnis ist in der Gegenwart noch spürbar (die Hände sind sauber).

	Handlung	Ergebnis

"May I **wash** Bonzo?"	"Look, **I've washed** him.	He's clean now."

"You must **clean** your room, Kate."	"You **haven't cleaned** your room yet.	It's still the same."

Ronny is going to **cook** the lunch.	He **has cooked** the lunch.	It is on the table now.

Mrs Griffin is going to **climb** the rocks.	"Look, she **has climbed** the rocks.	She's at the top."

Ronny and Kevin are going to **repair** Timmy's cars.	They **have repaired** his cars.	He can play with them again.

- Das *present perfect* wird gebildet mit *have/has* und dem *past participle;* die Verneinung lautet *haven't (have not)/hasn't (has not) + past participle.*
- Bei regelmäßigen Verben besteht das *past participle* aus der Stammform und der Endung *-ed.* (Bei den regelmäßigen Verben sind also Schreibung und Aussprache des *past participle* mit denen des *past tense* gleich: s. § 2.)

⚠ Beachte beim Übersetzen: Ronny has washed the car. Ronny hat das Auto gewaschen.
Ronny has jumped out of bed. Ronny ist aus dem Bett gesprungen.

§ 18 Das Present Perfect: unregelmäßige Formen — Unit 4 Step B
The present perfect: irregular forms

Viele Verben haben besondere, unregelmäßige Formen für das *past participle.*

infinitive	past participle	present perfect		
to come	**come**	The Road Safety Officer	has come	to the school.
to bring	**brought**	The children	have brought	their bikes.
to show	**shown**	He	has shown	them everything.
to see	**seen**	He	hasn't seen	Barbara's bike yet.
to take	**taken**	David	has taken	his mudguards off.

- Für die Bildung der unregelmäßigen Formen des *past participle* gibt es keine Regel. Deshalb müssen die einzelnen Formen gelernt werden.

⚠ Auf Seite 191 befindet sich ein Verzeichnis aller unregelmäßigen Verben, die in **Green Line 1** und **2** vorkommen. Alle anderen Verben in **Green Line 1** und **2** sind regelmäßig.

§ 19 Die Wortstellung beim Present Perfect
Word order with the present perfect

Frage (question)				short answer	Aussage (statement)			
Hv	S	V	O		S	Hv	V	O
Have	you	changed	the tyres?	Yes, I have.	I	have	changed	the tyres.
Has	Ronny	emptied	the bucket?	Yes, he has.	He	has	emptied	the bucket.
Have	you	washed	your hands?	No, I haven't.	I	haven't	washed	my hands yet.
Have	we	done	everything?	No, we haven't.	We	haven't	done	everything yet.

- Anders als im Deutschen steht im englischen Satz das Objekt **nach** dem *past participle.* Dies gilt sowohl für Aussage- als auch für Fragesätze:

Have you changed the tyres?	*Yes, I have.*	*I have changed the tyres.*

Hast du die Reifen ausgewechselt?	Ja.	Ich habe die Reifen ausgewechselt.

20 Der s-Genitiv und der of-Genitiv
The s-genitive and the of-genitive

Mrs Webb has got a new bus. **Mrs Webb's bus** looks very nice.	**The front of the bus** is green and white.
The Bennetts have changed the plugs. **The Bennetts' taxi** is O.K. now.	**The engine of the taxi** sounds much better.
The children are playing. Look at **the children's cars.**	**The wheels of the cars** look funny.

- Der *s*-Genitiv zeigt an, welcher Person etwas gehört.
- Der Genitiv mit *of* zeigt an, welcher Sache etwas zugeordnet ist.

Unit 5

21] ‚May' und ‚be allowed to' — Unit 5 Step A

May und *be allowed to* drücken beide eine Erlaubnis aus (auf deutsch: dürfen). *May not* und die verneinte Form von *be allowed to* drücken ein Verbot aus (auf deutsch: nicht dürfen). (Vgl. § 15)

- *May* und *may not* können nur im *present tense* verwendet werden. Für die anderen Zeiten muß man eine Form von *be allowed to* verwenden.

	present tense	past tense	
Du darfst…	You may… You are allowed to…	You were allowed to…	Du durftest…
Du darfst nicht…	You may not… You aren't allowed to…	You weren't allowed to…	Du durftest nicht

present tense	*past tense*
Peter: **"May** I take Bonzo to school, Mum?" *Mrs Wilson:* "No, you **may not.** You **aren't allowed to** take pets to school – you know that." *Peter:* "But we're going to go for a walk with Mr Edwards. And we **are allowed to** take our dogs." *Mrs Wilson:* "Oh, **are you** really? Well, have a nice time then."	And what about the school excursion? **Was** Peter **allowed to** take Bonzo then? No, he **wasn't.** He **wasn't allowed to** take him on the excursion. The children **were** only **allowed to** take their dogs on the walk.

- *May* und *may not* drücken aus, daß der Sprecher *selbst* um Erlaubnis bittet, etwas erlaubt oder etwas verbietet. *May* und *may not* werden hauptsächlich in Fragen und in Antworten auf diese Fragen gebraucht.
- Mit *be allowed to* wird festgestellt, daß allgemein eine Erlaubnis oder ein Verbot besteht. Es bleibt dabei offen, *wer* für die Erlaubnis oder das Verbot verantwortlich ist.

§ 22 ‚Must' und ‚have to'

Mit *must* oder einer Form von *have to* kann ausgedrückt werden, daß etwas notwendig ist oder getan werden muß (auf deutsch: müssen). (Vgl. § 16)

present tense	past tense

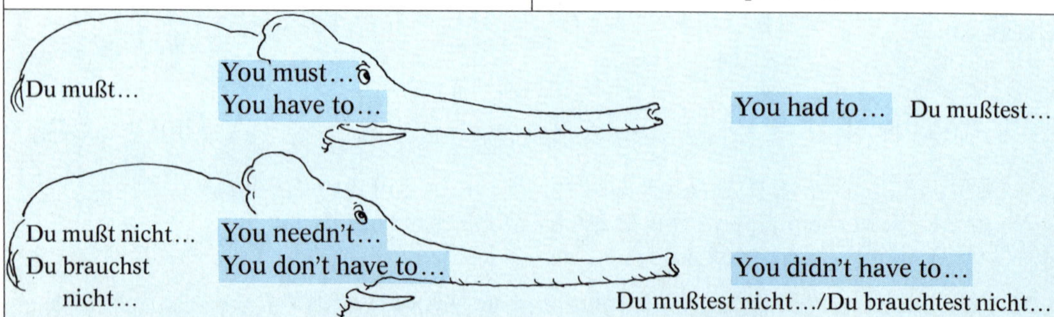

Paul: "**Must** you really go home now?" *Ben:* "Oh, perhaps I **needn't** go yet. I **don't have to** be home before 8." *Pam:* "But I **must** leave now. I **have to** be home by 7. When **does** Kevin **have to** be home?" *Paul:* "He **doesn't have to** go at all. He is going to stay the night."	*Helen:* **"Did** you **have to** leave the party early yesterday?" *Ben:* "No, I **didn't.** I **didn't have to** be home before 8." *Helen:* "What about Pam?" *Ben:* "She **had to** leave early. She **had to** be home by 7." *Helen:* "When **did** Kevin **have to** go?" *Ben:* "He **didn't have to** go at all. He stayed the night."

- *Must* kann nur im *present tense* verwendet werden. Für die anderen Zeitformen wird *have to* verwendet.
- Fragen und Verneinungen mit *have to* werden im *present tense* mit *do/does* und im *past tense* mit *did* gebildet.

23 ‚Should' und ‚shouldn't' — Unit 5 Step B

Should drückt wie das deutsche ‚sollte' einen Rat, eine Ermahnung oder eine Verpflichtung aus.

You	**should**	go to bed earlier.	Ihr solltet …
We know we	**should,**	but we always watch TV so long	… daß wir das (tun) sollten …
You	**shouldn't**	eat so much. Christine.	Du solltest nicht …
You are right. I	**shouldn't.**		… daß ich das nicht (tun) sollte …

- Die Form *should/shouldn't* ist bei allen Personen gleich.

24 ‚What?' und ‚which?'

What are you going to eat?	**Which** are you going to have – fish fingers or beans on toast?
What colour is your new car?	**Which** colour do you like better? Red or blue?
What subjects have you got at school?	**Which** of them do you like best.

- *What* fragt nach Sachen aus einer unbeschränkten Anzahl.
- *Which* fragt nach Sachen aus einer beschränkten Anzahl.

25 Das Simple Past und das Present Perfect — Unit 5 Step C

The simple past and the present perfect

Das Present Perfect The present perfect		**Das Simple Past mit Zeitangaben der Vergangenheit** The simple past with adverbials of time
What have they done?	(What is the result?)	**When** did they do it? **When** did it happen?
I **have cleaned** my bike.	(It looks good now.)	I **cleaned** it yesterday.
Ben **has seen** the film.	(He doesn't want to see it again.)	He **saw** it last night.
Miss Price **has put up** the notice.	(You can read it.)	She **put** it **up** a few hours ago.
We **have heard** the news.	(We know all about it.)	We **heard** the news after tea.
The boys **have bought** a present for Sharon.	(It's great.)	They **bought** it on Saturday.

- Das *present perfect* drückt aus, daß eine Handlung sich zwar in der Vergangenheit abgespielt hat, daß ihr Ergebnis aber noch in der Gegenwart wirksam ist. (Vgl. §§ 17–18)
- Das *present perfect* betont also nicht das Vergangene der Handlung, sondern ihr gegenwärtiges Ergebnis. Deshalb enthalten Sätze mit dem *present perfect* normalerweise **keine** Zeitangaben der Vergangenheit.
- Das *simple past* betont, daß Handlungen vorbei sind. (Vgl. §§ 1–5)
- Häufig wird das *simple past* mit Zeitangaben der Vergangenheit gebraucht. *Yesterday, last night, a few hours ago, in 1982* usw. sind Signalwörter, die darauf hinweisen, daß das *simple past* verwendet werden muß.

[§ 26] Das Stützwort ‚one/ones' beim Adjektiv
The prop-word 'one/ones' after adjectives

Timmy has got three cars – **a red one** and two blue ones.	…, ein rotes und zwei blaue.
"Which pencil do you want – **the long one** or **the short one**?"	…, den langen oder den kurzen?"
"Which of those men is your form master?" **"The big one."**	… Der große."

- Soll ein zählbares Nomen nicht wiederholt werden, so wird es durch *one* (im Plural *ones*) ersetzt.
- Anders als im Deutschen kann das Adjektiv meist nicht allein stehen.

Unit 6

§ 27 Das ‚will'-Futur The will-future

Unit 6 Step A

Das *will*-Futur verwendet man, um auszudrücken, was in der Zukunft passieren wird.

What	**will happen**	to Ben?
He	**will be**	all right.
He	**won't miss**	his flight.
In Enid the weather	**will be**	lovely,
and there	**won't be**	any rain.
Let's hope they	**will be**	happy in America.
Well, we	**'ll hear**	all about it.
Ben: "And I	**'ll write**	you a letter and
	send	you some photos."

- Das *will*-Futur wird aus *will* + Infinitiv gebildet. (In der 1. Person wird statt *will* gelegentlich auch *shall* gebraucht: z. B. I *shall* be in London next week, but I *shan't* be there long.)
- Häufig werden statt *will* und *will not* die Kurzformen *'ll* und *won't* [wəʊnt] verwendet.

⚠ Vergleiche: Wir **schicken** euch morgen die Fotos. We**'ll send** you the photos tomorrow.

28 Nebensätze mit ‚when' Clauses with 'when'

Nebensatz mit *when* (when-clause)	Hauptsatz (main clause)
When they **land** in Oklahoma City,	Mr MacDonald **will be** at the airport.
When Ben **sees** his father,	he **will explain** everything.
When they **get** to Enid,	they **won't know** anyone there.
simple present	will-future

- In Nebensätzen mit *when* wird kein *will*-Futur verwendet.

29 Das will-Futur und das going to-Futur **Unit 6 Step B**
The will-future and the going to-future

Bisher haben wir im Englischen zwei Zukunftsformen kennengelernt:
das *will*-Futur und das *going to*-Futur.
Die Form, die man wählt, hängt davon ab, welche Sprechabsicht man hat
(das heißt: was man ausdrücken möchte und welche Gesichtspunkte man besonders betonen will.)

1. Das *will*-Futur wird verwendet

a) zum Ausdruck einer **Vorhersage** oder einer **Vermutung**

Ben **will be** thirteen tomorrow.
I'm sure the sun **will shine** on his birthday.
I don't think **it'll rain** then.
Perhaps we'**ll go** for a picnic in the afternoon.
I hope we'**ll have** a good time.

- Man kann das *will*-Futur verwenden, um auszudrücken, daß zukünftige Ereignisse nicht von persönlichen Entscheidungen abhängen, sondern von äußeren Umständen (z. B. Geburtstag, Wetter usw.)
- Vermutungen werden häufig mit *I'm sure, I think, perhaps* + *will*-Futur ausgedrückt.
- Das *will*-Futur wird häufig im Zusammenhang mit *I hope* verwendet.

b) zum Ausdruck eines **spontanen Entschlusses.**

"Oh dear, my pullover is still upstairs."
– "I'**ll fetch** it for you."
"There's a good Western on TV."
– "I'**ll switch on.** O.K.?"
"I must get everything ready for the party."
– "We'**ll help** you."

- Das *will*-Futur kann verwendet werden, um einen Entschluß auszudrücken, der schnell, ohne langes Überlegen (d. h. spontan) gefaßt wird.
Es drückt in diesem Fall eine Bereitschaft oder ein Versprechen aus.

2. *Going to* wird verwendet,

um **Absichten, Vorhaben** und **Pläne** auszudrücken.
I'm going to visit a prairie castle on Monday. We**'re going to open** a lemonade stand this summer. Ben and Harry **are going to play** tennis after school.

- Anders als bei einem spontanen Entschluß (der mit dem *will*-Futur ausgedrückt wird), deutet der Gebrauch von *going to* darauf hin, daß die Absicht schon länger besteht. (Vgl. § 13)

§ 30 Shall I? Shall we?

"It's so hot in here.	**Shall I** open a window?"	Soll ich…
"The weather's lovely.	**Shall we** go for a walk?"	Sollen wir…?
"Yes, let's.	Where **shall we** go?"	Wohin sollen wir/wollen wir…?

- *Shall I?* und *Shall we?* werden in Fragesätzen verwendet, um den Wunsch eines anderen zu erfragen, einen Vorschlag zu machen oder einen anderen zu bitten, einen Vorschlag zu machen.

[§ 31] Die indirekte Rede I (Verb im Einführungssatz im Präsens) Unit 6 Step D
Reported speech I (introductory verb in the present)

Aussagen in der direkten Rede	Aussagen in der indirekten Rede
I've got some news. It'**ll be my** birthday on Sunday. **I'm going to** invite **you** to **my** party.	Ben says (that) **he has got** some news. He says (that) it **will be his** birthday on Sunday, and (that) **he is going to** invite **us** to **his** party.
I'm afraid I **can't** come. **We're going to** visit **my** aunt in Oklahoma City at the weekend.	Peggy says (that) **she can't** come. **They are going to** visit **her** aunt in Oklahoma City at the weekend.

- Wenn das einführende Verb im Präsens steht, so wird die Zeitform der direkten Rede beibehalten.
- Das einleitende *that* ist nicht notwendig und wird oft weggelassen.
- Zwischen Einführungssatz und indirekter Rede steht, anders als im Deutschen, **kein** Komma.
- Personalpronomen und Possessivpronomen müssen häufig verändert werden, d. h. sie werden in der indirekten Rede dem Standpunkt des Berichterstatters angepaßt. (*I* → *he/she; my* → *his/her* usw.)

Fragen in der direkten Rede	Fragen in der indirekten Rede
Have you invited Beverly? **Does she know** about the party? **What did Old Jeff say** about the weather?	Harry asks **if you have** invited Beverly. He asks **if she knows** about the party. He asks **what Old Jeff said** about the weather?

- Steht in der direkten Rede ein Fragewort (*who, what, which, how* usw.), so wird es in der indirekten Rede beibehalten.
- Steht kein Fragewort, so wird die indirekte Frage durch *if* eingeleitet.

Unit 7

Unit 7 Step A

32 Das Past Progressive

Neben dem *simple past* (vgl. §§ 1–5) kann man auch das *past progressive* verwenden, um auszudrücken, daß etwas in der Vergangenheit stattfand.

Hintergrundhandlung	Neu einsetzende Handlung
Harry **was dancing** about on the raft	when Ben took a photo.
Grandpa **was sleeping**	when Big Paws jumped on him.
Peggy and Nellie **were feeding** the hens	when their mother called them for lunch.
While they **were eating** lunch,	it started to rain.
While Ben **was washing up,**	he broke a plate.

Das *past progressive* wird gebildet aus dem *past tense* von *to be (was/were)* und der *ing*-Form.

- Das *past progressive* betont, daß ein Vorgang gerade ablief und noch nicht abgeschlossen war.
- Häufig beschreibt das *past progressive,* was gerade vor sich ging und noch nicht zu Ende war, als ein neues Ereignis eintrat. Es beschreibt also eine Art „Hintergrundhandlung“, während das *simple past* verwendet wird, um die neu einsetzende Handlung zu beschreiben. Im Deutschen gibt es diese Unterscheidung nicht:
  Vergleiche: *While the children* **were working,** *Ben* **took** *a photo.*
  Während die Kinder **arbeiteten, machte** Ben ein Foto.

33 Sätze mit Konjunktionen Clauses with conjunctions

Unit 7 Step B

Mit Hilfe von Konjunktionen kann man Sätze verknüpfen.

Hauptsatz (main clause)		Hauptsatz (main clause)	
Ben has come to the Whiteclouds' farm	**and**	Peggy is showing him everything.	…und…
"We haven't got many animals	**but**	we've got a few hens.	…aber…
You can feed the hens	**or**	you can look for eggs."	…oder…

- *And, but* und *or* verbinden gleichartige Sätze (z. B. zwei Hauptsätze) miteinander.

Hauptsatz (main clause)	Nebensatz (secondary clause)	
"Look, that's Rodney. He's won a prize	**because** he's so beautiful."	...weil...
We keep a cow	**so that** we don't have to buy any milk.	...so daß/ damit...
Let's look at the barn	**before** we have something to drink."	...bevor...
"Can we milk the cow?" "Let's wait	**until** Dad comes back."	...bis...
It started to rain	**when** they were leaving the lake.	...als...
One of the hens jumped on the table	**while** they were having lunch.	...während...

- *Because, so that, before, until, when* und *while* verbinden einen Hauptsatz mit einem Nebensatz.
  Because leitet einen Nebensatz des Grundes ein, *so that* einen Nebensatz des Zwecks.
  Die Konjunktionen *before, until, when* und *while* leiten Nebensätze der Zeit ein.

⚠ Anders als im Deutschen bleibt die Wortstellung S – V – O auch in untergeordneten Nebensätzen erhalten.

Vergleiche:

Wir halten Hühner, damit [S wir] jeden Tag [O Eier] [V haben.]

We keep hens so that [*S we*] [*V have*] [*O eggs*] *every day.*

Unit 8

§ 34 Could

Unit 8 Step A

Could hat zwei verschiedene Bedeutungen.

Could you see the men?	Konntet ihr...
No, we **couldn't** see them. It was too dark.	...konnten nicht...
But we **could** hear their voices.	...konnten...

- *Could/could not (past tense* von *can/cannot)* drücken aus, daß man in der Vergangenheit fähig oder unfähig war, etwas zu tun.

We **could** have a picnic next Sunday.	Wir könnten...
Couldn't we have the picnic near the lake?	Könnten wir nicht...
Could I have a piece of cake, please?	Könnte ich...
Could you tell me the way to the station?	Könnten Sie...

- *Could/couldn't* können gebraucht werden, um eine Möglichkeit auszudrücken oder um einen Vorschlag oder einen Plan zu machen.
  Die Frageform *Could...?* kann eine höfliche Frage oder eine Bitte einleiten.

35 Bedingungssätze Conditional sentences

Ein Bedingungssatz besteht aus einem *if*-Satz und einem Hauptsatz. Der *if*-Satz drückt eine Bedingung aus. Der Hauptsatz drückt aus, was passiert, wenn diese Bedingung erfüllt wird.

If-Satz (if-clause)	Hauptsatz (main clause)
If we **take** a taxi,	we'**ll get** to the airport early enough.
If Ben **doesn't hurry,**	they'**ll miss** their plane.
If they **miss** their plane,	they **won't arrive** in Oklahoma City on time.
If they **don't arrive** on time,	Mr MacDonald **will have** a nervous breakdown.

- Steht im Hauptsatz das *will*-Futur, so steht im *if*-Satz das *simple present.* (Vgl. *when*-Sätze § 28)
- Der *if*-Satz im *simple present* drückt aus, daß es möglich oder sogar wahrscheinlich ist, daß die Bedingung erfüllt wird.

⚠ Obwohl sich die Bedingung oft auf die Zukunft bezieht, darf im *if*-Satz nie das *will*-Futur stehen.

6] Das Adverb

Im Deutschen sind Adjektive und Adverbien formgleich, z. B.:
Sie ist **schön** (Adjektiv) – Sie singt **schön** (Adverb).
Im Englischen dagegen haben sie unterschiedliche Formen.

adjective	adverb
a **careful** driver	He drives **carefully.**
a **dangerous** corner.	The boy cycled round the corner **dangerously.**
She was **nervous.**	She talked **nervously.**
Don't be so **slow.**	He read the letter **slowly.**
This is **bad.**	You have done this **badly.**

- Adjektive geben an, wie jemand oder etwas ist.
- Ein Adjektiv steht vor einem Nomen oder nach dem Verb *to be.*

- Adverbien geben an, wie etwas getan wird. Sie geben Antwort auf Fragen mit *how*: *How does she drive? She drives* **carefully.**
- Adverbien der Art und Weise (adverbs of manner) werden meistens mit der Endung *-ly* von Adjektiven abgeleitet:
  careful + ly → carefully
  nice + ly → nicely

⚠ Beachte beim Schreiben:

adjective:	terrible	angry	noisy	happy
adverb:	terribly	angrily	noisily	happily

⚠ Beachte die Sonderformen:

good	fast
well	fast

[§ 37] Die Steigerung des Adverbs The comparison of adverbs

Die Steigerung der Adverbien gleicht der Steigerung der Adjektive (vgl. §§ 8, 10).

Firemen sometimes drive **dangerously**.
Bill Pushy drives **more dangerously.**
But Peggy drives **most dangerously** of all.

- Adverbien mit der Endung *-ly* haben zwei oder mehr Silben. Sie werden daher mit *more* und *most* gesteigert. (Vgl. § 10)

A cat can run very **fast.**
Some dogs can run **faster.**
But a cheetah can run **fastest** of all.

- Einsilbige Adverbien werden mit *-er*/*-est* gesteigert. (Vgl. § 8)

Harry can't swim very **well.**
Ben can swim much **better.**
And Peggy can swim **best** of all.

- Die Steigerungsformen von *well* lauten *better* und *best.* (Vgl. *good – better – best*)

Mrs Alassio sings **badly.**
Old Jeff sings even **worse.**
But Buddy sings **worst** of all.

- Die Steigerungsformen von *badly* lauten *worse* und *worst.* (Vgl. *bad – worse – worst*)

[§ 38] Das Gerund The gerund

Unit 8 Step B

Das Gerund wird aus der Stammform des Verbs und der Endung *-ing* gebildet.
Es nimmt eine Mittelstellung zwischen Verb und Nomen ein.

a) Das Gerund als Subjekt

Riding is fun. (Reiten macht Spaß)
Playing tennis is good exercise.
Helping on the farm can be hard work.
Working all day isn't always nice.

play + ing = playing

ride + ing = riding

sit + t + ing = sitting

- Das Gerund kann Subjekt eines Satzes sein und wird dann wie ein Nomen gebraucht.
  Vergleiche: **Horses** are nice. **Riding** is fun.
- Wie ein Verb kann das Gerund aber auch ein Objekt (*Playing tennis…*) oder eine Orts- und Zeitangabe (*Helping on the farm…*, *Working all day…*) bei sich haben.

b) Das Gerund als Objekt

I	like	**cooking.**		Ich koche gern.
He	hates	**writing**	letters.	Er schreibt sehr ungern Briefe.
She	enjoys	**reading**	comics.	Sie liest gern Comics.
We	love	**swimming**	in the lake.	Wir schwimmen sehr gern im See.
They	have stopped	**singing.**		Sie haben aufgehört zu singen.

- Nach bestimmten Verben kann entweder ein Nomen oder ein Gerund als Objekt stehen.
  Vergleiche: I like **books.** I like **reading.**
  He loves **the mountains.** He loves **climbing mountains.**
- Häufig verwendet man Verb + Gerund, um auszudrücken, was man gern oder ungern tut.

39] Contact clauses

Did you like **the story** **Peggy wrote** ?
(...die Geschichte, die Peggy schrieb?)

The fire-engine **Peggy drove** was very fast.
(Das Feuerwehrauto, das Peggy fuhr, ...)

The people **she rescued** were on the 21st floor.
(Die Leute, die sie rettete,...)

- *Contact clauses* werden direkt an ein Nomen angehängt.
- Sie geben wesentliche Informationen, ohne die man nicht wissen würde, wer oder was eigentlich gemeint ist. (Welche Geschichte? Welches Feuerwehrauto? Welche Leute?)

Übersichten

40 Langformen und Kurzformen
Long forms and short forms

long forms	short forms
to be	
I am	I'm
you are	you're
you are not	you aren't
she is not	she isn't
he is	he's
I was not	I wasn't
they were not	they weren't
do/did	
I do not mind	I don't mind
she does not mind	she doesn't mind
you did not mind	you didn't mind

long forms	short forms
have/have got	
I have got	I've got
he has got	he's got
I have not got	I haven't got
she has not got	she hasn't got
he has not finished	he hasn't finished
they have not finished	they haven't finished
will	
I will be 13	I'll be 13
he will not come	he won't come

41 Die Ordnungszahlen The ordinal numbers

1st	first	10th	tenth	30th	thirtieth
2nd	second	11th	eleventh	40th	fortieth
3rd	third	12th	twelfth	50th	fiftieth
4th	fourth	13th	thirteenth	60th	sixtieth
5th	fifth	15th	fifteenth	70th	seventieth
6th	sixth	20th	twentieth [twentɪəθ]	80th	eightieth
7th	seventh	21st	twenty-first	90th	ninetieth
8th	eighth [eɪtθ]	22nd	twenty-second	99th	ninety-ninth
9th	ninth [naɪnθ]	29th	twenty-ninth	100th	one hundredth

§ 42 Präpositionen
Prepositions

Vocabulary
Lautzeichen (Phonetic Symbols)

Vokale (Vowels)

[ɑ:] f**a**ther, c**a**rds; langes *a*, weiter hinten gesprochen als in *Vater*

[ʌ] m**o**ther, d**oe**s, br**u**sh; kurzes *a*, etwa wie in *Mann*

[e] p**e**n, h**ea**d; etwa wie das *e* in *nett*

[ə] **a** bar **o**f chocolate, sist**er**; kurzer, unbetonter Laut, wie der Endlaut in *bitte*

[ɜ:] g**ir**l, h**er**, w**or**d; etwa ein verlängertes [ə]. Dieser Laut wird weiter hinten gesprochen als das deutsche *ö* (Lippen nicht vorstülpen!)

[æ] fl**a**t, v**a**n; kurzes, ganz offenes *ä*, offener als in *Männer*

[ɪ] **i**t, buck**e**t; kurzes *i* wie in *Lippe*, doch weniger spitz, etwas zum [ə] hin

[i:] t**ea**cher, sh**e**, p**ie**ce; langes *i* wie in *tief*

[ɒ] sh**o**p, wh**a**t; kurzes, offenes *o*

[ɔ:] **o**r, s**aw**, f**our**; langes offenes *o* (Lippen leicht vorstülpen!)

[ʊ] p**u**llover, l**oo**k; kurzes *u* wie in *Schutt*

[u:] y**ou**, t**oo**, bl**ue**; langes *u*, etwa wie in *du* (Lippen kaum vorstülpen!)

Doppellaute (Diphthongs)

[aɪ] n**i**ne, b**y**, r**igh**t; wie *ai* in *Mai, Kaiser*

[aʊ] n**ow**, h**ou**se; helles *a* mit nachklingendem *u*, etwa wie in *Zauber*

[eə] th**ere**, ch**air**; kurzes, offenes *ä* mit nachklingendem [ə], etwa wie in *Bär*

[eɪ] n**a**me, th**ey**, **ei**ght; englisches [e] mit nachklingendem [ɪ]

[ɪə] h**ere**, id**ea**; etwa wie in *mir*

[ɔɪ] b**oy**; kurzes offenes *o* mit nachklingendem [ɪ], ähnlich wie in *Freude*

[əʊ] hell**o**, r**oa**d; [ə] mit nachklingendem [ʊ]

[ʊə] m**oo**rs, t**ou**rist; [ʊ] mit nachklingendem [ə]

Konsonanten (Consonants)

[j] **y**es; wie das deutsche *j*

[l] **l**isten, b**l**ue; am Wortanfang und vor Vokalen etwa wie das deutsche *l*
schoo**l**, she**l**f; am Wortende und vor Konsonanten wie das *l* der Rheinländer, z. B. in *Köln*

[ŋ] morni**ng**, lo**ng**; wie der *-ng*-Laut in *singen* (kein [g] sprechen!)

[ŋg] E**ng**lish; wie [ŋ] jedoch mit nachfolgendem gesprochenem [g]

[r] **r**ed, b**r**ush; Gaumen-*r*, Zungenspitze gegen Gaumen anheben und leicht zurückbiegen; der austretende Luftstrom erzeugt [r]

[s] **s**ister, thi**s**; stimmloses, d. h. hartes *s* wie in *Laus*

[z] i**s**, dog**s**; stimmhaftes, d. h. weiches *s* wie in *Rose*

[ʒ] gara**ge**; stimmhaftes *sch* wie in *Gelee*

[dʒ] **j**eans, **G**erman; [ʒ] mit vorausklingendem [d]

[ʃ] **sh**e, sta**ti**on; stimmloses *sch* wie in *Tisch*

[tʃ] tea**ch**er, **ch**ild; [ʃ] mit vorausklingendem [t]

[st/sp] **st**ory, **sp**ort; wird [st] und [sp] gesprochen, nicht [ʃt] und [ʃp]

[ð] **th**e, mo**th**er; stimmhafter Lispellaut (Zunge zwischen den Zähnen!)

[θ] **th**anks, no**th**ing; stimmloser Lispellaut (Zunge zwischen den Zähnen!)

[v] **v**an, o**f**; wie *w* in *Winter*

[w] **w**eek, **wh**ich, **o**ne; vom [ʊ] ausgehen und zum folgenden Laut hinübergleiten

ˈ = Hauptbetonung
ˌ = Nebenbetonung
(Die Betonungsstriche stehen immer **vor** der betonten Silbe.)
‿ = besonders enge Bindung zweier Wörter aneinander

° Die mit ° gekennzeichneten Wörter gehören zum rezeptiven Wortschatz. In Bundesländern, in denen ein rezeptiver Wortschatz nicht ausdrücklich verlangt wird, werden diese Wörter genauso behandelt wie der übrige Wortschatz.
⟨ ⟩ Stücke, deren Überschriften, und Übungen, deren Ziffern in Winkelklammern stehen, sind fakultativ.
s.th. = something
s.o. = someone

Unit 1

⟨Photo page: Holiday postcards⟩

postcard ['pəʊstkɑ:d]	Postkarte
Borrowdale ['bɒrəʊdeɪl]	*Ortsname*
Isle of Wight [ˌaɪl‿əv 'waɪt]	*Insel vor der Südküste Englands*
Newquay ['nju:ki:]	*Ortsname*

A The summer holidays

a)	**postcard** ['pəʊstkɑ:d]	Let's send them a *postcard.*	Postkarte
	Borrowdale ['bɒrəʊdeɪl]		*Ortsname*
	to **cycle** ['saɪkl]	to ride a bike	Fahrrad fahren
	We cycled ['saɪkld]		Wir fuhren ... mit dem Rad
	yesterday ['jestədeɪ]	Today is the day after *yesterday.*	gestern
	to climb, **climbed** [klaɪmd]		kletterte
	Great Gable [ˌgreɪt 'geɪbl]		*Name eines Berges*
	hardly ['hɑ:dlɪ]	Timmy has got a cold. He can *hardly* speak.	kaum
	Barton-on-Sea [ˌbɑ:tən‿ɒn 'si:]		*Ortsname*
	Hampshire ['hæmpʃə]		*Grafschaft in Südengland*
	to arrive, **arrived** [ə'raɪvd]		kam an
	aunt [ɑ:nt]	My mother's sister is my *aunt.*	Tante
	Isle of Wight [ˌaɪl‿əv 'waɪt]		*Insel vor der Südküste Englands*
	to **visit, visited** ['vɪzɪt(ɪd)]	to go and see	besuchen, besichtigen
	cousin ['kʌzn]	My aunt's children are my *cousins.*	Vetter, Kusine
	°**strange** [streɪndʒ]	That's a *strange* noise: what can it be?	°fremd, seltsam
	to happen, **happened** ['hæpnd]		geschah
b)	**diary** ['daɪərɪ]	Every day Helen writes something in her *diary.*	Tagebuch
	Newquay ['nju:ki:]		*Ortsname*
	Cornwall ['kɔ:nwəl]		*Grafschaft in Südwestengland*
	weather ['weðə]	The *weather* is wonderful. The sun is shining and it's nice and warm.	Wetter
	to be, is/are, **was/were** [wɒz/wɜ:]	It is hot today. It *was* cold yesterday.	war/waren
	to have, **had** [hæd]		hatte
	hot [hɒt]	very warm	heiß
	to stay, **stayed** [steɪd]		blieb

°**deck-chair** ['dek,tʃeə]	On the beach people often sit in *deck-chairs.*	°Liegestuhl
to do, **did** [dɪd]		tat, machte
all day [,ɔ:l 'deɪ]	from morning to night	den ganzen Tag
°to **go surfing** [,gəʊ 'sɜ:fɪŋ]	Let's *go surfing* – the wind is nice today.	°wellenreiten, surfen
to go, **went** [went]		ging
to rush, **rushed** [rʌʃt]		eilte
°to **collapse, collapsed** [kə'læps(t)]	to fall down	°zusammenbrechen
to **be asleep** [ə'sli:p]	Timmy *is asleep.* Don't wake him.	schlafen
to see, **saw** [sɔ:]		sah
to **drop, dropped** [drɒp(t)]	to let s.th. fall	fallenlassen
to try, **tried** [traɪd]		versuchte

Exercises

1 **lake** [leɪk]	The sea is big; a *lake* is small.	(ein) See
Lake District ['dɪstrɪkt]		*Seengebiet in Nordwestengland*
year [jɪə]	A *year* has twelve months.	Jahr
mountain ['maʊntən]	Great Gable is a *mountain* in the Lake District.	Berg
to **sail** [seɪl]	Can you *sail* against the wind?	segeln
thirty or forty miles **a day** [ə 'deɪ]		am Tag, pro Tag
°**camping-site** ['kæmpɪŋ ,saɪt]		°Campingplatz
5 **garage** ['gærɑ:ʒ]	You can keep a car in a *garage.*	Garage
Bolton Abbey [,bəʊltən‿'æbɪ]		*Klosterkirche*
near [nɪə]	not far from	nahe, in der Nähe von
Skipton ['skɪptən]		*Ortsname*
Daniel ['dænjəl]	Dan is short for *Daniel.*	*Vorname (männlich)*
London ['lʌndən]		*Hauptstadt von Groß-britannien*
6 **last year** [lɑ:st 'jɪə]	the year before this year	letztes Jahr

B Together again

°to **tour** [tʊə]	We *toured* Scotland in our car.	°eine Rundfahrt machen
all the way		den ganzen Weg
lots of ['lɒts‿əv]	a lot of	viele
hill [hɪl]	a small mountain	Hügel, Steigung
hard [hɑ:d]	It's *hard* to cycle up a hill.	schwer; schwierig, hart
work [wɜ:k]	Homework is *work.*	Arbeit
Scotland ['skɒtlənd]		Schottland
Perth [pɜ:θ]		*Stadt in Schottland*
uncle ['ʌŋkl]	My mother's brother is my *uncle.*	Onkel
farm [fɑ:m]	Kate's uncle has got a lot of hens on his *farm.*	Bauernhof, Farm
to rain **a lot**	very much	viel
to **learn** [lɜ:n]	Ronny is *learning* German at school.	lernen
Linda ['lɪndə]	a girl's name	*Vorname (weiblich)*
tennis ['tenɪs]	For a game of *tennis* you need two people or four people.	Tennis
to **go swimming**		schwimmen gehen
°**caravan** ['kærəvæn]	We didn't stay at a hotel. We had a *caravan.*	°Wohnwagen
fantastic [fæn'tæstɪk]	great, very exciting	phantastisch, großartig

°**adventure** [əd'ventʃə]	Something exciting happened to us – it was an *adventure!*	°Abenteuer
Carisbrooke Castle ['kærɪsbrʊk]	name of a castle	*Name einer Burg*
break [breɪk]	At school there is a *break* between two lessons.	Pause

Exercises

2 **weekend** ['wɪ:kend]	Saturday and Sunday	Wochenende
4 **What was ... like?**		Wie war ...?

C Did you know ...?

Ben Nevis [ben 'nevɪs]	name of a mountain in Scotland	*Name eines Berges*
high, **higher, highest** ['haɪə, 'haɪɪst]		höher, am höchsten
thousand ['θaʊzənd]	Ten hundreds are a *thousand.*	Tausend
1343	= one thousand, three hundred and forty-three	
°**metre** ['mi:tə]	The table is one *metre* long.	Meter
Karen Stevenson [ˌkærən 'sti:vnsn]		*Personenname*
fast [fɑ:st], **faster, fastest**	Let's take the *fast* train – it gets to London in only one hour.	schnell
baked beans [ˌbeɪkt 'bi:nz]		weiße Bohnen in Tomatensoße
°**eater** ['i:tə]	He eats fast: he is a fast *eater.*	°Esser
°**cocktail stick** ['kɒkteɪl ˌstɪk]		°Spieß
second ['sekənd]	There are sixty *seconds* in one minute.	Sekunde
big, **bigger, biggest**		größer, am größten
million ['mɪljən]	1,000,000	Million
small, **smaller, smallest**		kleiner, am kleinsten
Shetland ['ʃetlənd]		*Name einer Inselgruppe nördlich von Schottland; Ponyart.*
pony, *pl.* **ponies** ['pəʊnɪ(z)]	*Ponies* are small horses.	Pony
long, **longer, longest** ['lɒŋgə, 'lɒŋgɪst]		länger, am längsten
Humber Bridge [ˌhʌmbə 'brɪdʒ]	name of a bridge	*Name einer Brücke*
heavy, **heavier, heaviest** ['hevɪə, 'hevɪɪst]		schwerer, am schwersten
Luke McMasters [ˌlu:k mək'mɑ:stəz]		*Personenname*
to **weigh** [weɪ]	The baby *weighs* 7 pounds.	wiegen
°**kilo** ['ki:ləʊ]	Is a *kilo* heavier than two pounds?	°Kilo
world [wɜ:ld]	He wants to sail round the *world!*	Welt
(bigger) **than** [ðæn/ðən]	Horses are bigger *than* ponies.	(größer) als

Exercises

1 **the Nile** [naɪl]	name of a river	der Nil *(Fluß in Afrika)*
Mount Everest [ˌmaʊnt 'evərəst]	name of a mountain	*Berg im Himalaja*
Mexico City [ˌmeksɪkəʊ 'sɪtɪ]	name of a city	*Hauptstadt von Mexiko*
°**cheetah** ['tʃi:tə]	The *cheetah* is really a big cat.	°Gepard
3 young, **younger, youngest** ['jʌŋgə, 'jʌŋgɪst]		jünger, am jüngsten

D The dark tower

Nick [nɪk]	a boy's name	*Vorname (männlich)*
ago [əˈgəʊ]	Today is Friday: four days *ago* it was Monday.	vor (einiger Zeit)
part [pɑːt]	Rooms, walls, doors and windows are *parts* of a house.	Teil
Charles the First [ˌtʃɑːlz ðə ˈfɜːst]		*König von England (1600–1649)*
before [bɪˈfɔː]	Wash your hands *before* lunch.	vor (einem Zeitpunkt)
prisoner [ˈprɪznə]		Gefangener
°**execution** [ˌeksɪˈkjuːʃən]		°Hinrichtung, Exekution
entrance [ˈentrəns]	The front door is the *entrance* to a house.	Eingang
building [ˈbɪldɪŋ]	Houses, castles, museums are *buildings*.	Gebäude
inside [ɪnˈsaɪd]	Outside it's cold, but it's warm *inside* the house.	innen, drinnen, hinein
light [laɪt]	When you read at night, you need a *light*.	Licht
to **whisper** [ˈwɪspə]	I didn't hear her because she *whispered*.	flüstern
°**sword** [sɔːd]		°Schwert
thunder [ˈθʌndə]	You sometimes hear *thunder* when it rains.	Donner
nice, **nicer, nicest**		schöner, am schönsten
opposite [ˈɒpəzɪt]	Page 14 is *opposite* page 15.	gegenüber(liegend), entgegengesetzt
°to **bang** [bæŋ]	Close the door, but don't *bang* it.	°(zu)schlagen, (zu)knallen
shadow [ˈʃædəʊ]	The light throws *shadows* on the wall.	Schatten
figure [ˈfɪgə]	Is that *figure* in the picture a man or a woman?	Gestalt
lamp [læmp]	Take a *lamp*, because it's dark outside.	Lampe
to **touch** [tʌtʃ]	Don't *touch* that plate – it's hot.	berühren
°**fuse-box** [ˈfjuːz ˌbɒks]		°Sicherungskasten
good, **better, best** [ˈbetə, best]		besser, am besten

Exercises

1 **end** [end]	My birthday is at the *end* of the month – on the 31st.	Ende, Schluß
4 **Alec Jones** [ˌælɪk ˈdʒəʊnz]		*Personenname*
the day before yesterday	Today is Tuesday. *The day before yesterday* was Sunday.	vorgestern
5 **questionnaire** [ˌkwestʃəˈneə]	a piece of paper with a lot of questions on it	Fragebogen
6 **grandparents** [ˈgrænˌpeərənts]	Your father's or mother's parents are your *grandparents*.	Großeltern
grandfather [ˈgrænˌfɑːðə]	Your father's or your mother's father is your *grandfather*.	Großvater
grandpa [ˈgrænpɑː]		Opa
grandmother [ˈgrænˌmʌðə]	Your father's or your mother's mother is your *grandmother*.	Großmutter

	grandma ['grænmɑ:]		Oma
	husband ['hʌzbənd]	Mr Pearson is Mrs Pearson's *husband.*	Ehemann
	wife [waɪf]	Mrs Pearson is Mr Pearson's *wife.*	Ehefrau
	son [sʌn]	Kevin is Mr and Mrs Pearson's *son.*	Sohn
	daughter ['dɔ:tə]	Kate is Mr and Mrs Pearson's *daughter.*	Tochter
	nephew ['nevju:]	Your brother's or sister's son is your *nephew.*	Neffe
	niece [ni:s]	Your brother's or sister's daughter is your *niece.*	Nichte
	°**What relation is ... to ...?** [rɪ'leɪʃən]		°In welcher Verwandtschaftsbeziehung stehen ...?
	William Smith [ˌwɪljəm 'smɪθ]		*Personenname*
	grandchild ['græntʃaɪld] *pl.* **grandchildren**	You are the *grandchild* of your grandparents.	Enkel
	Mary ['meərɪ]	a girl's name	*Vorname (weiblich)*
	Mark [mɑ:k]	a boy's name	*Vorname (männlich)*
	Andrew ['ændru:]	Andy is short for *Andrew.*	*Vorname (männlich)*
	none [nʌn]	not any	keine (-r, -s)
7	**adjective** ['ædʒəktɪv]	'Big', 'red' and 'heavy' are *adjectives.*	Adjektiv
⟨9⟩	to pack [pæk]	to put in a bag, box, etc.	packen, einpacken
⟨10⟩	grand [grænd]		groß, großartig, bedeutend
	Duke [dju:k]		Herzog
	to march [mɑ:tʃ]	Quick, *march!* Left, right, left, right ...	marschieren, marschieren lassen
	half way ['hɑ:f ˌweɪ]	We're not near Leeds yet – we are only *half way* there.	auf halbem Weg
	neither ... nor ['naɪðə, nɔ:]	Mr Klein is *neither* English *nor* Danish. He's German.	weder ... noch
	to beat [bi:t], beat [bi:t]		schlagen
	drum [drʌm]	You beat a *drum* with a stick.	Trommel, Schlagzeug
	pipes [paɪps]	People in Scotland play them.	Dudelsack

Looking back

We arrived here **yesterday.**	... gestern.
Yesterday morning they climbed a mountain.	Gestern morgen ...
The weather was bad **the day before yesterday.**	Vorgestern ...
Last Tuesday Helen went surfing.	Letzten Dienstag ...
We didn't go away **last year.**	Letztes Jahr ...
My brother was here **two minutes ago.**	... vor zwei Minuten ...
A few weeks ago the weather was much better.	Vor einigen Wochen ...

Unit 2

A Welcome to Nottingham

Nottingham ['nɒtɪŋəm]	a city in England	*Stadt in England*
Broad Marsh ['brɔ:d ˌmɑ:ʃ]		*Name eines Einkaufszentrums*
most [məʊst]		am meisten, die meisten
modern ['mɒdən]	Their house is very old – it isn't a *modern* house.	modern
the **most modern**		am modernsten, der/die/das modernste
shopping centre	There are lots of shops in a *shopping centre.*	Einkaufszentrum
°**knitwear** ['nɪtweə]	cardigans, pullovers, socks, etc.	°Strickwaren
industry ['ɪndəstrɪ]		Industrie
important [ɪm'pɔ:tənt]		wichtig, bedeutend
Robin Hood [ˌrɒbɪn 'hʊd]		*Name eines Volkshelden*
statue ['stætju:]	You can walk round the *statue* to look at it.	Statue, Denkmal
famous ['feɪməs]	Everybody knows him: he's *famous.*	berühmt, bekannt
°**hero** ['hɪərəʊ]		°Held
°**folk hero** [fəʊk]	He is a *folk hero* – everybody remembers and likes him.	°Volksheld
cruel [krʊəl]	It is *cruel* to beat an animal.	grausam
enemy ['enəmɪ]	the opposite of 'friend'	Feind
°**sheriff** ['ʃerɪf]	In Robin Hood's time a *sheriff* was a very important man.	°Sheriff
bicycle ['baɪsɪkl]	a bike ('Bike' is short for 'bicycle'.)	Fahrrad
factory ['fæktrɪ]	People make things in a *factory.*	Fabrik
°**fair** [feə]	People buy and sell things at a *fair.*	°Markt, Jahrmarkt
Goose Fair [ˌgu:s 'feə]		*Name eines traditionellen Jahrmarkts (von* goose = Gans)
industrial [ɪn'dʌstrɪəl]	An *industrial* city has a lot of industry.	Industrie-, industriell
town [taʊn]	A *town* is bigger than a village, but smaller than a city.	Stadt
as ... as		so ... wie
poor [pʊə]	Some people are very *poor* and cannot buy food or clothes.	arm
rich [rɪtʃ]	the opposite of 'poor'	reich
°**powerful** ['paʊəfəl]	He's *powerful* – he can tell everybody what to do.	°mächtig
certainly ['sɜ:tənlɪ]		sicherlich, bestimmt, gewiß
more terrible		schrecklicher *(Komparativ)*
king [kɪŋ]	Charles the First was a *king.*	König
°to **hunt** [hʌnt]	to go after animals for food, or as a sport	°jagen
forest ['fɒrɪst]	a lot of trees together	Wald
Sherwood Forest ['ʃɜ:wʊd]	a forest near Nottingham	*Name eines Waldes*
°**deer** [dɪə]	Some people like to hunt *deer.*	°Hirsch, Reh; Rotwild

Exercises

2 to **agree** [əˈgriː]	to think the same	übereinstimmen, derselben Meinung sein
3 °**Northern** [ˈnɔːðən]		°Nord-, nördlich
England [ˈɪŋglənd]	*England* is part of Britain.	England
°to **pull down**		°niederreißen
4 **expensive** [ɪksˈpensɪv]	This shirt is much too *expensive* – it costs £20!	teuer
tourist [ˈtʊərɪst]		Tourist

B Robin Hood

history [ˈhɪstrɪ]	the story of what happened a long time ago	Geschichte
film [fɪlm]	I like to watch old *films* on TV.	Film
called [kɔːld]	People call her Linda – she is *called* Linda.	namens, genannt
ever [ˈevə]	Do you *ever* watch breakfast TV? – No, never.	jemals, irgendwann
truth [truːθ]	Where did you go yesterday? Tell me the *truth*.	Wahrheit
certain [ˈsɜːtn]	sure	sicher (Adjektiv)
°**outlaw** [ˈaʊtlɔː]		°Geächteter, Vogelfreier
Normandy [ˈnɔːməndɪ]		die Normandie
°to **conquer** [ˈkɒŋkə]		°erobern
°**Saxon** [ˈsæksən]		°sächsisch; Sachse, Sächsin
°**Norman** [ˈnɔːmən]	The people of Normandy were called *Normans*.	°normannisch; Normanne Normannin
to **begin** [bɪˈgɪn], **began** [bɪˈgæn]	to start	anfangen, beginnen
land [lænd]	My uncle's farm is big – he has a lot of *land*.	Land
°**goods** [gʊdz]		°Waren, Güter
right [raɪt]	An outlaw hasn't got any *rights*.	Recht
main [meɪn]	most important	Haupt-, hauptsächlich
to **hate** [heɪt]	I don't like it at all – I *hate* it!	hassen
money [ˈmʌnɪ]	Rich people have got a lot of *money*.	Geld
can, **could** [kʊd]		konnte
to **pay** [peɪ], **paid** [peɪd]	I haven't got any money – I can't *pay*.	bezahlen
to take, **took** [tʊk]		nahm
their **homes** [həʊmz]	The house where you live is your *home*.	ihre Häuser
to make, **made** [meɪd]		machte
to come, **came** [keɪm]		kam
to **become** [bɪˈkʌm], **became** [bɪˈkeɪm]	I want to *become* a teacher when I am older.	werden
somewhere [ˈsʌmweə]	I don't know where Kevin is, but he must be *somewhere*.	irgendwo
to **rob, robbed** [rɒb(d)]		rauben, berauben,

Exercises

2 **about** [əˈbaʊt]	I think there are *about* 500 boys and girls at our school.	ungefähr, etwa
New Forest [ˌnjuː ˈfɒrɪst]		*Waldgebiet in Südengland*
3 °**visitors' centre**		°Touristenzentrum, Besucherzentrum
4 **potato**, *pl.* **potatoes** [pəˈteɪtəʊ(z)]	I always have *potatoes* for lunch.	Kartoffel(n)

5 **purse** [pɜːs]	You keep your money in a *purse.*	Geldbörse, Geldbeutel 5
all right [ɔːlˈraɪt]	O. K.	in Ordnung, gut
anywhere [ˈenɪweə]	I can't find Timmy *anywhere.*	irgendwo, nirgendwo
anyone [ˈenɪwʌn]	Hello! Is *anyone* there?	(irgend) jemand
6 **Market Square** [ˌmɑːkɪt ˈskweə]	In the centre of a town there is often a *market square.*	Marktplatz
to complete [kəmˈpliːt]	to put in what is missing	vervollständigen
restaurant [ˈrestərɒnt]	You can have nice food at a *restaurant.*	Restaurant, Speiselokal
°**Information Centre** [ˌɪnfəˈmeɪʃn]		°Auskunft, Verkehrsbüro

C Robin Hood and the black cloak

1. °**cloak** [kləʊk]	Today, people wear coats, not *cloaks.*	°Umhang, Cape, (loser) Mantel
to **catch** [kætʃ], **caught** [kɔːt]	*Catch* the ball when I throw it to you!	fangen
Will Scarlet [ˌwɪl ˈskɑːlət]		*Name*
°**band** [bænd]	A *band* of people do something together.	°Schar, Gruppe, Bande
°**gallows** [ˈgæləʊz]		°Galgen
farmer [ˈfɑːmə]	The owner of a farm is a *farmer.*	Bauer, Landwirt
to bring, **brought** [brɔːt]		brachte
news [njuːz] *(sing.)*	Did you hear the *news* about Mrs Cook? – Yes, it was in the *news*paper this morning.	Nachricht(en), Neuigkeit(en)
to **rescue** [ˈreskjuː]	to help someone get free	retten, befreien
2. to think, **thought** [θɔːt]		dachte
to wear, **wore** [wɔː]		trug
°**bow** [bəʊ]	People in Robin Hood's time hunted with *bows* and *arrows.*	°Bogen
°**arrow** [ˈærəʊ]		°Pfeil
only [ˈəʊnlɪ]	This is the *only* chip shop in town – there are no others.	einzig
once [wʌns]	Were you ever in York? – Yes, I was there *once.*	einmal
Could you ...? [ˈkʊd juː]		Könnten Sie ...? Könntest Du ...?
to put, **put** (on) [pʊt]		zog an
God bless you! [gɒd ˈbles juː]		Gott segne dich!
already [ɔːlˈredɪ]	You can't be hungry *already* – it's too soon after breakfast!	schon
3. to stand, **stood** [stʊd]		stand
°**hangman** [ˈhæŋmən]		°Henker
crowd [kraʊd]	a lot of people together	(Menschen)menge
anybody [ˈenɪbɒdɪ]	anyone	(irgend)jemand
forward [ˈfɔːwəd]		nach vorne, vorwärts
shout [ʃaʊt]	He shouted, but nobody heard his *shout.*	Ruf, Schrei
egg [eg]	I always have an *egg* for breakfast.	Ei
to throw, **threw** [θruː]		warf
to **get on** with s.th.	Let's *get on* with our work!	*hier:* weitermachen; vorwärts-, vorankommen
to give, **gave** [geɪv]		gab
4. to **hurry (up)** [ˈhʌrɪ]	to do s.th. faster	sich beeilen

to **tighten** ['taɪtn]	Everything is falling out of that box – you must *tighten* the string.	anziehen, festziehen, straffen
5. to **kill** [kɪl]	When Robin Hood was hungry he *killed* an animal.	töten
to run, **ran** [ræn]		lief, rannte
to **shoot** [ʃu:t], **shot** [ʃɒt]	to make s.th. fly through the air	schießen
to fly, **flew** [flu:]		flog
enough [ɪ'nʌf]	Linda can't pay for her blouse. She hasn't got *enough* money.	genug

Exercises

3 to **compare** [kəm'peə]	to see how things are different or the same	vergleichen
boring ['bɔ:rɪŋ]	The book is not interesting. It's *boring.*	langweilig
bad, **worse, worst** [wɜ:s(t)]		schlechter, am schlechtesten (schlimmer, am schlimmsten)
4 to be **on**	There is a good film *on* tonight.	laufen *(Film),* auf dem Programm sein; vor sich gehen
Odeon ['əʊdɪən]		*Name eines Kinos*
cinema ['sɪnəmə]	You can see films at the *cinema.*	Kino
ticket ['tɪkɪt]		(Eintritts)karte
to hear, **heard** [hɜ:d]		hörte
to say, **said** [sed]		sagte
5 to **have a look at**	to look at	(kurz) anschauen
6 **pair** [peə]	These two socks belong together – they are a *pair.*	Paar
bird [bɜ:d]	Most *birds* can fly.	Vogel
°**hunter** ['hʌntə]	A *hunter* hunts animals.	°Jäger
toast [təʊst]	Some people only have tea and *toast* for breakfast.	Toast, Röstbrot
mouse [maʊs], *pl.* **mice** [maɪs]	a very small animal	Maus, Mäuse
snow [snəʊ]	*Snow* is cold and white.	Schnee
⟨8⟩ simple ['sɪmpl]		einfach, beschränkt
Simon ['saɪmən]	a boy's name	*Vorname (männlich)*
pieman ['paɪmən]	A *pieman* sells pies.	Pastetenverkäufer
to taste [teɪst]		schmecken, probieren
ware [weə]		Ware
unto ['ʌntʊ]	= to	zu *(veraltet)*
penny ['penɪ]	a hundred *pennies* = one pound	*englisches Geldstück*
Sir [sɜ:]		*höfliche Anrede (für einen Mann)*

⟨Authentic Britain: Industry in Nottingham⟩

Frank Bowden [ˌfræŋk 'bəʊdn]		*Personenname*
British ['brɪtɪʃ]		britisch
century ['sentʃərɪ]		Jahrhundert
William Lee [ˌwɪljəm 'li:]		*Personenname*
Calverton ['kælvətən]		*Ortsname*
machine [mə'ʃi:n]		Maschine
miner ['maɪnə]		Bergmann
chemical ['kemɪkl]		chemisch

No – any – some – every

no book(s)	**any** chair(s)	**some** boy(s)	**every** house
no one	**anyone**	**someone**	**everyone**
nobody	**anybody**	**somebody**	**everybody**
nothing	**anything**	**something**	**everything**
nowhere	**anywhere**	**somewhere**	**everywhere**

Nobody heard the burglar, because **everybody** was asleep.
Did you see **anybody** near the house? – Well, I didn't see **anybody** yesterday, but I saw **somebody** in the garden the day before yesterday.

Unit 3

A The check-up

1. **check-up** [ˈtʃekʌp]	Some people have a *check-up* every year. They want to be sure they are not ill.	Überprüfung, Kontrolle, ärztliche Untersuchung
to wake, **woke** (up) [wəʊk]		wachte auf
headache [ˈhedeɪk]	She doesn't feel well. She has got a *headache.*	Kopfschmerzen
temperature [ˈtemprətʃə]	I feel very hot – I think I have a *temperature.*	Temperatur, Fieber
pain [peɪn]	A headache is a *pain* in your head.	Schmerz
chest [tʃest]	You wear a pullover to keep your *chest* warm.	Brust
to **phone** [fəʊn]	= to telephone	anrufen
doctor [ˈdɒktə]	She's ill, so she needs a *doctor.*	Arzt, Ärztin
°**appointment** [əˈpɔɪntmənt]	Her *appointment* is for 3 o'clock on Tuesday.	°Verabredung, Termin
°to **make an appointment**		°eine Verabredung treffen, einen Termin vereinbaren
surgery [ˈsɜːdʒərɪ]	the rooms where a doctor works	Praxis
to **take s.o.'s temperature**	to see how high s.o.'s. temperature is	jds. Temperatur messen
to **examine** [ɪgˈzæmɪn]	What's the matter with me, doctor? – I don't know, I must *examine* you first.	untersuchen
I'm going to [ˈgəʊɪŋ tə]	*I'm going to* take your temperature.	ich werde ..., ich habe vor
hospital [ˈhɒspɪtl]	When you are very ill you must go to *hospital.*	Krankenhaus
°**prescription** [prɪˈskrɪpʃn]	A doctor writes *prescriptions.*	°Rezept
chemist [ˈkemɪst]	The *chemist* reads the doctor's prescription.	Apotheker(in), Drogist(in)
chemist's	= chemist's shop	Apotheke
medicine [ˈmedɪsɪn]	Mrs Bennett is very ill. She must take a lot of *medicine.*	Arznei, Medizin
for (your headache)	A walk is good *for* a headache.	*hier:* gegen
2. to get, **got** [gɒt]		bekam, wurde; *hier:* kam
to ring, **rang** [ræŋ]		klingelte

to **cook** [kʊk]	to make food ready to eat	kochen, (Speisen) zubereiten
meal [mi:l]	Breakfast and lunch are *meals.*	Mahl(zeit), Essen
to **worry** [ˈwʌrɪ]	She *worries* a lot about burglars.	sich Sorgen machen
Don't worry!		Mach dir keine Sorgen!
(doctor's) **set** [set]	The things in a *set* belong together. (Here, they are toys – you can play 'doctor' with them.)	(Arzt)ausrüstung *(als Spielzeug)*

Exercises

1 to **go to the doctor's**		zum Arzt gehen
3 to **do the shopping**	to go shopping, to buy what you need	einkaufen
5 **at the doctor's**		beim Arzt
to **act** [ækt]	Let's play 'school'. Who can *act* Mrs Griffin?	(eine Rolle, ein Stück) spielen, darstellen
°**I feel sick.** [sɪk]	I don't feel well at all – *I feel sick.*	°Ich fühle mich nicht wohl./Mir ist übel.
stomach [ˈstʌmək]	When you eat something, it goes into your *stomach.*	Magen, Bauch

B Keeping a pet

1. **outside** a shop		draußen vor ...
pet shop [ˈpet ʃɒp]	a shop where they sell pets	Tierhandlung
I needn't pay [ˈni:dnt]		ich brauche nicht zu zahlen
to **feed** [fi:d]	Pets need something to eat. You must *feed* them.	füttern
bone [bəʊn]	Dogs like *bones.*	Knochen
post office [ˈpəʊst‿ˌɒfɪs]	You go there to send letters to your friends.	Post(amt)
What for?	Why (must we go there)?	Wozu? Warum?
licence [ˈlaɪsəns]	You need a *licence* for a radio or TV, or to keep a dog, or to drive a car.	amtliche Genehmigung
2. **budgie** [ˈbʌdʒɪ]	a small bird	Wellensittich
hamster [ˈhæmstə]	A *hamster* looks like a mouse, but is a bit bigger.	Hamster
°**leaflet** [ˈli:flət]	A book has many pages – a *leaflet* has only one or two.	°Merkblatt, Prospekt
fresh [freʃ]	I don't like fruit in tins. I only like *fresh* fruit.	frisch
bird seed [si:d]	*Bird seed* is good for birds.	Vogelfutter
cage [keɪdʒ]	You keep budgies in a *cage.*	Käfig
sand [sænd]	On the beach there is a lot of *sand.*	Sand
himself [hɪmˈself]	He doesn't need any help. He can do it *himself.*	sich, sich selbst, selbst *(männlich)*
bird-bath [ˈbɜ:d ˌbɑ:θ]	Birds can have a bath in it.	Vogelbad

Exercises

1 **Gordon** [ˈgɔ:dn]	a boy's name	*Vorname (männlich)*
Nelson [ˈnelsn]	*Nelson* is the name of a famous hero.	*Name eines englischen Kriegshelden (hier als Hundename)*
3 **broken** [ˈbrəʊkən]	When you break something, it's *broken.*	gebrochen
tonight [təˈnaɪt]	later today, when it gets dark	heute abend

⟨5⟩ for fun [fə'fʌn]		zum Spaß ⟨5⟩
McTavish [mək'tævɪʃ]		*schottischer Familienname*
advertisement [əd'vɜ:tɪsmənt]		Anzeige
office ['ɒfɪs]		Büro
McGregor [mə'gregə]		*schottischer Familienname*
assistant manager [əˌsɪstənt 'mænədʒə]		stellvertretender Geschäftsführer
to smile [smaɪl]		lächeln

C Kate's story

1. **Tracy** ['treɪsɪ]		*Pferdename (auch weibl. Vorname)*
to **go near**		in die Nähe (von etwas) gehen
field [fi:ld]	There are many *fields* around a farm.	Feld, Weide
to **brush** [brʌʃ]	She *brushes* her dog every day.	bürsten
ride [raɪd]	You can go for a *ride* on a horse or on a bike.	Ritt, Fahrt
to **give s.o. a ride**		jdn. reiten/fahren lassen
2. to ride, **rode** [rəʊd]		ritt
to know, **knew** [nju:]		kannte, wußte
most of them		die meisten von ihnen
bread [bred]	I want to make a tomato sandwich, so I need *bread* and tomatoes.	Brot
even ['i:vn]	She's smaller than you. She's *even* smaller than your little sister.	sogar
fat [fæt]	Tracy had too much to eat. She is very *fat* now.	dick
to **put up**	I *put up* some pictures on the wall.	aufstellen, aufhängen
notice ['nəʊtɪs]	A *notice* tells you something important.	Schild, Hinweis
3. °**shock** [ʃɒk]	The bad news was a *shock* to him.	°Schock, Schreck
°**hoof** [hu:f] *pl.* **hooves** [hu:vz]	A horse's feet are called *hooves.*	°Huf
worried ['wʌrɪd]	I'm *worried* about Mum. She is very ill.	besorgt, beunruhigt
telephone box	There's a *telephone box* at the corner – you can phone me from there.	Telefonzelle
°**vet** [vet]	a doctor for animals	°Tierarzt (-ärztin)
4. **cloth** [klɒθ]		Stoff, Tuch
piece of cloth		Lappen
to **fill** [fɪl]	to put as much as possible into s.th.	füllen
wet [wet]	When it's raining, the streets are *wet.*	naß, feucht
°**badly** (swollen)	*here:* very	°*hier:* sehr, arg, heftig
°**swollen** ['swəʊlən]	Tracy's hooves are bigger than they usually are: they are *swollen.*	°geschwollen
°**injection** [ɪn'dʒekʃn]	A doctor sometimes gives you an *injection.* Most people don't like it.	Spritze, Injektion

Exercises

2	**group** [gru:p]	A number of people together is a *group* of people.	Gruppe
3	**games building**		Sporthalle
	playground ['pleɪgraʊnd]	Children can play games there.	Spielplatz, Schulhof
4	°**sign** [saɪn]	A *sign* helps you to find the right way or to do the right thing.	°Hinweis(schild); Zeichen
6	**test** [test]	In a *test,* you must show that you know something.	Prüfung, Klassenarbeit
	glass [glɑ:s]	You drink lemonade out of a *glass.*	Glas
	to **jump** [dʒʌmp]	The cat *jumped* off the wall.	springen
⟨8⟩	crow [krəʊ]	a black bird with a terrible voice	Krähe
	upon [ə'pɒn]	= on	auf
	frosty ['frɒstɪ]	very cold	frostig, eisig
	tall [tɔ:l]		groß, hochgewachsen
⟨9⟩	correct [kə'rekt]	That's right! Your answer is *correct.*	richtig
	take-off ['teɪkɒf]		Absprung, Start *(Flugzeug)*

⟨Authentic Britain: How to look after your cat⟩

ribbon ['rɪbən]	Girls sometimes wear *ribbons.*	Band, Borte
neck [nek]	Your head is on your *neck.*	Hals
natural ['nætʃərəl]	It's *natural* for cats to catch mice.	natürlich
regular ['regjʊlə]	*here:* at the same time every day	regelmäßig
chicken ['tʃɪkɪn]	a young hen	Hähnchen, Hühnchen
to dry [draɪ]	*Dry* your hands with this cloth.	(ab)trocknen
if [ɪf]		wenn, falls
comfortable ['kʌmftəbl]	I like to sit in this chair. It's very *comfortable.*	bequem
herself [hɜ:'self]		sich (selbst)
kitten ['kɪtn]	a young cat	Kätzchen, kleine Katze

Parts of the body ['bɒdɪ]

face	Gesicht	**head**	Kopf	**arm**	Arm
eye	Auge	**brain**	Hirn	**hand**	Hand
nose	Nase	**neck**	Hals	**finger**	Finger
mouth	Mund	**chest**	Brust	**leg**	Bein
ear	Ohr	**stomach**	Magen	**foot, feet**	Fuß, Füße

⟨Merry Christmas⟩

	merry ['merɪ]	happy	fröhlich
	Christmas ['krɪsməs]	December 25th	Weihnachten
2	Christmas Eve [ˌkrɪsməs‿'i:v]	December 24th	Heiligabend
	stocking ['stɒkɪŋ]	People wear *stockings* on their feet.	Strumpf
	Father Christmas	He gives presents to the children at Christmas.	Weihnachtsmann
	chimney ['tʃɪmnɪ]	The smoke from a house comes through the *chimney.*	Kamin

	Christmas Day	December 25th	1. Weihnachtsfeiertag
	dinner ['dɪnə]	a meal	(Festtags-, Mittag-, Abend-) essen
	turkey ['tɜ:kɪ]	a big bird	Truthahn
	roast potatoes [ˌrəʊst pə'teɪtəʊz]	You cook them together with the turkey.	Röst-, Bratkartoffeln
	plum pudding [ˌplʌm 'pʊdɪŋ]		Plumpudding *(kuchenartige Süßspeise)*
	coin [kɔɪn]	a small, hard piece of money	Münze, Geldstück
3	to wish [wɪʃ]	On April 21st they *wish* Sharon a happy birthday.	wünschen
	chorus ['kɔ:rəs]	The *chorus* is part of a song. You sing it again and again.	Refrain
	tidings ['taɪdɪŋz]	news	Kunde, Botschaft
	kin [kɪn]	family, relations	Verwandtschaft, Familie
	figgy pudding [ˌfɪgɪ 'pʊdɪŋ]		Feigenpudding
	we won't… [wəʊnt]		wir werden nicht…
4	Christmas card [kɑ:d]	It has a Christmas picture on the outside, and you write on the inside.	Weihnachtskarte
	scissors ['sɪzəz]	You can cut paper with them.	Schere
	glitter ['glɪtə]	It shines like little stars.	Glitzersterne, -material
	to fold [fəʊld]	When you *fold* a piece of paper in the middle it is half as big as before.	falten
	to draw [drɔ:]	You use a pencil to *draw* a picture.	zeichnen
	to decorate ['dekəreɪt]	People *decorate* the Christmas tree with glitter, etc.	schmücken, verzieren
	season ['si:zn]	A year has 4 *seasons.*	Jahreszeit
	greeting ['gri:tɪŋ]	'Hello' is a *greeting.*	Gruß
	Season's Greetings	the same as 'A Merry Christmas and a Happy New Year'	Fröhliche Weihnachten und ein gutes neues Jahr!
5	townspeople ['taʊnzˌpi:pl]	the people in a town	Städter, Stadtbewohner
	church [tʃɜ:tʃ]	Bells ring to call the people to *church* on Sundays.	Kirche
	beautiful ['bju:tɪfʊl]	very nice, lovely	schön
	sound [saʊnd]	When a bell rings, it makes a *sound.*	Klang
	they will… [wɪl]		sie werden…
	excited [ɪk'saɪtɪd]	On Christmas Eve, British children are very *excited.*	aufgeregt
	altar ['ɔ:ltə]	Every church has an *altar.*	Altar
	to promise ['prɒmɪs]	Ben *promised* to go shopping but he forgot.	versprechen
	one by one ['wʌn baɪ 'wʌn]	Go in *one by one* – not all at the same time.	einer nach dem anderen
	out of breath [ˌaʊt‿əv 'breθ]	You get *out of breath* when you run very fast.	außer Atem
	rags [rægz]	very old clothes	Lumpen
	to thank [θæŋk]	to say 'thank you'	(sich be) danken
	no one ['nəʊ ˌwʌn]	nobody	niemand
	side door [saɪd]	The *side door* is not as important as the main door.	Seitentüre

Unit 4

⟨Photo page: Bicycles and Cars⟩

cycle shop ['saɪkl ˌʃɒp]	*'Cycle'* is another word for 'bicycle'.	Fahrradladen
to check [tʃek]	to see if there is s.th. wrong with s.th.	(über)prüfen, kontrollieren
oil [ɔɪl]	Cars and bicycles need *oil.*	Öl

A A morning's work

1. to **check** [tʃek]	to see if there is s.th. wrong with s.th.	(über)prüfen, kontrollieren
check-list	a list of things to check	Kontrolliste
oil [ɔɪl]	Cars and bicycles need *oil.*	Öl
tyre [taɪə]	A car has got 4 *tyres.*	Reifen
°**plug** [plʌg]		°Zündkerze
the **inside** ['ɪnsaɪd]		Innenraum, Innere
to **empty** ['emtɪ]	opposite of 'to fill'	(aus)leeren
°**ash-tray** ['æʃˌtreɪ]		°Aschenbecher
to **polish** ['pɒlɪʃ]	The Bennetts first wash the car, then they *polish* it.	polieren
°**chrome** [krəʊm]	When you polish the *chrome* it shines in the sun.	°Chrom
busy ['bɪzɪ]	All the Bennetts are working – everyone is *busy.*	fleißig, beschäftigt
2. **engine** ['endʒɪn]	The *engine* is the most important part of a car.	Motor, Maschine
thin [θɪn]	My sister isn't fat – she's *thin.*	dünn
3. to **finish** ['fɪnɪʃ]	bring or come to an end	(be)enden, aufhören mit
yet [jet]	Have you finished that book *yet*?	(immer) noch, schon
not yet	No, I have*n't* finished it *yet.* I'm only at page 56.	noch nicht
to do, did, **done** [dʌn]		getan, gemacht

Exercises

2 to **matter** ['mætə]	to be important	von Bedeutung sein, darauf ankommen
it doesn't matter		es macht nichts
3 **cake** [keɪk]	Have some biscuits or a piece of *cake.*	Kuchen

B The Road Safety Officer

°**Road Safety Officer** [ˌrəʊd 'seɪftɪ ˌɒfɪsə]		°Verkehrssicherheitsbeamter
excited [ɪk'saɪtɪd]	Helen was very *excited* when she opened all her birthday presents.	aufgeregt
Mr **Edwards** ['edwədz]		*Familienname*
°**form master** ['fɔ:m ˌmɑ:stə]	A *form master* looks after one class. ('Form' is another word for 'class'.)	°Klassenlehrer
cycle ['saɪkl]	another word for 'bicycle' or 'bike'	
Mr **Haig** [heɪg]		*Familienname*
to come, came, **come** [kʌm]		gekommen

rule [ru:l]	It's against the *rules* to wear jeans at school.	Regel
rules of the road		Verkehrsregeln
to bring, brought, **brought** [brɔ:t]		gebracht
to **mark** [mɑ:k]	*Mark* the right box with an 'X'.	markieren, kennzeichnen
line [laɪn]	There are *lines* round the words in exercise 1, page 48.	Linie
to **practise** ['præktɪs]	I want to be good at tennis, so I must *practise* every day.	üben
to show, showed, **shown** [ʃəʊn]		gezeigt
to see, saw, **seen** [si:n]		gesehen
brakes [breɪks]	When you want to stop, you use your *brakes.*	Bremsen
handlebars ['hændlbɑ:z]	part of the bike where you put your hands.	Lenkstange
saddle ['sædl]	where you sit on a bicycle or on a horse	Sattel
sir [sɜ:]		(mein) Herr! *(respektvolle Anrede)*
°**scratch** [skrætʃ]	I played with a cat and now I have *scratches* on my hands.	°Kratzer
height [haɪt]	Ben Nevis is the highest mountain in Britain. Its *height* is 1,343 metres.	Höhe
°**mudguard** ['mʌdgɑ:d]	With *mudguards* on your bike, you don't get dirty.	°Schutzblech
to take, took, **taken off** ['teɪkən]		abgenommen, abmontiert
without [wɪ'ðaʊt]	opposite of 'with'	ohne
°**speedway bike** ['spi:dweɪ]		°Motorrad *(für Aschenrennbahn)*
°**frame** ['freɪm]	A *frame* keeps things together.	°Rahmen
rear light [rɪə]	the light at the back of a bike	Rücklicht
pedal ['pedl]	You use the *pedals* to make a bike go.	Pedal
front [frʌnt]	opposite of 'back'	Vorder-, Vorderseite
wheel [wi:l]	A bicycle has two *wheels,* a car has four.	Rad

Exercises

2 to **hold on** to [ˌhəʊld‿'ɒn]		(sich) festhalten (an)
3 **office** ['ɒfɪs]	The manager is in his *office.*	Büro
°**motor caravan** ['məʊtə ˌkærəvæn]	a caravan with an engine	°Campingbus, Wohnmobil
4 °**irregular** [ɪ'regjʊlə]	'To be' and 'to have' are *irregular* verbs.	°unregelmäßig
to **take a photo**		ein Foto machen, photographieren
5 to **lose** [lu:z], **lost, lost** [lɒst]	I've *lost* my pencil. I can't find it anywhere.	verlieren
°**bicycle pump** ['baɪsɪkl ˌpʌmp]	You need it to put air in the tyres of your bicycle.	°Luftpumpe, Fahrradpumpe.
°**ear-plugs** ['ɪə ˌplʌgz]	The noise is terrible – I need *ear-plugs.*	°Wattepfropfen, Ohrpfropfen

C The stolen bike

1. to **steal** [stɪ:l], **stole** [stəʊl], **stolen** ['stəʊlən]	Burglars *steal* things.	stehlen
to **pass** (a test) [pɑ:s]	The test wasn't hard – it was easy to *pass*.	(eine Prüfung) bestehen
almost ['ɔ:lməʊst]	nearly	fast, beinahe
everywhere ['evrɪweə]	David has looked *everywhere*, but he still can't find his bike.	überall
°to **report s.th.** [rɪ'pɔ:t]	to tell s.th. to s.o. (for example, to a teacher or to the police)	°(etwas) melden, anzeigen
police station [pə'li:s ˌsteɪʃən]	a building where the police work	Polizeirevier
policeman [pə'lɪ:smən]	A *policeman* wears a dark blue uniform.	Polizist
thief [θi:f], *pl.* **thieves** [θi:vz]	A *thief* steals things.	Dieb
2. to **go round**	*here:* to go to, s.o.'s house, to visit s.o.	*hier:* vorbeikommen (bei), jdn. besuchen
to **meet** [mi:t], **met, met** [met]	to come together	(sich) treffen
at least [ət 'li:st]	A good bike costs a lot of money – *at least* £100.	mindestens
luck [lʌk]	I have no *luck* at all – I always lose at cards.	Glück
3. **camera** ['kæmrə]	You can take photos with a *camera*.	Fotoapparat
club [klʌb]	The people in a *club* meet often to do something together.	Klub, Verein
snack bar ['snæk ˌbɑ:]	In a *snack bar* you can have things like sandwiches, chips and ice-cream.	Imbißstube
°**size** [saɪz]	These shoes are not the right *size* – they are too small.	°Größe
side [saɪd]		Seite
°**scratched** [skrætʃt]	with scratches on it	°zerkratzt
to **notice** ['nəʊtɪs]	to see or hear s.th. or s.o.	bemerken
4. to **follow** ['fɒləʊ]	to go after	(ver)folgen
to **paint** [peɪnt]	David's bike has got a new colour. They have *painted* it.	(be)malen, lackieren
°to **arrest** [ə'rest]	The police caught the thief and *arrested* him.	°festnehmen
for luck		als Glücksbringer

Exercises

2 **Grabbit** ['græbɪt]		*erfundener Name (von* grab it = schnapp es)
4 **butter** ['bʌtə]	You put it on bread.	Butter
fish *(sing.* and *pl.)* [fɪʃ]	*Fish* swim in the sea and in rivers.	Fisch(e)
6 **parrot** ['pærət]	A *parrot* is a bird. It can talk.	Papagei
Rex [reks]		*Hundename (auch männl. Vorname)*
Polly ['pɒlɪ]		*Papageienname (auch weibl. Vorname)*
〈9〉 horn [hɔ:n]		Hupe
to blare [bleə]	to be very loud	plärren

⟨Authentic Britain: Road Safety⟩

(to ride, rode) ridden ['rɪdn]	*here:* cycled	*hier:* gefahren
pavement ['peɪvmənt]	where people walk in the street	Bürgersteig
you may		*hier:* du könntest womöglich
to hurt s.o. [hɜ:t]	He fell and *hurt* himself.	jdn verletzen
to get into trouble ['trʌbl]		Ärger bekommen
cycleroute ['saɪkl,ru:t]	special road for bicycles	Fahrradweg

to be

My parents **are** busy.
Peter **is** hungry/thirsty.
His bike **is** old/dirty/scratched.
Don't **be** afraid.
I **was** late for school yesterday.
Be quiet!

to have

Kate **has** (got) a new bike.
I **had** a headache/a cold yesterday.
Let's see if you **have** (got) a temperature.
I'm going to **have** a bath.
Helen **had** a great idea.
Let's **have** a look at your photos.
Let's **have** a picnic/a party.
We always **have** breakfast in the kitchen.
What did you **have** for lunch?
We **had** chips and tea and cake.
Have a piece of chocolate!
We **had** a great time.

Unit 5

A At Fulford School

1. **language** ['læŋgwɪdʒ]	English and German are *languages.*	Sprache
°**language lab** [læb]	a room where you can practise languages	°Sprachlabor
French [frentʃ]	Can you speak *French*?	Französisch, französisch
foreign ['fɒrən]	For Kevin, German is a *foreign* language.	Fremd-, ausländisch
to **have to** do s.th.	'I *have to* go' means 'I must go'.	müssen
2. **rugby** ['rʌgbɪ]	It's a game like football, but the rules are different.	Rugby
you are allowed to [ə'laʊd]	you may	es ist erlaubt, du darfst, man kann
hockey ['hɒkɪ]	You play *hockey* with a stick.	Hockey
3. **pupil** ['pju:pl]	a boy or girl at a school	Schüler(in)
subject ['sʌbdʒɪkt]	What *subject* do you like best at school? – English, of course!	Fach
°**Home Economics** [ˌhəʊm i:kə'nɒmɪks]	a school subject	°Hauswirtschaftslehre
glad [glæd]	happy about s.th.	froh
4. °**outdoor** ['aʊtdɔ:]	Rugby and tennis are *outdoor* games. You play them outside.	°Freiluft-, im Freien
°**outdoor swimming-pool** ['swɪmɪŋˌpu:l]	You can swim there when the weather is warm.	°Freibad
°**term** [tɜ:m]	There are three *terms* in the English school year.	°Trimester

if [ɪf]	*If* the sun shines, we can go swimming.	wenn, falls
winter ['wɪntə]	It gets cold in *winter.*	Winter
°**public** ['pʌblɪk]	It's a *public* park – everyone can go there.	°öffentlich
°**public baths** [bɑ:ðz]	You can swim there in the winter, too.	°Hallenbad
5. **lesson** ['lesn]	They have an English *lesson* every day.	(Unterrichts)stunde
lunch hour ['lʌntʃ ˌaʊə]	They have lunch in the *lunch hour.*	Mittagspause
°rugby **practice** ['præktɪs]	What do they practise at rugby *practice?*	°Training, Übung
°**(food) mixer** ['mɪksə]	It's easy to make a cake if you've got a *mixer.*	°Mixer
to taste [teɪst]	Is that lemonade very sweet? – I don't know. *Taste* it.	schmecken, probieren
°**mixture** ['mɪkstʃə]	Put milk and water in one glass; now you have a *mixture* of milk and water.	°Mischung
finger ['fɪŋgə]	Your hand has five *fingers.*	Finger
idiot ['ɪdɪət]	When someone does something very silly, you could call him or her an *idiot.*	Idiot
to **switch on** [ˌswɪtʃ‿'ɒn]	*Switch on* the radio – I want to hear the news.	einschalten
Mrs **Walker** ['wɔ:kə]		*Familienname*
guitar [gɪ'tɑ:]	She can sing and play the *guitar.*	Gitarre

B School Lunch

a) °**cafeteria** [ˌkæfə'tɪərɪə]	A *cafeteria* is not as expensive as a restaurant.	°Kantine, Cafeteria
menu ['menju:]	a list of things to eat and drink in a restaurant	Speisekarte
fish fingers	Many children like *fish fingers.*	Fischstäbchen
°**Irish stew** [ˌaɪrɪʃ 'stju:]	*Irish stew* has a lot of potatoes in it.	°*irisches Eintopfgericht aus Fleisch, Kartoffeln und Zwiebeln*
vegetable ['vedʒətəbl]	Beans and carrots are *vegetables.*	Gemüse
peas [pi:z]	*Peas* are small and green.	Erbsen
mashed potatoes [ˌmæʃt pə'teɪtəʊz]	I like *potatoes* only if they are *mashed.*	Kartoffelbrei
pudding ['pʊdɪŋ]	You eat it at the end of a meal. (Sometimes, *pudding* means fruit, ice-cream, etc.)	(kuchenartige) Pudding, Nachspeise
vanilla [və'nɪlə]	*Vanilla* ice-cream is white.	Vanille
cheese [tʃi:z]	If you don't want anything sweet after your meal, you can have *cheese.*	Käse
you should [ʃʊd]	*You should* always eat a good breakfast.	Du solltest …
both of them [bəʊθ]	the two of them, not just one or the other	(alle) beide
°**devil** ['devl]		°Teufel
°**Be a devil!**		°Sei mal gut zu dir! Riskier's!
b) Mrs **Wood** [wʊd]		*Familienname*

which...? [wɪtʃ]	*Which* is better: the mashed potatoes or the chips?	Welcher/welche/ welches?
would you like...?	*Would you like* an ice-cream? – Oh, yes, please.	möchtest du ...?
I'd like [ˌaɪd ˈlaɪk]	= I would like	Ich möchte
favourite [ˈfeɪvrɪt]	It's her *favourite* pudding: she likes it best.	Lieblings-
to **be thirsty** [ˈθɜ:stɪ]	When you *are thirsty,* you need something to drink.	Durst haben, durstig sein
cup [kʌp]	In England, you always get tea in a *cup,* not in a glass.	Tasse

Exercises

1 **fault** [fɔ:lt]	Our budgie flew away. It was my *fault* – I left the window open.	Schuld
4 **slow** [sləʊ]	not fast	langsam
5 **coffee** [ˈkɒfɪ]	In Germany, people drink more *coffee* than tea.	Kaffee
⟨6⟩ waiter [ˈweɪtə]		Kellner
soup [su:p]		Suppe
steak [steɪk]		Steak
fork [fɔ:k]		Gabel
spoon [spu:n]		Löffel
⟨7⟩ cockles [ˈkɒklz] and mussels [ˈmʌslz]		Muscheln *(zwei Sorten)*
Dublin [ˈdʌblɪn]		*Hauptstadt von Irland*
fair [feə]		schön
pretty [ˈprɪtɪ]		hübsch
to set one's eyes on	to see	erblicken
Molly Malone [ˌmɒlɪ məˈləʊn]		*Personenname*
to wheel [wɪ:l]	*here:* to push	*hier:* schieben
wheelbarrow [ˈwɪ:lˌbærəʊ]		Schubkarren
broad [brɔ:d]		breit
narrow [ˈnærəʊ]		eng
alive [əˈlaɪv]		lebendig
fishmonger [ˈfɪʃˌmʌŋgə]	A *fishmonger* sells fish.	Fischverkäufer(in)
'twas [twɒz]	= it was	es war
no wonder [nəʊ ˈwʌndə]		kein Wunder
to die, died [daɪ(d)]		sterben
fever [ˈfi:və]		Fieber
to save [seɪv]		retten

C Have you heard?

team [ti:m]	In football and in hockey, two *teams* play against each other.	Mannschaft
°**National Cup** [ˌnæʃnəl ˈkʌp]	What team won the *Cup* last year?	°Landespokal
Queen Margaret's [ˌkwi:n ˈmɑ:grɪts]	name of a school	*Name einer Schule* ("Königin-Margaret-Schule")
to qualify, qualified [ˈkwɒlɪfaɪ(d)]	to show that you are good enough (*here:* to win against other teams)	sich qualifizieren
°**finals** [ˈfaɪnlz]	The best teams meet in the *finals.*	°Endrunde

°**reserve** [rɪ'zɜ:v]	If someone in the team can't play, they ask a *reserve* to play.	°Ersatzspieler
there's **room** [ru:m]	Is there *room* in your bag for two more books?	(genug) Platz
°**supporter** [sə'pɔ:tə]	She's a Fulford *supporter:* she goes to all their games.	°Anhänger(in), Fan
I've put my name down.	I've written my name on the list.	Ich habe mich eingetragen.
anyway ['enɪweɪ]	It doesn't matter if I can't go – I don't like hockey *anyway.*	sowieso
to move [mu:v]	to go somewhere else to live	umziehen
America [ə'merɪkə]	York is in England, but New York is in *America.*	Amerika, *hier:* die USA

Exercises

2 **essay** ['eseɪ]	We have to write an *essay* on 'What I did in the holidays'.	Aufsatz
3 **pen-friend** ['pen ˌfrend]	She has never met her German *pen-friend.*	Brieffreund(in)

D Come on, Fulford

Miss Price [ˌmɪs 'praɪs]		*Personenname* („Fräulein Price")
M 1 [ˌem 'wʌn]	To go from Northern England to London, you drive down the *M 1.*	*eine Autobahn*
south [saʊθ]	Nottingham is *south* of York.	Süd-, südlich, Süden
to look out for	to keep your eyes open for	Ausschau halten nach
Buckingham Palace [ˌbʌkɪŋəm 'pæləs]	The Queen lives there.	*Residenz der Königin*
the only ones ['əʊnlɪ ˌwʌnz]	Have you got any other comics? – No, these are *the only ones.*	die einzigen
nervous ['nɜ:vəs]	worried and afraid	nervös
even so [ˌi:vn 'səʊ]	We lost – but it was a good game, *even so.*	trotzdem
hockey stick ['hɒkɪ ˌstɪk]	You play hockey with a *hockey stick.*	Schläger
a new one ['nju: ˌwʌn]	If you've lost your pen, you must buy *a new one.*	einen neuen
°**sports ground** ['spɔ:ts ˌgraʊnd]	They play many different sports there.	°Sportplatz
°**round** [raʊnd]	All the teams play in the first *round;* the winners then play in the second *round.*	°Runde
St Anne's [snt 'ænz]	name of a school	*Name einer Schule*
match [mætʃ]	a game where it is important who wins	Spiel
loud [laʊd]	I can't hear you – the radio is too *loud.*	laut
°to **appreciate** [ə'pri:ʃɪeɪt]	to like, to know how good s.o. or s.th. is	°schätzen
°to **dribble** ['drɪbl]	to push the ball (with your feet or with a stick) towards the goal.	°dribbeln
to **score** [skɔ:]	*here:* to put the ball in the goal	*hier:* ein Tor schießen
to **go mad** [mæd]	to get very excited	aus dem Häuschen geraten, verrückt werden

to **have a chance** [tʃɑ:ns]	We would like to win, but I don't think we *have a chance.*	eine Chance haben
not ... much chance		kaum eine Chance
°**half-time** [ˌhɑ:fˈtaɪm]	the break in the middle of a match	°Halbzeit
You're on.	Now you must play! It's your turn!	Du bist dran!
to **believe** [bɪˈli:v]	to think s.th. is the truth	glauben
Sarah Wiley [ˌseərə ˈwaɪlɪ]		*Personenname*
°**injury** [ˈɪndʒərɪ]	Ben couldn't play the guitar because he had a hand *injury.*	°Verletzung
Sue Evans [ˌsu:‿ˈevənz]	*Sue* is short for Susan.	*Personenname*
to hit, hit, hit [hɪt]	In hockey, you *hit* the ball with a stick.	schlagen
°to **bounce** [baʊns]	When you drop a ball, it *bounces.*	°springen, abprallen
to **pass** (the ball) to s.o. [pɑ:s]	to give (the ball) to s.o. near you	jdm (den Ball) zuspielen
quick [kwɪk]	fast	schnell
°**whistle** [ˈwɪsl]	I didn't hear the *whistle* at the end of the match.	°Pfeife, Pfiff, Abpfiff
Well done! [ˌwel ˈdʌn]	You say this if you think someone has *done* something very *well.*	Gut gemacht! Bravo!

Exercises

1 °**interview** [ˈɪntəvju:]	In an *interview,* a reporter asks someone a lot of questions.	°Interview
Sheila [ʃi:lə]	a girl's name	*Vorname (weiblich)*
°to **interview** s.o.	The reporter *interviewed* the famous writer.	°jdn interviewen
2 **Southgate** [ˈsaʊθgeɪt]	name of a school	*Ortsname, Name einer Schule*
Yorkshire [ˈjɔ:kʃə]		Grafschaft York
notice-board [ˈnəʊtɪsˌbɔ:d]	Is there any new notice on the *notice-board?*	Schwarzes Brett
5 to **set the table** [set]	to put things on the table for a meal	den Tisch decken
salt [sɔ:lt]	You put it on an egg.	Salz
sugar [ˈʃʊgə]	It makes your tea sweet.	Zucker
marmalade [ˈmɑ:məleɪd]	You put it on your toast at breakfast.	Orangenmarmelade
teapot [ˈti:pɒt]	You make tea in it.	Teekanne
saucer [ˈsɔ:sə]	You put your cup on it.	Untertasse
(tea)spoon [(ˈti:)spu:n]	You put sugar in your tea with it.	(Tee)Löffel
knife [naɪf], *pl.* **knives** [naɪvz]	You cut bread with it.	Messer
fork [fɔ:k]	I don't eat with my fingers, I use a knife and *fork.*	Gabel
meat [mi:t]	There's *meat* in Irish stew.	Fleisch
7 **meaning** [ˈmi:nɪŋ]	'Hot' means 'very warm'. This is its *meaning.*	Bedeutung

⟨Authentic Britain: A trip through London⟩

trip [trɪp]	Fahrt, Reise
Marble Arch [ˌmɑ:bl‿ˈɑ:tʃ]	*Name eines Triumphbogens*
Hyde Park [ˌhaɪd ˈpɑ:k]	*Name eines Parks*
Parliament [ˈpɑ:ləmənt]	*Parlament*

Have you noticed? Some verbs and nouns are the same:

to **answer**	– an **answer**	to **score** a goal	– the **score**
to **brush** the horse	– a **brush**	to **shout**	– a **shout**
to **dream**	– a **dream**	to **telephone**	– the **telephone**
to **end**	– the **end** of s.th.	to **test** s.th.	– a **test**
to **help** s.o.	– some **help**	to **walk**	– a **walk** in the park
to **look**	– a **look** at s.th.	to **work**	– hard **work**
to **notice**	– a **notice**	*But be careful:*	
to **ride** a bike/horse	– a **ride**	to **practise**	– rugby **practice**

Be careful how you write it:

American – British – Danish – English – French – German – Irish

I met two **American** girls in the park.
They're not **Danish**, they're **German**, and they all speak **English**.
I don't understand this **French** sentence: what's it in **English**?
Do you like **Irish** stew? It's an **Irish** meal, but many **British** people eat it, too.

⟨Revision⟩

1	Ireland ['aɪələnd]		Irland
	O'Connor [əʊ'kɒnə]		*irischer Familienname*
	bonnet ['bɒnɪt]	Babies wear *bonnets* on their heads.	Babymütze
	Irishman ['aɪrɪʃmən]	a man from Ireland	Ire
2	fun [fʌn]	Christine had a lot of *fun* in her holidays.	Spaß
	circus ['sɜ:kəs]	In a *circus* people and animals do tricks.	Zirkus
	elephant ['elɪfənt]	a very big animal	Elefant
	sick [sɪk]	ill	krank
	Tarzan ['tɑ:zæn]		Tarzan
	jumbo ['dʒʌmbəʊ]	very big	Riesen-, riesig
	jet [dʒet]	a very fast plane	Jet, Düsenflugzeug
	jungle ['dʒʌŋgl]	Tarzan lives in the *jungle.*	Urwald
4	zoo [zu:]	You can see a lot of animals in the *zoo.*	Zoo
8	Sandra ['sændrə]		*Vorname (weiblich)*
	Philip ['fɪlɪp]		*Vorname (männlich)*

Unit 6

⟨Photo page: Heathrow⟩

Heathrow ['hi:θrəʊ]		*größter Flughafen von London*
terminal ['tɜ:mɪnəl]		Terminal
airport ['eəpɔ:t]		Flughafen
reception hall [rɪ'sepʃn ˌhɔ:l]		Abflughalle
background ['bækgraʊnd]		Hintergrund

A Oklahoma, here we come

	Oklahoma [ˌəʊklə'həʊmə]		*amerikanischer Bundesstaat*
a)	**rainy** ['reɪnɪ]	with a lot of rain	regnerisch
	airport ['eəpɔ:t]	You go there to get on a plane.	Flughafen
	they will [wɪl, wəl]		sie werden
	we'll [wi:l]	= we will	wir werden
	°**flight** [flaɪt]	*here:* plane to somewhere	°Flug
	we won't [wəʊnt]	= we will not	wir werden nicht
	impossible [ɪm'pɒsɪbl]	opposite of 'possible'; *here:* terrible, very silly	unmöglich
	ticket ['tɪkɪt]		*hier:* Flugschein
	Indian ['ɪndɪən]	The *Indians* lived in America long before the white people came.	*hier:* Indianer
	to **land** [lænd]	Most flights to London *land* at Heathrow.	landen
	counter ['kaʊntə]	Someone stands behind it to sell you something, or to check your ticket.	Schalter, Ladentisch
	in time	We're not late : we'll be there *in time.*	rechtzeitig
	he'll [hi:l]	= he will	er wird
	to **explain** [ɪks'pleɪn]	If you don't understand, I'll *explain.*	erklären
	°**nervous breakdown** [ˌnɜ:vəs 'breɪkdaʊn]	If you worry too much you'll have a *nervous breakdown!*	°Nervenzusammenbruch
	to **find out**	If you want to *find out* what a word means, look in the vocabulary.	herausfinden
b)	**Mr Pushy** ['pʊʃɪ]		*erfundener Personenname (von* push*)*
	°**Congratulations!** [kənˌgrætjʊ'leɪʃnz]	You say this if something good has happened to someone.	°Wir gratulieren! Herzlichen Glückwunsch!
	°**ten millionth** ['mɪljənθ]		°zehnmillionste

Exercises

3	**Enid** ['i:nɪd]	a town in Oklahoma	*Ortsname*
	to **take off**	The plane *took off* from Heathrow.	starten
	stewardess [ˌstjʊə'des]	She helps the passengers on a plane.	Stewardeß
	at first [ət 'fɜ:st]	*At first* he was nervous, but then he began to like the flight.	zunächst
4	**wow!** [waʊ]		*Ausruf*
	cowboy ['kaʊbɔɪ]	Let's play '*cowboys* and Indians'.	Cowboy
5	**the United States** [jʊˌnaɪtɪd 'steɪts]	= United States of America	die USA
	Atlantic Ocean [ətˌlæntɪk‿'əʊʃən]		der Atlantik, der atlantische Ozean

p.m. [piːˈem]	in the afternoon/evening	nachmittags/abends
Africa [ˈæfrɪkə]		Afrika
Chicago [ʃɪˈkɑːgəʊ]		*Großstadt in den USA*
New York [njuː ˈjɔːk]		*Großstadt in den USA*
Ireland [ˈaɪələnd]		Irland
U.K. [juːˈkeɪ]	= United Kingdom of Great Britain and Northern Ireland	das Vereinigte Königreich
country [ˈkʌntrɪ]	Germany, Britain and Ireland are *countries.*	Land
miles per hour (mph) [maɪlz pɜːrˈaʊə]	We can cycle at about 10 *miles per hour.*	Meilen pro Stunde

B Ben's letter

Glenwood Drive [ˌglenwʊd ˈdraɪv]		*Name einer Straße*
°**trip** [trɪp]	We went on a *trip* to London in our new car.	°Fahrt, Reise
°**article** [ˈɑːtɪkl]	A reporter writes newspaper *articles.*	°Artikel
spring [sprɪŋ]	*Spring* is between winter and summer.	Frühling
windy [ˈwɪndɪ]	with a lot of wind	windig
storm [stɔːm]	bad weather with a lot of wind	Sturm
thunderstorm [ˈθʌndəˌstɔːm]	a storm with thunder	Gewitter
not ... any more		nicht mehr
north [nɔːθ]	opposite of 'south'	(nach) Norden, Nord-, nördlich
east [iːst]	In the morning the sun is in the *east.*	(nach) Osten, Ost-, östlich
°**wheat** [wiːt]	It grows in fields, and people use it to make bread.	°Weizen
°**capital** [ˈkæpɪtl]	most important city	°Hauptstadt
°**prairie** [ˈpreərɪ]	land in the middle of the U.S. with no hills and no trees	°Prärie
flat [flæt]	The country is *flat* – there are no hills.	flach
for miles and miles	very far	meilenweit
sky [skaɪ]	When the sun shines, the *sky* is blue.	Himmel
Peggy Whitecloud [ˌpegɪ ˈwaɪtklaʊd]		*Personenname*
Cherokee [ˈtʃerəkiː]		*Indianerstamm*
Ralph Jones [ˌrælf ˈdʒəʊnz]		*Personenname*
Harry Hopper [ˌhærɪ ˈhɒpə]		*Personenname*
magic tricks [ˈmædʒɪk]	These tricks are hard to understand.	Zauberkunststücke
crazy [ˈkreɪzɪ]	mad	verrückt
°**lemonade stand** [stænd]	In America, children often make lemonade and sell it at a *lemonade stand.*	°Limonadenstand
postman [ˈpəʊstmən]	He brings the letters every day.	Postbote
Shall I...? [ʃæl]		Soll ich ...?
autumn [ˈɔːtəm]	*Autumn* is between summer and winter.	Herbst
°**fall** [fɔːl]	an American word for 'autumn'	°Herbst

Exercises

2 **table tennis** [ˈteɪbl ˌtenɪs]	It's like tennis, but you play it on a table.	Tischtennis

C Looking at the Weather

announcer [ə'naʊnsə]	The TV *announcer* tells you what is on TV next.	Ansager(in)
weatherman ['weθəmæn]	He tells you what the weather will be like.	Meteorologe (im Fernsehen)
Doyle [dɔɪl]		*Familienname*
Panhandle ['pæn,hændl]	This part of Oklahoma looks like one on the map.	*„Pfannenstiel"*
Tulsa ['tʌlsə]		*Stadt in Oklahoma*
Red River	name of a river	*Fluß zwischen Oklahoma und Texas*
sunny ['sʌnɪ]	When the sun is shining, it's *sunny.*	sonnig
cloudy ['klaʊdɪ]	When it's *cloudy,* you cannot see the sun.	wolkig
rain [reɪn]	It's wet and falls from the sky. (*verb:* 'to rain')	Regen
lightning ['laɪtnɪŋ]	When there's thunder, you can often see *lightning* in the sky.	Blitz
cool [ku:l]	opposite of 'warm'	kühl
northwest [,nɔ:θ'west]		Nordwesten, Nordwest-, nordwestlich
dry [draɪ]	opposite of 'wet'	trocken
west [west]	opposite of 'east'	Westen, West-, westlich
around 86 degrees [dɪ'gri:z]	about 86° F	um die 86 Grad Fahrenheit (= 30° C)

Exercises

1 **weather report** ['weðə rɪ,pɔ:t]	This tells you what the weather is like.	Wetterbericht
°**central** ['sentrəl]	in the middle, the middle part of	°Zentral-, Mittel-
2 **Mabel** ['meɪbl]	a girl's name	*Vorname (weiblich)*
Arnie ['ɑ:nɪ]	a boy's name	*Vorname (Kurzform von 'Arnold')*
3 **icy** ['aɪsɪ]	very cold	eisig
snowy ['snəʊɪ]	with a lot of snow	schneereich
stormy ['stɔ:mɪ]	with a lot of wind and rain	stürmisch
fog [fɒg]	If there is *fog,* you cannot see very far.	Nebel
foggy ['fɒgɪ]	with a lot of fog	neblig

D The Bet

bet [bet]	If you think you know who will win a match, you could make a *bet.*	Wette
Beverly Snyder [,bevəlɪ 'snaɪdə]		*Personenname*
neighbourhood ['neɪbəhʊd]	part of town where s.o. lives	Nachbarschaft
to **decide** [dɪ'saɪd]	to say what you want to do	entscheiden
kids [kɪdz]	young people, children	junge Leute, Kinder
especially [ɪ'speʃəlɪ]	in a special way, more than the others	besonders
Buddy ['bʌdɪ]		*Vorname oder Spitzname (männlich)*
to play a trick on s.o.	to do s.th clever to make s.o. look silly	jdm einen Streich spielen

	Pete [pi:t]	short for 'Peter'	*Vorname (männlich)*
	to **move** [mu:v]	to go or come (nearer or away from s.th.)	(näher-/weg-)rücken, (sich) bewegen
	close, closer [kləʊs(ə)]	near, nearer	nah, näher
	next to	very near	direkt neben
	to give a signal ['sɪgnəl]	to do s.th. as a sign	ein Zeichen geben
	to **turn on**	To start the water, you must *turn* it *on.*	andrehen, einschalten
	Uhhh [ɜ:]		*Ausdruck der Unsicherheit*
	°**hose** [həʊz]	It is useful in the garden in dry weather.	°Schlauch
	°**sprinkler** ['sprɪŋklə]	The *sprinkler* at the end of a hose goes round and round.	°Sprinkler, Rasensprenger
	lawn [lɔ:n]	short grass in a garden	Rasen
	°**right where...**	Stay *right where* you are.	°gerade da, wo...
	to **smile** [smaɪl]	She didn't laugh out loud, she only *smiled.*	lächeln
	°**brain** [breɪn]	You think with your *brain.*	°Gehirn
	°to **have s.th. on the brain**	to think all the time about s.th.	°von etwas besessen sein, eine fixe Idee haben
	to **bet, bet, bet** [bet]		wetten
	dollar ['dɒlə]	In America, you pay in *dollars.*	Dollar
	each other [i:tʃ 'ʌðə]	H. looked at B. and B. looked at H. They looked at *each other.*	sich (gegenseitig), einander
	°to **jump about**	to jump around (the garden)	°herumspringen
	wild [waɪld]	A cheetah is a *wild* animal.	wild
	above [ə'bʌv]	over	über
	to **turn off**	To stop the water, you must *turn* it *off.*	abdrehen, ausschalten
	Hey! [heɪ]		He!
	°to **switch** (two things) [swɪtʃ]	to put one thing where another should be	°vertauschen
	°**penny** ['penɪ]		*eine Münze*
	°**the penny dropped**	He/she/they understood at last.	°der Groschen fiel

Exercises

1	**fact** [fækt]	It is a *fact* that Oklahoma is in the USA.	Tatsache
2	**magician** [mə'dʒɪʃn]	A *magician* can do magic tricks.	Zauberer
	policewoman [pə'li:sˌwʊmən]	She does the same work as a policeman.	Polizistin
3	the **day after tomorrow**	If today is Monday, the *day after tomorrow* is Wednesday.	übermorgen
⟨4⟩	abracadabra [ˌæbrəkə'dæbrə]	a magic word	Abrakadabra
	huh? [hə]		*hier:* ..., nicht?
5	**Hi,** Grandma [haɪ]	another way to say 'hello'	*informelle Begrüßung*
6	**Jeff** [dʒef]	a boy's name	*Vorname (männlich)*
	rodeo ['rəʊdɪəʊ]	Cowboys show what they can do at a *rodeo.*	Rodeo
8	**T-shirt** ['ti:ʃɜ:t]	I like to wear a *T-shirt* with jeans.	T-shirt
	bank [bæŋk]	People keep their money there.	Bank
	Spot [spɒt]	a dog's name	*Hundename*
	sofa ['səʊfə]	You can sit or lie on a *sofa.*	Sofa
10	**Frontier City** ['frʌnˌtɪə]		*Ortsname*
	Indian City		*Ortsname*
	Salt Plains [ˌsɔ:lt 'pleɪnz]		*eine Salzwüste*

⟨12⟩	to blow [bləʊ]	to make a long sound	*hier:* pfeifen
	Lord [lɔ:d]	= God	Herr (Gott)
	back [bæk]		Rücken
[13]	to **snow** [snəʊ]	It's *snowing* = Snow is falling.	schneien
	to **get s.th. wrong**	not to understand s.th. right	etwas falsch auffassen, einen Fehler machen
	board [bɔ:d]	There's one in every classroom.	Tafel
⟨14⟩	pin [pɪn]		Stecknadel
	balloon [bə'lu:n]		Luftballon
	to burst [bɜ:st]		platzen

⟨Authentic America: Ben's photos⟩

ranch [ræntʃ, rɑ:ntʃ]	Ranch
tent [tent]	Zelt
Anadarko [ˌænə'dɑ:kəʊ]	*Ortsname*
wicki-up ['wɪkɪˌʌp]	*eine Art Hütte*

Jobs

a radio/TV **announcer**	Ansager(in)	a **milkman**	Milchmann
a **butcher**	Metzger(in)	a **policeman/-woman**	Polizist(in)
a **chemist**	Apotheker(in)	a **shop-assistant**	Verkäufer(in)
a **doctor**	Arzt/Ärztin	a **stewardess**	Stewardeß
a **farmer**	Bauer, Bäuerin	a **taxi driver**	Taxifahrer(in)
a **greengrocer**	Obst- und Gemüsehändler(in)	a **teacher**	Lehrer(in)
		a **vet**	Tierarzt/-ärztin

Unit 7

A The raft

°**raft** [rɑ:ft]	Peggy and the boys made a *raft.*	°Floß
to **invite** [ɪn'vaɪt]	to ask s. o. to come and see you	einladen
°**jetty** ['dʒetɪ]	You tie your raft to a *jetty.*	°Landungssteg
problem ['prɒbləm]	I've got a *problem* – I don't know what to do!	Problem
tool [tu:l]	You make things with *tools.*	Werkzeug
°**oil-drum** ['ɔɪlˌdrʌm]		°Ölfaß
°**board** [bɔ:d]	You make a raft out of *boards.*	°Brett
while [waɪl]		während
nail [neɪl]	Peggy and Ben used *nails* to put the boards together.	Nagel
hammer ['hæmə]	A *hammer* is a tool.	Hammer

drink [drɪŋk]	When people eat something, they usually have a *drink*, too.	Getränk
to **take a picture**	to take a photo	photographieren
Sure! [ʃʊə]		*Ausdruck der Zustimmung*
to **hide** [haɪd], **hid** [hɪd], **hidden** [ˈhɪdn]	When you *hide*, no one can see you.	sich verstecken
to **untie** [ˌʌnˈtaɪ]	opposite of 'to tie'	losbinden

Exercises

2 **Nellie** [ˈnelɪ]	a girl's name	*Vorname (weiblich)*
°**paw** [pɔ:]	People have hands, but cats have *paws*.	°Pfote
Big Paws		*Katzenname*

B Looking at the farm

to **show s.o. around** [əˈraʊnd]	to take s.o. to see all the different parts of s.th.	herumführen
Boy!		*Ausdruck des Erstaunens*
What a lot of...		Was für eine Menge...
machine [məˈʃi:n]	A lot of work is easier if you have a *machine* to help you.	Maschine
tractor [ˈtræktə]	A tractor is a farm machine	Traktor
windmill [ˈwɪndmɪl]	*Windmills* only work when there is a strong wind.	Windmühle
own [əʊn]	When something belongs to you it is your *own*.	eigen
°**flour** [ˈflaʊə]	You make bread with *flour*.	°Mehl
°to **pump** [pʌmp]		°pumpen
°**well** [wel]	You *pump* water up from a *well*.	°Brunnen
watermelon [ˈwɔ:təˌmelən]	a big round fruit	Wassermelone
barn [bɑ:n]	Farmers keep their animals in the *barn*.	Scheune
hay [heɪ]	Horses eat *hay* in winter.	Heu
Emily [ˈemɪlɪ]	a girl's name	*Vorname (weiblich)*
so that [ˈsəʊ ˌðæt]		so daß
pig [pɪg]	a fat farm animal.	Schwein
bacon [ˈbeɪkn]	Pigs give us *bacon* for breakfast.	Speck
sheep *(sing.* and *pl.)* [ʃi:p]	a farm animal	Schaf(e)
bull [bʊl]	*Bulls* can be dangerous.	Stier
Rodney [ˈrɒdnɪ]	a boy's name	*Vorname (männlich)*
prize [praɪz]	Rodney won a *prize* last year.	Preis
beautiful [ˈbju:tɪfʊl]	very, very nice to look at	schön
Elsie [ˈelsɪ]	a girl's name	*Vorname (weiblich)*
cow [kaʊ]	A *cow* gives us milk.	Kuh

Exercises

1 to **lay** [leɪ], **laid, laid** [eɪ]	Hens *lay* eggs.	legen
2 **dinner** [ˈdɪnə]	the big meal of the day	Mittag-, Abendessen
4 **because of** [bɪˈkɒzəv]		wegen

C How Rabbit brought fire to the people

	fire [ˈfaɪə]	You need a *fire* if it's cold.	Feuer
1.	**earth** [ɜ:θ]	We all live on the *earth.*	Erde
	Thunderbirds [ˈθʌndəˌbɜ:dz]		„Donnervögel"
	island [ˈaɪlənd]	a piece of land in the middle of a lake	Insel
	°**weasel** [wi:zl]		°Wiesel
	deep [di:p]	going down a long way	tief
2.	to **suffer** [ˈsʌfə]	to feel very bad because you are hungry or cold or have pains	leiden
	°to **freeze** [fri:z], **froze, frozen** [əʊ]	to be very, very cold	°(er)frieren
	°**mole** [məʊl]	This animal is small and lives in a hole in the earth.	°Maulwurf
	also [ˈɔ:lsəʊ]	I can *also* dance. = I can dance, too.	auch
	across [əˈkrɒs]	to the other side of s.th.	hinüber
	°**pine tar** [ˈpaɪnˌtɑ:]		°Kienteer
	hair [ˈheə]	You have *hair* on your head.	Haar(e)
	to **stand, stood, stood** [ʊ] **up**		*hier:* nach oben stehen
3.	**circle** [ˈsɜ:kl]	A *circle* is round.	Kreis
	°to **bow** [baʊ]	The weasels *bowed* to the fire.	°sich neigen, sich verbeugen
	Yahoo! [jæˈhu:]		*Ausruf*
	to **lead** [li:d], **led, led** [led]	Rabbit *led* the dance.	führen
	ahead of [əˈhed]	in front of	vor, voran
	low [ləʊ]	opposite of 'high'	niedrig
	to **catch fire** [ˌkætʃ ˈfaɪə]	The pine tar *caught* fire.	Feuer fangen
4.	**chase** [tʃeɪs]	A *chase* is when someone runs after someone else.	Jagd
	to **call out** [ˌkɔ:l‿ˈaʊt]	to shout loudly	ausrufen
	except [ɪkˈsept]	Everyone else *except* you!	außer
5.	°**tepee** [ˈti:pi:]	An Indian lives in a *tepee.*	°(Indianer-) Zelt
	°**courage** [ˈkʌrɪdʒ]	Rabbit showed a lot of *courage.*	°Mut

Exercises

2	corn [kɔ:n]		Mais
	fox [fɒks]		Fuchs
	goose [gu:s]		Gans
	belongings *(pl.)* [bɪˈlɒŋɪŋz]	Your own things are your *belongings.*	Sachen, Besitz
3	to **break down** [ˌbreɪk ˈdaʊn]	The car *broke down* because it was very old.	kaputtgehen, eine Panne haben
4	**doggy** [ˈdɒgɪ]	little dog	Hündchen
	Freddy [ˈfredɪ]	a boy's name	*Vorname (männlich)*
	Doc [dɒk]	short for 'Doctor'	*Spitzname*
	perfect [ˈpɜ:fɪkt]		perfekt
5	**Alice** [ˈælɪs]	a girl's name	*Vorname (weiblich)*
	Ellis [ˈelɪs]	a boy's name	*Vorname (männlich)*
	Ellen [ˈelən]	a girl's name	*Vorname (weiblich)*
	Alan [ˈælən]	a boy's name	*Vorname (männlich)*
	worm [wɜ:m]	Birds eat *worms.*	Wurm
	Ernie [ˈɜ:nɪ]	a boy's name	*Vorname (männlich)*
⟨10⟩	chick [tʃɪk]	a baby hen	Küken
	geese [gi:s]	plural of 'goose'	Gänse
⟨11⟩	neck [nek]	Your head is on your *neck.*	Hals

⟨12⟩ to love [lʌv]	to like very, very much	lieben
settler ['setlə]		Siedler
Chapman ['tʃæpmən]		*Familienname*
New England		Neuengland *(nordöstliche Staaten der USA)*
apple seed [si:d]		Apfelkern
to plant [plɑ:nt]		pflanzen

⟨Photo page: Farming in America⟩

farming ['fɑ:mɪŋ]	Landwirtschaft
to harvest ['hɑ:vəst]	ernten
to round up [ˌraʊnd‿'ʌp]	zusammentreiben
cattle ['kætl]	Vieh
cattle drive ['kætl ˌdraɪv]	Viehtrieb

Ausrufe: grüßen und Gefühle äußern

Hello.	**What!** You drove the tractor?	**Be a devil!**
Hi, Grandma.	**Hey!** That's my bike!	**Come on, Fulford!**
O.K./All right.	**Wow!** What a big bull!	**Well done!**
Sure!	**Boy!** It's hot.	**Congratulations!**
No problem.	**What a lot of wheat!**	**God bless you!**

to do	to make	to take
What are you **doing**?	Can you **make** a cake?	Someone has **taken** my pen!
We have a lot of jobs to **do**.	They **make** their own flour.	We can walk or **take** the bus.
I haven't **done** my homework.	The girls have **made** a kite.	They **took** turns to drive.
He **did** the wrong exercise.	Ronny **made** breakfast today.	I must **take** a photo of the castle.
Can you **do** magic tricks?	Don't **make** so much noise!	He **took** my temperature.
We can **do** the shopping later.	**Make** a new sentence.	I must **take** my medicine.

Unit 8

⟨Authentic America: In town⟩

fireman ['faɪəmən]	Feuerwehrmann
pretzel ['pretsəl]	Bretzel
skates [skeɪts]	Rollschuhe

A No Problem!

Mrs **Alassio** [ə'læsɪəʊ]	*italienischer Familienname*
into town	in die Stadt

to **post** [pəʊst]	to send (a letter) away	einstecken, zum Briefkasten bringen
to **love** [lʌv]	to like very much	lieben, mögen, gern tun
I love cycling		ich fahre gern Rad
40**c** = 40 **cents** [sents]	There are 100 *cents* in a dollar.	Cent
the rest [rest]	what is left	der Rest
°**cheque** [tʃek]	Can I pay by *cheque?*	°Scheck
Italy ['ɪtəlɪ]	a country south of Germany	Italien
to **go off**	to go away, to start (on a trip)	abgehen (*Brief*), losgehen (*Person*),
France [frɑ:ns]	a country west of Germany	Frankreich
°**clerk** [klɑ:k]	man or woman behind the counter in an office	°Büroangestellte(r)
envelope ['envələʊp]	You put a letter in one.	Umschlag
°**by airmail** ['eəmeɪl]	Letters from Britain to the USA go *by airmail.*	mit Luftpost
to **enjoy** [ɪn'dʒɔɪ]	to like (doing s. th.)	genießen
$2.72	= two dollars, seventy-two cents	zwei Dollar, zweiundsiebzig Cent
°**airmail sticker** ['stɪkə]	a small blue piece of paper, to put on an airmail letter	°Luftpostaufkleber
mistake [mɪs'teɪk]	I did something wrong: it was a *mistake.*	Fehler, Versehen

Exercises

2 **brains** [breɪnz]	She has *brains* – she's very clever.	Intelligenz, Grips
4 Sally **Kahn** [kɑ:n]		*Familienname*
[5] **slowly** ['sləʊlɪ]		langsam *(Adverb)*
carefully ['keəfəlɪ]		vorsichtig *(Adv.)*
badly ['bædlɪ]		schlecht *(Adv.)*
Bill [bɪl]	a boy's name	*Vorname (männlich)*
dangerously ['deɪndʒərəslɪ]		gefährlich *(Adv.)*
easily ['i:zɪlɪ]		leicht *(Adv.)*
real [rɪəl]		echt

B Fire at the Oxford Hotel

°**tall story** ['tɔ:l 'stɔ:rɪ]	A *tall story* is too fantastic to believe.	°Lügengeschichte, „Märchen"
fire-station ['faɪə ˌsteɪʃn]	You can't leave the car in front of the *fire-station.*	Feuerwehrhaus
fireman ['faɪəmən]	He rescues people from fires.	Feuerwehrmann
fire-engine ['faɪər‿ˌendʒɪn]	The firemen drive to the fire in it.	Feuerwehrauto
°**alarm bell** [ə'lɑ:m ˌbel]	It rings if there is a fire somewhere.	°Alarmglocke
all alone [ˌɔ:l ə'ləʊn]	with nobody else there	ganz allein
to **grab** [græb]	to catch and pull away	(er)greifen, packen
She had a lot of nerve! [nɜ:v]		Die hatte vielleicht Nerven!
°**siren** ['saɪrən]	If you hear a *siren,* you know a police-car or fire-engine is coming.	°Sirene
to **do 150 mph**	to drive (fly, ...) at 150 mph	*hier:* 150 fahren
flame [fleɪm]	*Flames* are very hot.	Flamme
to **scream** [skri:m]	to cry in a high voice	schreien
to **lose one's head**	to get too excited and do s.th. silly	den Kopf verlieren
the 21st **floor** [flɔ:]	What *floor* is your room on?	Stockwerk, Etage

	to **put out** a fire	They *put out* the fire with water.	löschen
	to **raise** [reɪz]	to put up high	hochheben, aufstellen, *hier:* ausfahren
	ladder [ˈlædə]	You need it to get up to a high window.	Leiter
	stupid [ˈstjuːpɪd]	silly, not clever	dumm
	trouble [ˈtrʌbl]	problems	Ärger, Schwierigkeiten
	to **be in trouble**		Ärger bekommen

Exercises

3	**Mickey** [ˈmɪkɪ]		*Spitzname*
	°**fire department** [dɪˈpɑːtmənt]	They put out fires.	°Feuerwehr
[4]	**person** [ˈpɜːsən]	a man, woman, boy or girl	Person
	hobby [ˈhɒbɪ]	You do it because you enjoy it.	Hobby
[8]	**mine** [maɪn]		meine (-s, -r)
	yours [jʊəz]		deine/eure/Ihre (-s, -r)
	his [hɪz]		seine (-s, -r)
	hers [hɜːz]		ihre (-s, -r)
	ours [aʊəz]		unsere (-s, -r)
	theirs [ðeəz]		ihre (-s, -r) *(Plural)*
	What a mess! [mes]		Was für ein Durcheinander!
⟨9⟩	California [kælɪˈfɔːnjə]		*amerikanischer Bundesstaat*
	redwood [ˈredwʊd]	*Redwood* trees get very old and very big.	Redwood *(kalifornischer Nadelbaum)*
	Gulf Stream [ˈgʌlf ˌstriːm]	The *Gulf Stream* is in the Atlantic. It brings warm water from Mexico to Britain and Ireland.	Golfstrom
	ribbon [ˈrɪbn]	A road can look like one.	Band
	highway [ˈhaɪweɪ]	a long road	Straße, Autobahn
	endless [ˈendləs]	with no end	endlos
	skyway [ˈskaɪweɪ]	*here:* sky	*hier:* Himmel
	golden [ˈgəʊldən]		golden, Gold-
	valley [ˈvælɪ]	low land between mountains	Tal

⟨Photo page: American cities⟩

skyline [ˈskaɪlaɪn]		Silhouette, Skyline
New Orleans [njuː ˈɔːliːəns]		*Stadt im Süden der USA*
cable car [ˈkeɪbl kɑː]		Drahtseilbahn
Fifth Avenue [fɪfθ‿ˈævənjuː]		*bedeutende Geschäftsstraße in New York*

In town: shops and other buildings

supermarket	Supermarkt	**bank**	Bank	**offices**	Büros
sweet shop	Süßwarenladen	**post office**	Postamt	**flats**	Wohnungen
cycle shop	Fahrradladen	**railway station**	Bahnhof	**cinema**	Kino
pet shop	Tierhandlung	**bus station**	Busbahnhof	**museum**	Museum
bookshop	Buchhandlung	**fire station**	Feuerwache	**public baths**	Hallenbad
the butcher's	Metzgerei	**hospital**	Krankenhaus	**hotel**	Hotel
the greengrocer's	Gemüseladen	**school**	Schule	**restaurant**	Restaurant
the chemist's	Apotheke	**factory**	Fabrik	**snack bar**	Imbißstube

Alphabetical Word List

– Die Zahlen verweisen auf das erstmalige Vorkommen der Wörter,
z. B. **airport 6 A** 77,a) = Unit 6 A, Seite 77, Paragraph a)
to **act 3 A** 34,5 = Unit 3 A, Seite 34, Übung 5
– Das Zeichen ° vor einer Angabe bedeutet, daß das Wort zum rezeptiven Wortschatz zählt.

earth 7 C 95,1.
east 6 B 80
°**eater 1 C** 13
egg 2 C 27,3.
⟨elephant 73,2⟩
to **empty 4 A** 47,1.
end 1 D 16,1
⟨endless **8 B** 111,9⟩
enemy 2 A 20
engine 4 A 47,2.
to **enjoy 8 A** 103
enough 2 C 27,5.
entrance 1 D 15
envelope 8 A 103
especially 6 D 83
essay 5 C 65,2
even 3 C 38,2.
even so 5 D 66
ever 2 B 23
everywhere 4 C 52,1.
to **examine 3 A** 32,1.
except 7 C 96,4.
excited ⟨45,5⟩ **4 B** 49
°**execution 1 D** 15
expensive 2 A 22,4
to **explain 6 A** 77,a)

F

fact 6 D 84,1
factory 2 A 20
°**fair 2 A** 20
⟨fair *(schön)* **5 B** 63,7⟩
°**fall** *(Herbst)* **6 B** 80
famous 2 A 20
fantastic 1 B 11
farm 1 B 11
farmer 2 C 26,1.
⟨farming **7** 101⟩
fast 1 C 13
fat 3 C 38,2.
⟨Father Christmas 44,2⟩
fault 5 B 62,1
favourite 5 B 61,b)
to **feed 3 B** 35,1.
⟨fever **5 B** 63,7⟩
field 3 C 38,1.
⟨figgy pudding 44,3⟩
figure 1 D 16
to **fill 3 C** 39,4.
film 2 B 23
°**finals 5 C** 64
to **find out 6 A** 77,a)
finger 5 A 59,5.
to **finish 4 A** 47,3.
fire 7 C 95,1.
°**fire department 8 B** 108,3
fire-engine 8 B 106
fireman ⟨8 102⟩ **8 B** 106
fire station 8 B 106
fish ⟨3 43⟩ **4 C** 55,4
fish fingers 5 B 61,a)
⟨fishmonger **5 B** 63,7⟩
flame 8 B 106
flat *(flach)* **6 B** 80
°**flight 6 A** 77,a)
floor *(Stock)* **8 B** 106
°**flour 7 B** 92
fog 6 C 82,3
foggy 6 C 82,3
⟨to fold 45,4⟩
°**folk hero 2 A** 20
to **follow 4 C** 53,4.
°**food mixer 5 A** 59,5.
for *(gegen)* **3 A** 32,1
foreign language **5 A** 58,1.
forest 2 A 21
fork ⟨**5 B** 63,6⟩ **5 D** 70,5
°**form master 4 B** 49
forward 2 C 27,3.
⟨fox **7 C** 96,2⟩
°**frame 4 B** 49
°to **freeze 7 C** 95,2.
French 5 A 58,1.
fresh 3 B 35,2.
front wheel **4 B** 49
⟨frosty **3 C** 42,8⟩
⟨fun **3 B** 37,5⟩
°**fuse-box 1 D** 16

G

°**gallows 2 C** 26,1.
games building 3 C 40,3
garage 1 A 10,5
⟨geese **7 C** 100,10⟩
to **get on** with **2 C** 27,3.
⟨to get into trouble **4** 57⟩
[to **get s.th. wrong 6 D** 88,13]
glad 5 A 58,3.
glass 3 C 41,6
⟨glitter 45,4⟩
to **go**
to go mad **5 D** 66
to go near **3 C** 38
to go off **8 A** 103
to go round to **4 C** 52,2.
°to go surfing **1 A** 9,b)
to go swimming **1 B** 11
going to **3 A** 32,1
God bless you 2 C 26,2.
⟨golden **8 B** 111,9⟩
°**goods 2 B** 23
⟨goose **7 C** 96,2⟩
to **grab 8 B** 106
⟨grand **1 D** 19,9⟩
grandchildren 1 D 18,6
grandfather 1 D 18,6
grandma 1 D 18,6
grandmother 1 D 18,6
grandpa 1 D 18,6
grandparents 1 D 18,6
⟨greeting 45,4⟩
group 3 C 40,2
guitar 5 A 59,5.

H

hair 7 C 95,2.
⟨half way up **1 D** 19,10⟩
°**half-time 5 D** 67
hammer 7 A 90
hamster 3 B 35,2.
handlebars 4 B 49
°**hangman 2 C** 27,3.
hard 1 B 11
hardly 1 A 8,a)
⟨harvest **7** 101⟩
to **hate 2 B** 23
to **have a look at 2 C** 29,5
to **have to 5 A** 58,1.
hay 7 B 92
headache 3 A 32,1.
height 4 B 49
°**hero 2 A** 20
°folk **hero 2 A** 20
[**hers 8 B** 111,8]
⟨herself **3** 43⟩
Hi! 6 D 85,5
to **hide 7 A** 90
⟨highway **8 B** 111,9⟩
hill 1 B 11
himself 3 B 35,2.
[**his** *(pron.)* **8 B** 111,8]
history 2 B 23
to **hit 5 D** 67
[**hobby 8 B** 109,4]
hockey 5 A 58,2.
hockey stick **5 D** 66
to **hold on to 4 B** 50,2
our **home 2 B** 23
°**Home Economics 5 A** 58,3.
°**hoof/hooves 3 C** 39,3.
⟨horn **4 C** 56,9⟩
°**hose 6 D** 83
hospital 3 A 32,1.
hot 1 A 9,b)
⟨huh? **6 D** 84,4⟩
°to **hunt 2 A** 21
°**hunter 2 C** 30,6
to **hurry** (up) **2 C** 27,4.
⟨to hurt **4** 57⟩
husband 1 D 18,6

I

icy 6 C 82,3
idiot 5 A 59,5.
if ⟨3 43⟩ **5 A** 59,1
important 2 A 20
impossible 6 A 77,a)
Indian 6 A 77,a)
industrial 2 A 21
industry 2 A 20
information centre 2 B 25,6
°**injection 3 C** 39,4.
°**injury 5 D** 67
inside 1 D 15
the **inside 4 A** 47,1.
°**interview 5 D** 68,1
°to **interview 5 D** 68,1
in trouble 8 B 106
to **invite 7 A** 90
⟨Irishman 72,1⟩
Irish stew 5 B 61,a)
irregular 4 B 51,5
island 7 C 95,1.

J

⟨jet 73,2⟩
°**jetty 7 A** 90
⟨jumbo 73,2⟩
to **jump 3 C** 41,6
°to jump about **6 D** 83
⟨jungle 73,2⟩

K

kids 6 D 83
to **kill 2 C** 27,5.
°**kilo 1 C** 13
⟨kin 44,3⟩
king 2 A 21
⟨kitten **3** 43⟩
knife 5 D 70,5
°**knitwear 2 A** 20

L

ladder 8 C 106
lake 1 A 8,1
lamp 1 D 16
land 2 B 23
to **land 6 A** 77,a)
foreign **language 5 A** 58,1.
°**language lab 5 A** 58,1.
last year **1 A** 10,6
lawn 6 D 83
to **lay 7 B** 93,1
to **lead 7 C** 95,3.
leaflet 3 B 35,2.
to **learn 1 B** 11
at **least 4 C** 52,2.
lesson 5 A 59,5.
licence 3 B 35,1.
light 1 D 15
lightning 6 C 82
what was it **like**? **1 B** 12,4
line 4 B 49
to have a **look** at **2 C** 29,5
to **look out for 5 D** 66
⟨Lord **6 D** 87,12⟩
to **lose 4 B** 51,5
to lose one's head **8 B** 106
a lot 1 B 11
lots of 1 B 11
loud 5 D 66
to **love** ⟨**7 C** 100,12⟩ **8 A** 103
low 7 C 95,3.
luck 4 C 52,2.
for luck **4 C** 53,4.
lunch hour 5 A 59,5.

M

machine ⟨2 31⟩ **7 B** 92
mad 5 D 66
magician 6 D 84,2
magic tricks 6 B 80
main 2 B 23
⟨manager **3 B** 37,5⟩
⟨to march **1 D** 19,10⟩
to **mark 4 B** 49
market square 2 B 25,6
marmalade 5 D 70,5
mashed potatoes 5 B 61,a)
match 5 D 66
to **matter 4 A** 48,2
⟨you may hurt **4** 57⟩
meal 3 A 32,2.
meaning 5 D 70,7
meat 5 D 70,5
medicine 3 A 32,1.
to **meet 4 C** 52,2.
menu 5 B 61,a)
⟨merry 44⟩
[what a **mess! 8 B** 111,8]
°**metre 1 C** 13,1.
mile 6 A 79,5
for miles and miles **6 B** 80
miles per hour **6 A** 79,5
million 1 C 13
millionth 6 A 77,b)
[**mine 8 B** 111,8]
⟨miner **2** 31⟩
Miss Price 5 D 66
mistake 8 A 103
food **mixer 5 A** 59,5.
°**mixture 5 A** 59,5.
modern 2 A 20
°**mole 7 C** 95,2.
money 2 B 23
more terrible 2 A 21
most modern 2 A 20
most of 3 C 38,2.
°**motor** caravan **4 B** 50,3
mountain 1 A 8,1
mouse/mice 2 C 30,6
to **move** *(umziehen)* **5 C** 64
to **move closer 6 D** 83
°**mudguard 4 B** 49
⟨mussels **5 B** 63,7⟩

N

nail 7 A 90
⟨narrow **5 B** 63,7⟩
°**national 5 C** 64
⟨natural **3** 43⟩
near 1 A 10,5
to go near **3 C** 38,1.
⟨neck **3** 43⟩
you **needn't 3 B** 35,1.
neighbourhood 6 D 83
⟨neither … nor **1 D** 19,10⟩
nephew 1 D 18,6
to have a lot of **nerve 8 B** 106
nervous 5 D 66
°**nervous breakdown 6 A** 77,a)
news 2 C 26,1.
next to 6 D 83
niece 1 D 18,6
none 1 D 18,6
⟨no one 45,5⟩
°**Norman 2 B** 23
north 6 B 80
°**Northern 2 A** 22,3
not … yet 4 A 47,3.
notice 3 C 38,2
to **notice 4 C** 53,3.
notice-board 5 68,2

O

ocean 6 A 79,5
to go **off 8 A** 103
office ⟨**3 B** 37,5⟩ **4 B** 50,3
oil ⟨**4** 46⟩ **4 A** 47,1.
°**oil-drum 7 A** 90
to be **on 2 C** 29,4
you're **on 5 D** 67
once 2 C 26,2.
the only **one/ones 5 D** 66
⟨one by one 45,5⟩
only 5 D 66
the only 2 C 26,2.
opposite 1 D 16
[**ours 8 B** 111,8]
°**outdoor swimming-pool 5 A** 58,4
°**outlaw 2 B** 23
outside *(prep.)* **3 B** 35,2.
own 7 B 92

P

⟨to pack **1 D** 19,9⟩
pain 3 A 32,1.
to **paint 4 C** 53,4.
pair 2 C 30,6
parrot 4 C 56,6
part 1 D 15
to **pass a test 4 C** 52,1.
to **pass the ball 5 D** 67
⟨pavement **4** 57⟩
°**paw 7 A** 91,2
to **pay 2 B** 23
pea 5 B 61,a)
pedal 4 B 49
pen-friend 5 C 65,3
°**penny** ⟨**2 C** 30,8⟩ **6 D** 83
perfect 7 C 97,4
[**person 8 B** 109,4]
pet shop 3 B 35,2.
to **phone 3 A** 32,1.
piece of cloth 3 C 39,4.
⟨pieman **2 C** 30,8⟩
pig 7 B 92
⟨pin **6 D** 88,14⟩
°**pine tar 7 C** 95,2
⟨pipes **1 D** 19,10⟩
⟨to plant **7 C** 100,12⟩
to **play a trick on** s.o. **6 C** 83
player 5 D 66
playground 3 C 40,3
°**plug** *(Zündkerze)* **4 A** 47,1.
⟨plum pudding 44,2⟩
p.m. 6 A 79,5
policeman 4 C 52,1
police station 4 C 52,1.
policewoman 6 D 84,2
to **polish 4 A** 47,1.
pony 1 C 13
poor 2 A 21
to **post 8 A** 103
postcard ⟨1 7⟩ **1 A** 8,a)
postman 6 B 80
post office 5 B 35,1.
potato 2 B 25,4
mashed potatoes **5 B** 61,a)
⟨roast potatoes 44,2⟩
°**powerful 2 A** 21
practice 5 A 59,5.
to **practise 4 B** 49
prairie castle 6 B 80
°**presciption 3 A** 32,1.
⟨pretty **5 B** 63,7⟩
⟨pretzel **8** 101⟩
prisoner 1 D 15
prize 7 B 92
problem 7 A 90
⟨to promise 45,5⟩
°**public baths 5 A** 58,4.
pudding 5 B 61,a)
°to **pull down 2 A** 22,3
°to **pump up 7 B** 92
pupil 5 A 58,3.
purse 2 B 25,5
to **put**
to put one's name down **5 C** 64
to put out a fire **8 B** 106
to put up **3 C** 38,2.

Q

to **qualify 5 C** 64
questionnaire 1 D 18,5
quick 5 D 67

R

°**raft 7 A** 90
⟨rags 45,5⟩
rain 6 C 82
rainy 6 A 77,a)
to **raise 8 B** 106
⟨ranch **6** 89⟩
rear light **4 B** 49
⟨reception hall **6** 76⟩
⟨redwood **8 B** 111,9⟩
⟨regular **3** 43⟩
°**relation 1 D** 18,6
report 6 C 82,1
°to **report 4 C** 52,1.
to **rescue 2 C** 26,1
°**reserve 5 C** 64
rest 8 A 103
restaurant 2 B 25,6
⟨ribbon **3** 43⟩
rich 2 A 21
ride 3 C 38,1.
right 2 B 23
°**right where 6 D** 83
°**Road Safety Officer 4 B** 49
⟨roast potatoes 44,2⟩
to **rob 2 B** 23
rodeo 6 D 85,6
there's **room 5 C** 64
°**round 5 D** 66
⟨to round up 101⟩
rugby 5 A 58,2.
rule 4 B 49
[**runner 8 A** 105,5]

S

saddle 4 B 49
to **sail 1 A** 8,1
salt 5 D 70,5
sand 3 B 35,2.
saucer 5 D 70,5
⟨to save **5 B** 63,7⟩
°**Saxon 2 B** 23
⟨scissors 45,4⟩
to **score 5 D** 66
°**scratch 4 B** 49
°**scratched 4 C** 53,3.
to **scream 8 B** 106
⟨season 45,4⟩
second 1 C 13
doctor's **set 3 A** 32,2.
to **set a table 5 D** 70,5
⟨to set one's eyes on **5 B** 63,7⟩
⟨settler **7 C** 100,12⟩
shadow 1 D 16
shall 6 B 80
sheep 7 B 92
°**sheriff 2 A** 20
°**shock 3 C** 39,3.
to **shoot 2 C** 27,5.
to do the **shopping 3 A** 33,3
shopping centre 2 A 20
should 5 B 61,a)
shout 2 C 27,3.
to **show s.o. around 7 B** 92
⟨sick 73,2⟩
°to feel **sick 3 A** 34,5
side ⟨45,5⟩ **4 C** 53,3.
°**sign 3 C** 41,4

signal 6 D 83
⟨simple **2 C** 30,8⟩
sir ⟨**2 C** 30,8⟩ **4 B** 49
°**siren 8 B** 106
°**size 4 C** 53,3.
⟨skates **8** 101⟩
sky 6 B 80
⟨skyline **8** 112⟩
⟨skyway **8 B** 111,9⟩
slow 5 B 62,4
[**slowly 8 A** 105,5]
smile 7 A 90
to **smile** ⟨**3 B** 37,5⟩ **6 D** 83
snack bar 4 C 53,3.
snow 2 C 30,6
[to **snow 6 D** 88,13]
snowy 6 C 82,3
so that 7 B 92
sofa 6 D 86,8
somewhere 2 B 23
son 1 D 18,6
⟨sound 45,5⟩
⟨soup **5 B** 63,6⟩
south 5 D 66
°**speedway bike 4 B** 49
spoon ⟨**5 B** 63,6⟩ **5 D** 70,5
°**sports ground 5 D** 66
spring 6 B 80
°**sprinkler 6 D** 83
stamp 8 B
°**stand 6 B** 80
to **stand up 7 C** 95,2.
statue 2 A 20
⟨steak **5 B** 63,6⟩
to **steal 4 C** 52,1.
hockey **stick 5 D** 66
°cocktail **stick 1 C** 13
stewardess 6 A 78,3
⟨stocking 44,2⟩
stomach 3 A 34,5
storm 6 B 80
stormy 6 C 82,3
°**strange 1 A** 8,a)
stupid 8 B 106
subject 5 A 58,3.
to **suffer 7 C** 95,2.
sugar 5 D 70,5
sun hat 1 A 9
sunny 6 C 82
°**supporter 5 C** 64
Sure! 7 A 90
to go **surfing 1 A** 9,b)
surgery 3 A 32,1.
[**swimmer 8 A** 105,5]
to go **swimming 1 B** 11
swimming-pool 5 A 58,4.
°to **switch** *(tauschen)* **6 D** 83
to **switch on 5 A** 59,5.
°**swollen 3 C** 39,4.
°**sword 1 D** 15

T

table-tennis 6 B 81,2
to **take**
to take a photo **4 B** 51,5
to take a picture **7 A** 90
to take s.o.'s temperature **3 A** 32,1.
⟨take-off **3 C** 42,9⟩
to take off **6 A** 78,3
⟨tall **3 C** 42,8⟩
°**tall story 8 B** 106
to **taste** ⟨**2 C** 30,8⟩ **5 A** 59,5.
team 5 C 64
teapot 5 D 70,5
teaspoon 5 D 70,5
telephone box 3 C 39,3.
temperature 3 A 32,1.
tennis 1 B 11
⟨tent **6** 89⟩
°**tepee 7 C** 96,5.
°**term 5 A** 58,4.
⟨terminal **6** 76⟩
test 3 C 41,6
bigger **than 1 C** 13
⟨to thank 45,5⟩
[**theirs 8 B** 111,8]
thief/thieves 4 C 52,1.
thin 4 A 47,2.
thirsty 5 B 61,b)
thousand 1 C 13
thunder 1 D 15
thunderstorm 6 B 80
ticket 2 C 29,4
⟨tidings 44,3⟩
to **tighten 2 C** 27,4.
in **time 6 A** 77,a)
toast 2 C 30,6
tonight 3 B 37,3
tools 7 A 90
to **touch 1 D** 16
°to **tour 1 B** 11
tourist 2 B 25, 6
town 2 A 21
into town **8 A** 103
⟨townspeople 45,5⟩
tractor 7 B 92
°**trip** ⟨**5** 71⟩ **6 B** 80
trouble 8 B 106
in trouble **8 B** 106
⟨to get into trouble **4** 57⟩
truth 2 B 23
T-shirt 6 D 86,8
⟨turkey 44,2⟩
to **turn**
to turn off **6 D** 83
to turn on **6 D** 83
⟨'twas **5 B** 63,7⟩
tyre 4 A 47,1.

U

uncle 1 B 11
to **untie 7 A** 90
⟨unto **2 C** 30,8⟩
to put **up 3 C** 38,2.
⟨upon **3 C** 42,8⟩

V

⟨valley **8 B** 111,9⟩
vanilla 5 B 61,a)
vegetables 5 B 61,a)
°**vet 3 C** 39,3.
to **visit 1 A** 8,a)
°**visitors' centre 2 B** 24,3

W

⟨waiter **5 B** 63,6⟩
⟨ware **2 C** 30,8⟩
watermelon 7 B 92
°**weasel 7 C** 95,1.
weather 1 A 9,b)
weatherman 6 C 82
weekend 1 B 12,2
to **weigh 1 C** 13
°**well 7 B** 92
well done 5 D 67
west 6 C 82
wet 3 C 39,4.
what a 7 B 92
what for? 3 B 35,1.
°**wheat 6 B** 80
wheel 4 B 49
⟨to wheel **5 B** 63,7⟩
⟨wheelbarrow **5 B** 63,7⟩
which? 5 B 61,a)
while 7 A 90
to **whisper 1 D** 15
°**whistle 5 D** 67
⟨wicki-up **6** 89⟩
wife 1 D 18,6
wild 6 D 83
will/won't 6 A 77,a)
windmill 7 B 92
windy 6 B 80
winter 5 A 58,4.
⟨to wish 44,3⟩
without 4 B 49
⟨no wonder **5 B** 63,7⟩
work 1 B 11
world 1 C 13
worm 7 C 97,5
worried 3 C 39,3.
to **worry 3 A** 32,2.
worse 2 C 28,3.
worst 2 C 28,3
would 5 B 61,b)
Wow! 6 A 79,4

X

Y

Yahoo! 7 C 95,3.
year 1 A 8,1
yesterday 1 A 8,a)
yet 4 A 47,3.
[**yours 8 B** 111,8]

Z

⟨zoo 73,4⟩

Boy's names

Alan ['ælən]
Alec ['ælɪk]
Andrew ['ændru:]
Arnie ['ɑ:nɪ]
[Bill [bɪl]]
Buddy ['bʌdɪ]
Charles [tʃɑ:lz]
Daniel ['dænjəl]
Ellis ['elɪs]
Ernie ['ɜ:nɪ]
Freddy ['fredɪ]
⟨Frank [fræŋk]⟩
Gordon ['gɔ:dn]
Harry ['hærɪ]
Jeff [dʒef]
Luke [lu:k]
Mark [mɑ:k]
Mickey ['mɪkɪ]
Nick [nɪk]
Pete [pi:t]
⟨Philip ['fɪlɪp]⟩
Ralph [rælf]
Rex [reks]
Robin ['rɒbɪn]
Rodney ['rɒdnɪ]
⟨Simon ['saɪmən]⟩
Will [wɪl]
William ['wɪljəm]

Girl's names

Alice ['ælɪs]
Anne [æn]
Beverly ['bevəlɪ]
Ellen ['elən]
Elsie ['elsɪ]
Emily ['emɪlɪ]
Karen ['kærən]
Linda ['lɪndə]
Mabel ['meɪbl]
Margaret ['mɑ:grɪt]
Mary ['meərɪ]
⟨Molly ['mɒlɪ]⟩
Nellie ['nelɪ]
Peggy ['pegɪ]
Polly ['pɒlɪ]
⟨Sandra ['sændrə]⟩
Sarah ['seərə]
Sheila ['ʃi:lə]
Sue [su:]
Tracy ['treɪsɪ]

Surnames

Alassio [ə'læsɪəʊ]
⟨Bowden ['bəʊdn]⟩
⟨Chapman ['tʃæpmən]⟩
Doyle [dɔɪl]
Edwards ['edwədz]
Evans ['evənz]
Haig [heɪg]
Hopper ['hɒpə]
Jones [dʒəʊnz]
Kahn [kɑ:n]
⟨Lee [li:]⟩
⟨McGregor [mə'gregə]⟩
McMasters [mək'mɑ:stəz]
⟨McTavish [mək'tævɪʃ]⟩
⟨Malone [mə'ləʊn]⟩
Nelson ['nelsn]
⟨O'Connor [əʊ'kɒnə]⟩
Price [praɪs]
Smith [smɪθ]
Snyder ['snaɪdə]
Stevenson ['sti:vənsn]
Walker ['wɔ:kə]
Whitecloud ['waɪtklaʊd]
Wiley ['waɪlɪ]
Wood [wʊd]

Geographical names

Africa ['æfrɪkə]
America [ə'merɪkə]
⟨Anadarko [ˌænə'dɑ:kəʊ]⟩
Atlantic Ocean [ətˌlæntɪk‿'əʊʃən]
Barton-on-Sea [ˌbɑ:tən‿ɒn 'si:]
Ben Nevis [ˌben 'nevɪs]
Bolton Abbey [ˌbəʊltən‿'æbɪ]
Borrowdale ['bɒrəʊˌdeɪl]
Broad Marsh ['brɔ:dˌmɑ:ʃ]
Buckingham Palace [ˌbʌkɪŋəm 'pæləs]
⟨California [ˌkælɪ'fɔ:njə]⟩
⟨Calverton ['kælvətən]⟩
Carisbrooke Castle [ˌkærɪsbrʊk 'kɑ:sl]
Chicago [ʃɪ'kɑ:gəʊ]
Cornwall ['kɔ:nwəl]
⟨Dublin ['dʌblɪn]⟩
England ['ɪŋglənd]
Enid ['i:nɪd]
France [frɑ:ns]
Frontier City [ˌfrʌntɪə 'sɪtɪ]
Glenwood Drive ['glenwʊd]
Great Gable [ˌgreɪt 'geɪbl]
⟨Gulf Stream ['gʌlf ˌstri:m]⟩
Hampshire ['hæmpʃə]
Heathrow ['hi:θrəʊ]
⟨Houses of Parliament [ˌhaʊzɪz‿əv 'pɑ:ləmənt]⟩
Humber Bridge [ˌhʌmbə 'brɪdʒ]
⟨Hyde Park [ˌhaɪd 'pɑ:k]⟩
Ireland ['aɪələnd]
Isle of Wight [ˌaɪl‿əv 'waɪt]
Italy ['ɪtəlɪ]
Lake District ['leɪk ˌdɪstrɪkt]
London ['lʌndən]
⟨Marble Arch [ˌmɑ:bl‿'ɑ:tʃ]⟩
M 1 [ˌem 'wʌn]
Market Square [ˌmɑ:kɪt 'skweə]
Mexico City [ˌmeksɪkəʊ 'sɪtɪ]
Mount Everest [ˌmaʊnt‿'evərəst]
⟨New England [nju: 'ɪŋglənd]⟩
⟨New Orleans [nju: 'ɔ:lɪənz]⟩
New York [nju: 'jɔ:k]
Newquay ['nju:ki:]
the Nile [naɪl]
Normandy ['nɔ:məndɪ]
Northern England [ˌnɔ:ðən 'ɪŋglənd]
Nottingham ['nɒtɪŋəm]
Oklahoma (City) [ˌəʊklə'həʊmə]
Oxford ['ɒksfəd]
the Panhandle ['pænˌhændl]
Perth [pɜ:θ]
Red River [ˌred 'rɪvə]
Salt Plains [ˌsɔ:lt 'pleɪnz]
Scotland ['skɒtlənd]
Shetland (Islands) ['ʃetlənd]
Sherwood Forest [ˌʃɜ:wʊd 'fɒrɪst]
Skipton Castle [ˌskɪptən 'kɒ:sl]
Southgate ['saʊθgeɪt]
Tulsa ['tʌlsə]
U.K. [ˌju:'keɪ]
United States [ju:ˌnaɪtɪd 'steɪts]
U.S.(A.) [ˌju:'es/ˌju:es'eɪ]
Yorkshire ['jɔ:kʃə]

Other names

Big Paws ['bɪg ˌpɔ:z]
Charles the First [ˌtʃɑ:lz ðə 'fɜ:st]
Cherokee (Indians) ['tʃerəˌki:]
Doc [dɒk]
⟨Father Christmas [ˌfɑ:ðə 'krɪsməs]⟩
Goose Fair [ˌgu:s 'feə]
Grabbit ['græbɪt]
Odeon ['əʊdɪən]
Mr Pushy ['pʊʃɪ]
Queen Margaret's [ˌkwɪ:n 'mɑ:grɪts]
Robin Hood [ˌrɒbɪn 'hʊd]
Spot [spɒt]
St Anne's [snt 'ænz]
⟨Tarzan ['tɑ:zæn]⟩
Thunderbirds ['θʌndəˌbɜ:dz]
William of Normandy [ˌwɪljəm‿əv 'nɔ:məndɪ]
Will Scarlet [ˌwɪl 'skɑ:lət]

⟨Useful phrases in class⟩

What you can say to your friends or to the teacher

Good morning/Goodbye.	Guten Morgen/Auf Wiedersehen.
Thanks. Thank you (very much).	Danke. Vielen Dank.
• I'm sorry.	Tut mir leid.
I'm sorry I'm late.	Tut mir leid, daß ich mich verspätet habe.
I'm not feeling well.	Ich fühle mich nicht gut.
I've got a headache.	Ich habe Kopfweh.
What's the matter with you?	Was fehlt dir denn?
Are you feeling ill?	Fühlst du dich krank?
Are you better now?	Geht's dir jetzt besser?
Can I open the window?	Darf ich das Fenster aufmachen?
• What's this in English/German?	Was heißt dies auf englisch/deutsch?
What does ... mean?	Was bedeutet ... ?
• Can I ask a question, please?	Kann ich bitte eine Frage stellen?
How do you do this exercise?	Wie macht man/geht diese Übung?
Can/Could you help me, please?	Können Sie/Kannst du mir bitte helfen?
This question is difficult.	Diese Frage ist schwierig.
I don't know the answer.	Ich weiß die Antwort nicht.
I'm not sure.	Ich bin nicht sicher.
Is this right?	Ist das richtig?
Could you repeat the question?	Könnten Sie die Frage wiederholen?
Could you look at my exercise book?	Könnten Sie mein Heft anschauen?
I don't understand this word/sentence.	Ich verstehe dieses Wort/diesen Satz nicht.
Pardon?	Wie bitte?
Could you write it on the board?	Könnten Sie es an die Tafel schreiben?
I can't see the board.	Ich kann die Tafel nicht sehen.
What must we do for homework?	Was haben wir als Hausaufgabe auf?
• Can we read this story?	Können wir diese Geschichte lesen?
Let's act the story.	Wir möchten die Geschichte spielen.
Can we sing a song?	Können wir ein Lied singen?
• Where's my ruler/biro/... ?	Wo ist mein Lineal/Kugelschreiber/... ?
Has anyone seen my ... ?	Hat irgend jemand mein ... gesehen?
Have you got/seen/taken my ... ?	Hast du mein ... ?/... gesehen/genommen?
Have you looked for it in the hall/... ?	Hast du auf dem Gang/... schon gesucht?
• This story is good/great/interesting.	Diese Geschichte ist gut/toll/interessant.
I like it.	Ich mag sie.
This story isn't interesting.	Diese Geschichte ist nicht interessant.
I think it's terrible!	Das ist furchtbar!
I don't agree.	Das finde ich nicht.

What the teacher may say to you

• Open your books at page ...	Öffnet eure Bücher auf Seite ...
Close your books.	Schließt eure Bücher.
Turn to page	Schlagt Seite ... auf.
Read the story on page	Lies den Text auf Seite ....
We're going to do exercise ... on page	Wir werden die Übung ... auf Seite ... machen.
• Please fetch me some chalk.	Bitte hol mir Kreide.
Would you collect the exercise books?	Würdest du die Übungshefte einsammeln?
Do this exercise for homework.	Macht diese Übung als Hausaufgabe.
Have you done your homework?	Habt ihr eure Hausaufgaben gemacht?
Write the answers in your exercise book.	Schreibt die Antworten in eure Übungshefte.
• That's right. That's wrong.	Das ist richtig. Das ist falsch.
Good. Very good. That's good. Well done.	Gut! Sehr gut! Das ist gut. Gut gemacht.
That's not very good. Try again.	Das ist nicht sehr gut. Versuch es noch einmal.
• Be quiet.	Seid ruhig.
Sit down, please.	Setzt euch bitte.
Please speak up.	Sprich lauter bitte.